Liz

100
THINGS

Explore Your Potential

☐

Seb

Explore Your Potential

100
THINGS

WHAT'S ON YOUR LIST?

SEBASTIAN TERRY

EBURY
PRESS

An Ebury Press book
Published by Random House Australia Pty Ltd
Level 3, 100 Pacific Highway, North Sydney NSW 2060
www.randomhouse.com.au

First published by Ebury Press in 2011

Addresses for companies within the Random House Group can be found at
www.randomhouse.com.au/offices

National Library of Australia
Cataloguing-in-Publication Entry

Terry, Sebastian.
100 things / Sebastian Terry.

ISBN 978 1 74275 153 5 (pbk.)

Goal (Psychology).
Motivation (Psychology).
Conduct of life – Miscellanea.

153.8

Cover design by Christa Moffitt, Christabella Designs
Internal design by Midland Typesetters, Australia
Typeset in Sabon 11.5/15.5 pt by Midland Typesetters, Australia
Printed in Australia by Griffin Press, an accredited ISO AS/NZS 14001:2004
Environmental Management System printer

To anyone who's ever dreamed

Introduction

'SEBASTIAN, DO YOU TAKE Chevali to be your lawfully wedded wife? Do you vow to treat her right and to be her Tiger Man?'

'I do.'

'Chevali, do you take this hunk, *a hunk of burnin' love*, to be your husband from this day on?'

'I do.'

'Well, then, by the powers vested in me by the state of Nevada, I, Elvis Presley, now pronounce you husband and wife. Sebastian, you may kiss your bride.'

Considering I'd only met Chevali three days ago, you could say that we'd decided to tie the knot quite quickly, but if the truth be known, I was only marrying Chevali because my intended bride, Crystal, had stood me up twenty minutes earlier. I'd only find out later the horrific reason why this was.

Let me explain myself. You see, I'd always wanted to marry a stranger in Las Vegas. I'm not sure why exactly, but I guess it was just one of those things that I'd always wanted to do.

That's the sole reason I was in Vegas at the time; I was wife hunting.

As it happened, it only took one day to find someone willing to marry me once I touched down in Vegas, but never in my wildest dreams did I think I'd end up marrying the receptionist at my hostel.

The funniest thing was that when the Elvis impersonator asked us to kiss, this would be the first and last time we would ever do so. I had to leave the country the next day to return to Australia. Luckily for me, Chevali had a great sense of humour.

Two nights prior to spontaneously marrying Chevali, I'd found myself at a bar along the infamous Strip of Las Vegas. The sign out the front read 'Dirty Girls Mud Wrestling' and, since I was looking for a potential bride, it seemed like a good place to start my search. Inside, as you might expect, was a bar full of blokes drinking and shouting; by smell alone, it appeared that they hadn't left the bar for the better part of a week. In the middle of the room, on a sunken level, was a big inflatable swimming pool, filled to the brim with mud. This was why everyone was there.

Typically not being one to go to a bar by myself, I bought a beer and stood inconspicuously at the back of the room, where I felt the most comfortable.

Then came the announcement: 'Ladies and gentlemen, welcome! I'm your referee for the evening.'

The man who had just announced himself to the smoky room via his microphone was indeed dressed like a referee and as he circled the pool of mud, he went on to explain the rules of the evening. Apparently we were in for a dirty night of wrestling whereby the only rule was that photos were not allowed. This was easy enough to understand.

'Before we start though, I need a volunteer,' said the referee.

Like a badly timed Mexican wave, every hand in the room went up as one, mine included. None of us knew exactly what we were volunteering for, but even the slight possibility that it might get us nearer to the ring was enough for us all to jockey for attention. The atmosphere immediately changed from excitement to one of fierce competition: men pushing, yelling and jostling for eye contact with the referee. Given I was standing at the back of the room, my hopes weren't high, but this was Vegas: anything was possible.

'You, sir, at the back of the room, come on down!'

As unlikely as it seemed, I had been picked. Every other man in the room instantly turned to look at me with envy as I began to push towards the ring. I was the chosen one. Moments later I found out what this in fact meant: I had been given the honour of circling the ring and pushing the girls back in, should they stray too close to the edge during battle. Things were falling into place just as I had hoped; surely I'd find a bride this way.

As I familiarised myself with the ring dimensions, the referee then beckoned two scantily clad girls from the nearby change rooms into the arena. The crowd's response was ravenous, to the point where I questioned if any of the men had seen a girl since the mid 1980s. The room was worked up, to say the least. The girls, ever the professionals, jumped into the ring and flaunted about as if performing at a gentlemen's club. As it turned out, when not mud wrestling these girls were indeed strippers.

Ding, ding.

'Seconds out, round one.'

Before the bell had stopped vibrating, the girls sprang from their corners, sliding on all fours into the centre of the ring. Mud sprayed everywhere. Glistening, bouncing and contorting, the girls certainly weren't holding anything back and with each moan came an even louder cheer from the crowded room. Some men, so affected by the sheer beauty of the sport, were unable to make a noise of any type.

Again circling the ring at the end of round one, the referee who sported a cheesy smile and a horrible moustache was successfully whipping the crowd into a testosterone-fuelled frenzy. As he walked past me, a sudden idea filled me with excitement. I had to act quickly. All I had to do was ask the referee to make an announcement on my behalf and see if there were any takers. This he agreed to enthusiastically.

'Okay, everybody, listen here now! I've got an announcement to make for this young fella here.'

The crowd, as well as the half-nude wrestlers, all fell silent. It was perfect. I had everyone's attention.

'Now this guy is from Australia, and he's come here tonight for one thing.'

Everyone leaned in, curious to hear what it was.

'His name is Sebastian and he's flown all the way to Vegas searching for a wife!'

The room began to applaud, but as I looked around there were no girls with raised hands. This didn't surprise me. But I hoped that I'd at least planted a seed. Only time would tell.

Ding, ding.

'Seconds out, round two.'

As the rounds progressed, the wrestlers, like the crowd, became dirtier and by the end of the night I was covered in mud. Somehow amid all the mayhem, a mud-wrestling champion was announced; her name was Crystal. Though this didn't seem to matter too much to the crowd who, shortly after applauding the decision, all left the bar. The masses were satisfied.

The referee, who since announcing the winner had switched off his microphone, then walked over to me and offered me a beer.

He liked Australians and as such showed me to the bar, handed me a Budweiser, and left me there to plot my next move.

As I sipped my beer and wiped the mud splatter from my clothes, a girl approached from the change rooms and introduced herself. It was Crystal, the newly crowned champion of the ring. I could tell this because she still had mud on her face.

'So, were you serious about wanting to marry someone?' she asked with a curious smile.

'Absolutely! I've always wanted to marry someone here in Vegas. Just for twenty-four hours, though.'

'Sounds like fun!'

Was this girl actually showing interest in the idea? Could she be the one?

After chatting for a further thirty minutes, I'd convinced myself that indeed she was, and so naturally I asked for her hand in marriage.

'Sure!' came the immediate reply.

And that's how Crystal and I got engaged. Five minutes later, she left the bar; she had to get back home to her three kids. Before she did though, she gave me her email address.

'Send me a message tomorrow. Let me know the details!'

What was I going to tell my mum?

Having found a bride to marry, my next job was to find a venue to get married in. Vegas being Vegas, I assumed this wouldn't be a problem. The next morning I began searching for an ideal chapel.

The first place I tried gave me little hope.

'How can I help you?' asked the quiet priest at the reception desk of a small white chapel known for offering the cheapest and quickest weddings in Vegas.

'I'm here for the quickest and cheapest wedding in Vegas,' I replied with a straight face. Judging by his steely gaze, he didn't seem overly supportive. Purposefully he scanned me up and down before responding.

'Well, where is your fiancée?'

I began to explain that I wasn't quite sure, but I told him that I knew where she mud wrestled every Tuesday.

'I also have her email address,' I added.

The old man's forehead tightened as he stood up and planted his hands on his hips. It was clear that we had got off on the wrong foot. Then, in the tone of an angry father questioning his disobedient son after returning home late from a school disco, he loudly responded, 'How long have you been seeing this girl?'

'Well, almost twelve hours now.' I knew he wouldn't like this answer.

After a moment of silence, he delivered his next sentence, 'Marriage is not something to joke about, you know!'

With that, an Elvis impersonator casually strolled through the foyer, chewing on a sandwich as he walked past.

Of course, marriage is no joking matter, but I couldn't quite help but wonder why this man seemed so surprised with my request. Was he somehow unaware that he worked in a Las Vegas wedding chapel offering 'Drive-thru weddings in under 20 minutes!'?

It was time to try elsewhere.

Thankfully the next place I visited, another drive-through wedding chapel, was a lot more helpful. Not only did they give me a great deal – which included being married at the express drive-through window – but they also threw in a stretch Hummer as well as Las Vegas's number-one Elvis impersonator who would sing three songs at the ceremony. Perfect.

Happily, I parted with my money. I couldn't believe it: I was going to get married the next day after only seventy-two hours in town. It had all happened so quickly.

After running back to my hostel and telling everyone who cared to listen that they were all invited to the wedding the following day, I sent Crystal an email with the details of our nuptials as promised; after all she was pivotal to the day. This was all it would take to confirm our commitment to each other.

By midday the next day, the sun was out and everyone was getting ready for the wedding. Having made a few friends whilst staying at the hostel, there was genuine excitement about the occasion. In all, there were about thirty people in our makeshift wedding party, but even so there was one glaring problem: I hadn't heard back from Crystal. Had she got cold feet?

As the clock ticked on, a mild sense of worry had turned into the onset of panic and with less than an hour until the ceremony, I cursed the fact that I hadn't taken Crystal's number. All I could do was send her a second email entitled: 'Urgent – your wedding'.

Lester, a friendly Aussie who by virtue of nationality alone I'd asked to be my best man, looked discreetly at his watch with thirty minutes to go. Things were not looking good and with every passing second, it seemed more and more likely that Crystal was going to stand me up. Lester pointed out the obvious, as a best man should. 'You need to find another bride, mate.'

He was right.

There was only one option left, and her name was Chevali. The first girl I met in Vegas was the receptionist of the hostel I checked into when I arrived in town. Chevali was a friendly girl with a big laugh, and happened to be the only other person I could think of with a sense of humour large enough to consider marrying me. With just twenty minutes until the ceremony was due to start, I called her.

'Chevali, it's Seb here. Remember me?'

'Sure. How are you, Seb?' This was a good start.

'Look, this might seem a bit sudden, but I was just wondering if you wanted to marry me?'

I'd told Chevali on my first day the reason for my trip to Vegas and I remembered that she'd laughed loudly. At this point I had convinced myself that due to this she would at least consider my proposal, but the silence on the other end of the line worried me. After a moment I could hear her giggling with a friend who must have been standing next to her.

'You're crazy! Sure, I'll marry you.'

'Really?' I was shocked.

'Yeah, I've wanted to get married in Vegas for ages as well! When shall we do it?'

'How about in twenty minutes?'

Another silence made me wince before Chevali again agreed. Somehow my wedding was back on track! What were the chances?

'What shall I wear, though?' she asked.

'Just something casual, I guess.'

Twenty minutes later, Chevali and I were seated on top of the stretch Hummer, ready for the ceremony to begin. And for the first time, I took a moment to think about what I was doing. I'd flown to Vegas on a whim and had spent three days consumed in the search for a bride. Now I was about to marry a complete stranger under the watchful eye of Elvis and a rogue bunch of backpackers, none of whom I'd known for longer than a day or two. Despite every piece of logic telling me that I was doing something of extreme stupidity, for some reason I felt more alive than I ever had before. I wasn't quite sure why, but I just knew I was doing the right thing.

I glanced around and noticed everyone was smiling and as I looked over to Chevali, I could tell that she too was having fun. We all were.

'Sebastian, do you take Chevali to be your lawfully wedded wife? Do you vow to treat her right and to be her Tiger Man?'

'I do.'

'Chevali, do you take this hunk, *a hunk of burnin' love*, to be your husband from this day on?'

'I do.'

'Well, then, by the powers vested in me by the state of Nevada, I, Elvis Presley, now pronounce you husband and wife. Sebastian, you may kiss your bride.'

I had done it; I had married a stranger.

The next day I flew home.

A week later, I received an email entitled 'Re: Urgent – your wedding'; it was from Crystal, asking if I still wanted to get married. It appeared that she hadn't stood me up, after all. It turned out that she'd been hit by a car on the way to the wedding and had only just got out of hospital. Thankfully she was okay.

Chapter 1

I KNOW WHAT YOU'RE thinking. You think I'm crazy, don't you? I don't mind; in fact, I'd probably assume the same thing if I'd just read about someone marrying a stranger in Vegas on a whim. In reality, though, this was not a spur-of-the-moment decision fuelled by alcohol, immaturity or even an unsound mind. Rather it was a very deliberate choice, the upshot of a set of significant events in my life at that time, the saddest of which involved the loss of a close friend's life.

Without a doubt, the events leading up to the wedding in Vegas completely changed the way I viewed the world and myself. And in a moment of clarity whilst sitting upon that stretch Hummer saying my vows to Chevali, I felt something inside me click. It was this feeling that sparked an incredible journey that is still continuing to this day. I think without further delay I should probably explain in a little more detail why I found myself in Las Vegas in the first place.

As far back as I can recall, I remember living a fairly normal life; I had loving parents, a little sister to joke with and we even enjoyed a bit of travel as we followed my dad's work around the world. By the time I was four years old, I'd lived in four countries and, like all young kids, was leading the life that was handed to me. By my teens, the natural progression of growing up had led me into high school with no major hiccups and with a healthy diet of good parenting and a love of team sports, you could say that I was a well-balanced kid, a product of a solid upbringing. On paper everything was just right.

In honesty, like most, my life up to until the end of school was fairly easy; I didn't have to think too hard and everything just happened systematically. The first decision that I ever had to make was whether, after graduating from Year Twelve, to start a career or further my study. Between you and me, neither of these options really appealed to me and although there was also a third option to travel, it was suggested to me that this would in no way aid in the process of achieving what had been deemed as paramount to a good life: financial security. Without financial security, the ideals that had been instilled into me, such as being able to afford a car, a house and even one day a family, would be jeopardised. So, in what was ultimately a process of elimination, I ended up committing the next three years of my life to a university degree in Human Movement simply because the notion of starting a career with no idea of what career path I wanted to follow seemed even more ridiculous.

Three years later, after obtaining a degree and accumulating some $17,000 in student loans, I still felt no true calling. I was twenty-two years old and confused. I'd accomplished all that society had encouraged me to do but in reality I remained lost. The overwhelming expectation that I become financially secure was still ringing loudly in my ears but by this stage I'd developed a curiosity that I couldn't shake: why did financial security seem to take precedence over everything else?

My quick-fix solution was to travel and so I spent the next few years of my life drifting aimlessly overseas as I tried to search for an answer to one simple question: What do I want to do with my life? This, though, remained unanswered and so, by the time I'd completely run out of money at the age of twenty-four, somewhere in the middle of Canada I might add, I'd begun readying myself to return home to Australia in preparation for the inevitable next step of finding a career. I saw no other alternative.

One week before my flight home, I noticed what I thought was a mistake on my bank statement. They had swindled me out of $200! Naturally I got in touch with the bank to reclaim the last of my money but, within minutes of speaking to the gentleman at the other end of the line, learned that the only mistake was that of my own maths – I was not owed anything. Just as I was about to hang up the phone in embarrassment, the man added, 'Sebastian, by the way, my computer is telling me that I can extend your credit card limit by $3500, on the spot. Does this interest you?'

It did, and within ten minutes of hanging up the phone, I had made plans to visit one more place before flying home. You see, I'd always wanted to go to Las Vegas and I saw this moment as possibly the last opportunity to do it before securing a proper job and, that old chestnut, financial stability.

It was on the eve of flying out that I heard the news about Chris.

Chris, or Detho, as everyone knew him, was a close friend of mine. We grew up together in high school. We played rugby together, rowed together and shared beers together. Detho was everyone's best mate. He was a legend in his own right. Detho had lived his whole life in the same house, only minutes from our school, and closer again to our surf club. Not only was he a great person, but so too are his family. They all played a large part within a close-knit community.

The phone call I received from a mutual friend back in Australia stopped me in my tracks; Detho had died overnight. He was twenty-four years old. I fell silent on the phone. To be honest, I can't recall what was said after that.

Chris was a big kid at heart and always enjoyed the fun, carefree side of life. He had been partying all night with good friends, as he loved to do. The partying had continued into the next morning, when they found themselves in a friend's backyard. An exuberant game of roof-jumping then ensued, each person attempting to outdo the other, as boys do. Detho, in pushing the limits, tragically lost his life. He died at the scene. Coincidentally, the first responding ambulance officer was one of his good friends. Everyone knew Detho.

Logistically, I couldn't get back in time for the funeral and as such was left in North America, feeling useless. All I could do was think and before long I decided to start writing. I wrote down all my thoughts on pages and pages of scrap paper as a way of trying to make some sense of what had happened.

My parents of course attended the funeral back in Sydney. They, along with hundreds of others, had to stand outside the church, due to the sheer number of people grieving the loss.

Death sparks reflection, first of the deceased, and then of yourself. There were many questions in my head at that time but there was one in particular that I couldn't look past: If Detho knew that that particular day was going to be his last, would he have changed anything? Would he have changed his last week, his last month or even his last year? Ultimately, given another chance, would Detho have changed the way he lived up to that point, full stop?

Although I could only guess, I think Detho's answer would have been no; he wouldn't have changed a thing. His life revolved around his friends, family and good times. He surrounded himself with the things he loved until his last day and as I saw it, he was happy because of it.

With this same question in mind, I pondered my own situation. Could I say the same thing? If I knew I was to die next year, next month, next week or even that very day, would I change anything? I thought about this long and hard, first considering everything I had done and then taking into account how I felt inside.

Unlike Detho, my answer was yes; I would change something.

This wasn't just a question that disappeared from my consciousness after a moment's thought. It stuck with me, and does to this day. With my affirmative answer came a realisation that there was a huge problem: I was not living as I wanted to; fundamentally, I wasn't happy. I was furious with myself. Who would allow such a thing? The answer was *me*! I had never felt so angry. For the first time I had seen my own life with absolute clarity, and I realised I wasn't who I wanted to be.

Immediately I began to question everything. Why was I not out there achieving all my true dreams and desires – the things that *I* wanted to do? In my eyes I had been wasting my life up to that point in an effort to walk a path of comfort, a path that society had dictated for me.

The next question was obvious as it was pivotal in my life: If given another chance, what would I do differently?

I fetched another piece of paper and again started to write.

Death puts things into perspective. We only have one life.

After scribbling frantically for a while, I put the pen back on the table and looked at what I'd written. It was a list of 100 things that I had always wanted to do, dreams and goals that would test me on all kinds of levels – physical, mental and emotional. As I peered down at the plethora of challenges before me, I was suddenly filled with possibilities and excitement. I had even left room on the list for things I was yet to discover. I labelled these 'TBA'.

Calmness soon replaced my anger as I grasped something just as important as the question itself: I was not dead, I was alive. I had a chance to make a change. With this realisation I immediately felt empowered, flooded with energy and a determination not to waste my life from that day on. There in front of me, on that piece of paper, was the key to my self-fulfilment. This was my chance to answer no; I wouldn't change a thing.

The next day I flew to Vegas and three days later I married a stranger.

Although at face value, marrying a stranger was certainly an odd thing to do, it was the first time I remember feeling like I'd accomplished something of meaning. This sense of achievement was something I'd never felt before. It wasn't so much the fact that it involved a stretch Hummer, wedding vows and a celebrity impersonator, but more so the underlying fact that for the first time in my life I'd simply achieved a goal that I'd identified as important to me. Although seemingly a bizarre goal to pursue in light of Detho's passing, it was something I felt compelled to do because of it.

By sheer coincidence, Detho's funeral occurred on the very same day as my Vegas wedding. I think this was a sign. It was at that moment I decided that I would complete my list.

One item down, ninety-nine to go.

100 THINGS

1. Running with Bulls
2. Marry a Stranger
3. Bet $1000 on Black (Roulette)

4. Raise Money for Charity
5. Save a Life
6. Complete a Triathlon
7. Feature in a Bollywood Movie
8. Olympic Ski Jump
9. Be in a Dance Video Clip
10. Chase a Tornado
11. Whale Shark Swim
12. Visit a Death Row Inmate
13. Be in a Medical Trial
14. Burning Man Festival
15. Stand-Up Comedy Routine
16. Street Performance
17. Surf Safari
18. Hit a Hole in One
19. Guinness World Record
20. Say Yes to Everything for One Week
21. Speed Dating
22. Participate in a Boxing Match
23. Deliver a Baby
24. Publish an Article
25. Catch a Thief
26. Help a Stranger
27. TBA
28. Visit a Fortune Teller
29. One Week's Silence
30. Join a Protest
31. Build Something
32. Learn Salsa
33. Be a Contestant on a TV Game Show
34. Kiss a Celebrity
35. Find My Family Tree
36. Walk Across a Country

37. Be a Horse Jockey
38. Be in a Hollywood Movie
39. Read the National TV Weather Report
40. Sail the Seas
41. Buy a Stranger Lunch
42. Cycle Through Cuba
43. Work at an Orphanage
44. Represent a Country at Something
45. Sumo Wrestling
46. Learn French
47. Go to Timbuktu
48. Act in a Play
49. Be a Matador
50. Throw a Party
51. Endurance Tandem Bike Ride
52. Sports Streak
53. Ice Fishing
54. Scooter Across Australia
55. Own a Company
56. Tantric Lesson
57. Cross a Desert
58. Skydive Naked
59. Attend an Extreme Religious Ceremony
60. Throw a Dart at a Map and Visit the Country It Lands On
61. Ultimate Prank
62. Live on the Streets
63. Get a Tattoo
64. Challenge a World Champion
65. Dad's Dream Car
66. Treacherous Trek
67. Live on a Desert Island for One Week
68. Invent Something

69. Join a Cattle Drove
70. Meet Another 'Sebastian Terry'
71. Naked Rugby
72. Stay Awake for Seventy-Two Hours
73. Get Shot
74. Crazy Bid
75. Pose Nude
76. Surf River Wave
77. Be a Team Mascot for a Day
78. Write and Perform a Song
79. Live with a Tribe for One Week
80. Have Something Named After Me
81. Make a Beefeater Laugh
82. Hitchhike
83. Foreign Aid
84. Face a Shane Warne Over
85. Go on an Adventure
86. Marathon
87. Meditation
88. Grow a Beard
89. Playboy Mansion
90. Land Diving
91. Plant a Tree
92. Haunted House
93. TBA
94. TBA
95. TBA
96. TBA
97. TBA
98. Crash a Red Carpet
99. TBA
100. Publish a Book

Chapter 2

WITH A HEAD FULL of ideas but a wallet devoid of coins, I realised that before I could start achieving my list, I needed a little money in my pocket; I had none. In an effort to make some cash fast, I decided to set up a business with two friends in Sydney, one of whom was my best mate Tank. The business itself was based on the quirky idea of offering giant inflatable movie screens for outdoor cinema nights. Essentially, we were an events company.

Admittedly it was a novel idea but, with no business nous to speak of and being cursed with the foresight of a nine-year-old, I failed to realise the commitment of time needed to make a business work. Luckily the others seemed to know what they were doing and so after borrowing $100,000 and purchasing the necessary business licences, equipment and uniforms, we were ready to operate. It was time to make some money.

For me the risk of committing to a large debt through the business was overshadowed by the notion that it would be an adventure shared with two friends. However, only one month into operation, the third partner announced that he wanted to walk away from the business. Not only this but he had also decided to go out on his own – in competition with us, no less. As we had not signed any legal documents in the establishment of our partnership, there was nothing Tank or I could do to stop him. Sadly for us, our misguided trust had resulted in what was now a tricky situation. We were gutted, victims of naivety.

Without our third partner we were in trouble; our model for success hinged on the fact that it would take three of us to help out. With this fairly large metaphorical spanner being thrown into the works, Tank and I were left with only one choice: we had to cast aside our personal lives and devote every spare moment we had to the business and paying off the debt. Not only was this going to be hard with one man down but as Tank also had a full-time job, the survival of the business rested almost entirely on my shoulders. Consequently, I tossed my list of 100 things in a drawer and focused my efforts solely on the business.

With a completely new mindset and just one simple goal, soon enough, as the days went by, business increased and we began to cut into our debt. This was encouraging of course, but behind the scenes I was beginning to struggle. I had regressed into a lifestyle that I knew I hated, but my hands were tied and there was nothing I could do.

Running the business from my bedroom, I worked from the early hours of the morning until bedtime every day, seven days a week. I had no time for my family, friends or even myself. Ultimately, the business took priority over everything in my life and although we were heading in the right direction, we still owed a lot of money.

Eighteen months later, the reality of my situation hit me one night in the back of a taxi. I'd just left a dinner function in the city that Tank had invited me to. He'd offered to cover my portion of the bill seeing as I couldn't afford it. Throughout what had been a lavish meal involving his friends, I'd barely said a word to anyone; I felt useless. Apologetic and somewhat embarrassed, I excused myself early from the meal and quietly asked Tank if he could lend me some money so that I could get a taxi home. Avoiding eye contact, I thanked him again and left the restaurant. As I rode home, I stared vacantly out of the rear side window. What had happened to me? I felt pathetic and lost. And with a heavy feeling in my chest, I just burst out crying.

At that moment I recognised that I'd lost my freedom, and I'd found myself in a place I promised I wouldn't ever be again. I'd forgotten about my list of dreams and, as such, my happiness. I'd even turned my back on my family and friends in a desperate attempt to keep the business afloat. Somehow my life was now focused on money – something that I knew I didn't actually care for.

Thankfully, though, it's often these dark moments in life that allow us to see the light. I needed to make a change.

The next day, before starting work, I ran into town and bought a huge wall map of the world. When I got home I opened up my desk drawer and pulled out my list of 100 things. Five minutes later, I'd mounted the map above my desk and placed 100 tags on the map, each tag displaying one of my goals. The tags were scattered across the world, from Asia to Europe, South America to North America. Taking a step back to look at my creation, I felt my heart beating harder than it had in a long time. The previous night, I'd used my time in the taxi to think about my life once again. I concluded quite simply that I needed to take a leap into the unknown.

That day I met up with Tank to talk about how I felt. Tank, of course, understood; he was my best mate. I told him that once the company debt was paid off, I needed to sort my life out, outside of the business. We both knew that this would put into doubt the future of the company but I'd decided that my life was far more important to me.

With a rekindled desire to pay off the debt, I worked harder than ever, every day glancing up at the map that now hung directly in front of me. A fresh perspective made it seem ridiculous that for almost two years I'd been putting all my effort and energy into something I didn't care about.

With my new drive, I soon began to wonder if there were things from my list that I could start planning or ticking off immediately. Why wait? And so in between work emails and phone calls, I began to put pen to paper and created action plans.

As I saw it, there were a handful of items that I could begin to look at:

- Number 4: Raise Money for Charity
- Number 6: Complete a Triathlon
- Number 9: Be in a Dance Video Clip
- Number 12: Visit a Death Row Inmate
- Number 15: Stand-Up Comedy Routine
- Number 21: Speed Dating
- Number 33: Be a Contestant on a TV Game Show
- Number 78: Write and Perform a Song

It was just a matter of doing.

Without so much as a moment's hesitation, I enrolled in the Mooloolaba Triathlon and began training straightaway. Tank decided to register for the race as well and after running, swimming and cycling everywhere in preparation, we took on the challenge and completed the event. Enriched with a sense of progress, I then emailed every Australian TV game show requesting to be a contestant. Immediately I got a response from *Taken Out*, a confronting dating show, offering me a spot in an upcoming episode. After googling 'death row penpals', I wrote a letter to an inmate on Oklahoma's death row, named J-Loc, who replied within two weeks. We were now penpals. At the same time I started to carry a notepad around in my pocket and whenever I noticed something even remotely humorous, I would jot it down as potential material for a stand-up comedy routine.

As the days rolled by, the items from my list began to take shape organically, each one transforming from an idea in my head to a tag on the map and then finally into an imminent event in my life. By the time I ticked off Number 9: Be in a Dance Video Clip, and consequently embarrassed myself nationally by dancing terribly in a Young Divas music video, I could feel a transition taking place within me. The thrill I got as I ticked off each item was immense, as if my whole body had been pumped with adrenaline. This was addictive. For the first time since tying the knot with Chevali, I felt alive!

The tipping point took place at Tank's house one morning when, whilst checking the company's bank balance, we noticed that we had $2000 in profit. Although not quite threatening the likes of financial heavyweights Microsoft or Facebook, we had reached a huge milestone with the business; we had successfully paid off our debt, all $100,000. In my eyes, we were the most successful company in the world. I'd be lying if I said we didn't celebrate by smoking a cigar and spraying champagne on each other before heading into town to party for the better part of two days, but a little lie won't hurt; let's just say we shook hands and had a quiet evening.

With the debt now paid off, I'd honoured my commitment to the business and as such I was free to make my next move – but in which direction? With just $9000 to my name, I knew I wanted to pursue my list, I just wasn't sure where to begin.

It would take a big step off the beaten track, based purely on my gut instinct.

One morning, I flicked through the mail and noticed another letter from J-Loc. After almost twelve months of correspondence, it was easy to recognise his handwriting. I always looked forward to reading his letters; he was a funny bloke who was keen to learn about Australia and even me. Occasionally I would send him photos of Manly Beach, where I lived. I felt guilty about sending photos of such a picturesque place as I knew that he lived in a tiny cell three floors underground, but he insisted he wanted them.

When I got upstairs to my bedroom office, I sat down, opened the envelope and began reading his news. He had just come out of a six-day stint in solitary confinement – a tiny room with no light – as a punishment from a guard who simply didn't like him. As always he wasn't angry – J-Loc lived with a well-balanced understanding of his predicament – he was just upset. After sharing his refreshing outlook on this recent experience, he asked a series of questions about what I'd been up to before suggesting something that took me by surprise.

Hey homie, I think it would be cool if you came and saw me.

J-Loc had invited me to visit him in Oklahoma. I sat back in my chair in disbelief. I was nervous and intimidated, but most of all excited. With no plans in my life other than wanting to tick items on my list, this seemed like a timely invite.

Although I didn't know it then, J-Loc's invitation was the most invaluable invitation I had ever received, and it came at a time when I was at a crossroads in my life. On the one hand I had just paid off a company that seemed destined to make money and could very well lead me to the encouraged goal of financial security, whilst on the other hand lay an opportunity to meet a man whose life would soon be taken from him for a crime that he claims he never committed. The sensible choice was obvious but this wasn't about being sensible, this was about something far more important: self-discovery.

Immediately I booked a one-way flight to the US.

Chapter 3

THE WEEK BEFORE I flew out of Sydney, Tank and I decided to have a bite to eat down on Woolloomooloo Bay, a great spot on Sydney's harbour foreshore. The sun was out and neither of us was wearing a watch; time didn't matter.

As the sun peaked in the sky, we spoke of all kinds of things, including the eventful last few years. The weight of debt was now off our shoulders and with the excitement of the unknown ahead, we had one of those afternoons where our only regret was that it didn't last longer. It was a great way to say goodbye.

After a few beers, we befriended a couple in their forties who were sitting at a table next to us. We soon found out that they were actually on a date but, having consumed a few wines themselves, they were not hiding the fact that they had run out of conversation.

As the usual line of questioning pertaining to careers and hobbies began, I fidgeted in my seat, readying myself to explain my impending journey. By now I had told the majority of my own friends what I was about to do, but I hadn't as yet had to explain my intentions to complete strangers, especially inebriated forty-something-year-olds who I imagined were well along their chosen career paths and financially stable.

'So, what do you do, Sebastian?' asked the inquisitive woman.

I wriggled in my seat awkwardly as I prepared to let rip with something I've repeated many times since. 'Well, I've got a list of 100 things that I've always wanted to do, and I'm leaving next week to go and do them.'

'Excuse me?' came the delayed response from the woman.

The couple glanced at each other in confusion, then busied themselves swilling their wine. I turned to Tank for some form of backup, but all he offered was a smile as he raised his glass to me.

'Where are you off to, then?' came another question, this time from the man whose squinting eyes suggested that he thought I was quite possibly crazy.

'I'm off to Oklahoma,' I said casually.

'Oh, what are you doing there?'

'I'm visiting a guy on death row, actually.'

This, I think, only strengthened his opinion.

'So, how long are you going for?' asked the woman, who was now looking at me as if waiting for me to announce that it was all a joke.

'I don't know,' I said.

'But how much money do you have?'

'Not much.'

The conversation continued in a similar manner for the remainder of the afternoon and by the time the sun had begun to disappear over the distant Blue Mountains to the west, I felt happy, as though I'd passed a test of some sort. Although my actions might have sounded strange to the middle-aged couple and despite all the raised eyebrows and awkward pauses in our conversation, I knew that deep down I was doing the right thing. Thankfully I wasn't after understanding.

Against all theories of logic and normality, I was chasing something intangible. I wanted to grow, to experience more and enrich myself with the possibilities of dreaming, believing and achieving.

I suppose you could say that embarking on this trip was the biggest decision that I had ever made, but I also found it to be the easiest.

Chapter 4

EMBARRASSINGLY, ONE THING I had never done up until this stage of my life was donate money to charity. For this reason it became one of the first items that I added to my list; however, with just two days left before I left Australia, there were two minor problems I needed to address:

1. I had no idea *how* I would raise the money for a charity.
2. I had no idea *which* charity I would raise money for.

Of all the casual jobs that I had previously held, I always liked the ones, such as surf instructing, where I got to help kids. Considering this, I knew that I wanted to support an organisation that benefited kids and Camp Quality was the first charity that came to mind. Camp Quality helps kids and families affected by cancer. Essentially, through providing a fun form of therapy, they bring happiness to families throughout Australia and beyond.

With my new-found energy and enthusiasm, I sent an email to Camp Quality, asking if I could raise money for them. A day later, not only had they said yes, but they had somehow got me an interview on the national TV breakfast show, *Sunrise*. This took me by surprise – why would a TV show want to interview *me*?

At six o'clock the next morning, I turned up at the city-based TV studio where I'd organised to meet Maraya from Camp Quality for the first time. After giving her a big hug, she welcomed me on board and led me into the studio. On the way, I asked Maraya how much she'd like me to raise, to which she replied with a smile, 'How about $10,000?' Although it was ambitious, I couldn't see why not and so straightaway this became my goal: Number 4: Raise $10,000 for Camp Quality.

In a studio busy with producers, stylists, cameramen and stagehands, I couldn't believe how quickly everything was happening. As the first commercial ran, I was led to a chair that sat centrestage and introduced to Mel and Kochie, the two hosts of the show. Whilst confident on the outside, my insides were communicating a different story. The only comforting factor was that behind me on a large wall hung my map, adorned with 100 tags. The producer had asked me to bring it in as a prop. Other than that, I was alone and only seconds away from being beamed onto TV screens in homes all across Australia.

Cue intro music and a lead-in by Mel.

'The phenomenon of a bucket list has become popular in recent years, has even prompted a movie, but how many lists include things like marrying a stranger, betting $1000 on roulette or delivering a baby?'

Wow, that is a crazy list, I thought to myself.

'You've had lots of adventures! . . . Tell us about Vegas,' inquired a curious Kochie.

For the next sixty seconds of a three-minute interview, Mel and Kochie laughed at the fact that some bloke had flown to Vegas to marry a stranger. Even I laughed at how ridiculous it sounded. The fact that I had been successful in my mission blew them away, but amid the laughter I began to wonder if the only reason I had been invited onto the show was to be a token circus freak, someone to laugh at. Would they see beyond the frivolity of a twenty-four-hour marriage?

As the interview continued, any nerves associated with being on TV quickly left my body and soon enough I began to enjoy myself. Over the remaining next two minutes of the interview, I shared my reasoning for my trip as well as my immediate plans to visit J-Loc on death row, and as I did so I noticed a genuine sense of excitement and support building in the studio. It was then I learned that the *Sunrise* team even wanted to help me out.

'While you're completing all these tasks, you're raising money though, aren't you?' asked Mel.

With Maraya looking on from behind a camera, it felt great to announce that I was raising money for Camp Quality. I still had no idea *how* I would be doing this, but the thought alone made me smile.

'Absolutely,' I replied.

Mel concluded the interview by saying that they would be making a donation on my behalf to Camp Quality. And with that, I'd raised my first $150 courtesy of the generous guys at *Sunrise*.

I was ecstatic. Not only had I completed my first television interview, but I had also received my first donation simply because they liked what I was doing! Perhaps there was something to this . . . ?

The website that I'd created was just a blogging platform. I'd decided that this would be the easiest way to keep my friends and family up to date with my progress. Little did I know that within an hour of completing the interview, my blog would receive over 10,000 hits! On top of this, my inbox was full. At first I feared that I may have fallen victim to a barrage of junk email suggesting that I increase the size of certain body parts, but I was amazed to find that instead I'd been flooded with letters of support from strangers around the country. From young kids to the elderly, they had all seen me on *Sunrise*.

I read each message twice. I even pulled my mum over to take a second look. She was speechless.

Every email was slightly different: some offered kind words of encouragement, whilst others shared personal stories of anguish, belief or accomplishment. I had somehow connected with thousands of people whom I'd never met.

Incredibly there were even three messages from pregnant women who, having heard that Number 23 on the list was to Deliver a Baby, were offering me the chance to deliver theirs!

What the hell had the *Sunrise* interview started?

There were also heaps of emails simply asking, 'How can we donate to Camp Quality?'

I had stumbled on a way to raise money for a charity and so immediately I posted a link to the fundraising page.

I wasn't a token circus clown. People were pouring their hearts out to me and wishing me luck. They recognised that there was a lot more to this than an impromptu wedding in Vegas. There was some kind of genuine interest beyond my novel, ambitious list. It seemed that my story touched many people in some way. Why exactly this was I wasn't sure yet and so after replying to everyone, I did the only thing that I knew felt right: I headed overseas to get stuck into my list.

I left on 9 June 2009, my twenty-eighth birthday.

Chapter 5

From a distance, I could see a ten-metre-high wall wrapping around the heavily concreted Oklahoma State Penitentiary, a reminder to all that this was a maximum-security prison of the highest order. This was death row.

I walked into the building through a heavily guarded entrance and signed in at 8 am, surrendering all my belongings including my camera. Waiting nervously in the reception area, I made conversation with a friendly Dutch woman who sat in the corner of the room; she told me she was here to see her husband. Our conversation was cut short though as a guard called my name and quickly ushered me down a tight concrete corridor and through a series of heavy steel doors that powerfully opened and then slammed shut behind us as we walked deeper into the fortress. I was now in death row – there was no turning back. The prison guard escorting me had no expression on her face.

We soon reached a small room with eight glass windows facing us, four to my right and four to my left. Each window had a stool in front of it. This was the meeting room. I was led to window number two and sat down nervously. To my right was a phone attached to the wall. There was no keypad; instead it connected directly to a phone on the opposite side of the reinforced glass. I peered through the window and noticed a vacant stool in an otherwise empty concrete room. At the back of the room was a steel door with a tiny window positioned halfway up. I hated to think what happened beyond it. Suddenly, the door swung open. I jumped to my feet. It was J-Loc. I recognised him from a photo. My heart raced.

By the time the steel door closed again, he'd walked straight up to the window in front of me. I took a step forwards. We were only centimetres apart. Our eyes locked.

I felt the urge to shake his hand, but the thick glass separating us denied this. Instead, I made a fist with my right hand and placed it against the window. With a big smile, J-Loc did the same. This was as close as we could get. He was happy to see me. I was speechless.

Following his lead, I slowly sat down on my stool and picked up the phone that connected us. I had absolutely no idea about what was about to unfold.

'What's up, Seb?' J-Loc asked in an upbeat tone.

After a moment, I replied, 'Mate, I can't believe we finally meet.'

It had taken me a day of commuting from LA to reach J-Loc in the heart of America. Oklahoma State Penitentiary lies in the small country town of McAlester. There is not much there other than cheap motels and dead raccoons, both of which lined the bumpy bitumen road through town. Approaching McAlester, I managed to lose my way at an intersection and when I looked to the nearest signpost for direction, it read: 'Do not pick up hitchhikers as they may be escaped prisoners.'

I knew I must be near.

Finally I came to a long and windy road that nervously stretched to the maximum-security prison. Surprisingly, family homes with kids' toys in the front yards sat only minutes from one of the most daunting places in America. After driving a further few hundred metres up the road, I noticed something glistening in the distance but only after I squinted my eyes could I make out what it was; it was a large white building on a hill, with razor wire that shimmered under the hot sun. Oklahoma's death row.

'What's up, homie?' came another question from behind the big smile that J-Loc now sported.

'Hey, mate! How are you going in there?'

'Hot, man! Very hot!' J-Loc said.

J-Loc was thirty-two years old. He stood at about 175 centimetres, and was a good-looking guy; this much I could tell from his online profile. However, in person, I was struck by a huge smile and friendly eyes that made me feel comfortable.

Twelve months prior to this meeting, J-Loc sent me his first letter. He asked that I be his eyes and ears to the outside world. He wanted to escape his 'world of darkness', as he called it, and live vicariously through others on the outside. He shared ideas and philosophies as insightful as they were refreshing.

Always controlled, J-Loc tried to avoid talking of his plight on death row as it got him down, but occasionally he would open up. He was never bitter, just sad. On one occasion he wrote:

> How can an innocent man be behind bars? But it's all good, homie. I believe in justice and God will free me.

Everything was going well until his third letter when I realised that J-Loc was blatantly flirting with me! I quickly replied asking him if he knew that I was a male. His reply simply read:

Ha ha, sorry homie, I thought you was a chick! It's all good, at least I don't have to worry about all that emotional stuff now.

J-Loc's right hand gripped a white face cloth. He was sweating profusely and used the cloth first to wipe his shaved head and then his dripping face. The cloth was already drenched. It was ridiculously hot inside the prison.

'Mate, I was going to complain about it being hot out in the reception area but I think you win!' I joked.

'It's all good, man; I just came from basketball. It's hot down there, dawg!' Again he smiled.

'Basketball? Were you winning?' I asked.

'I always win, dawg!'

We both started laughing. This set the tone for our chat.

J-Loc wore damp grey gym shorts and an even damper grey T-shirt that read 'Prison Run Against Child Abuse 2007'.

Ironically, it was the death of a child that landed J-Loc behind that window.

On the morning of 23 July 2000, J-Loc told me, he gave his girlfriend a lift to work, as he had done many times before. Due to the short nature of the trip, they decided to leave his girlfriend's two children, from a previous relationship, in bed. They got in the car at 7.30 am but his girlfriend had forgotten something so she ran back into the house quickly. After she got back in the car, J-Loc drove her to work, dropping her off at 8 am, returning home by 8.30 am.

Once back at the house, he noticed that the younger child had a black eye and was complaining of a sore head. She seemed disorientated and unresponsive. Something was wrong.

He immediately rang his girlfriend at work to ask what to do but there was no answer. Soon after this, the child died.

Doctors at the scene concluded that the child had died from trauma to the head. This trauma led to brain haemorrhaging occasioning death.

A case of whodunnit immediately arose. Both J-Loc and his girlfriend were arrested.

J-Loc was charged with murder in the first degree, child abuse and sexual abuse of a child. His girlfriend was charged with murder in the first degree and child abuse. Since that day, he has argued his innocence.

J-Loc has been sentenced to death via lethal injection whilst his girlfriend serves a life term at a separate penitentiary.

'Man, I seen her slappin' her kids before, you know, and said nothin'. Damn, they're her kids! And when she went back in the house to get something, she must have done somethin' then.'

I just sat and listened; there was nothing I could say. I had been let into a world that was entirely unfamiliar. All my senses were heightened.

'The doctor says that a haemorrhage takes a certain amount of time to occur and seeing as I rang her at 8.30 am to tell her about the symptoms, they say the blow must have happened roughly two hours prior, which means something happened at about 6.30 am, right?'

I nodded.

J-Loc continued. 'So then she says to the police that she's been at work that day since 6 am, so it couldn't have been her! I know I dropped her off at 8 am and so I got them to check her sign-in card at work and sure enough it say 8 am. We caught her lying, dawg.'

Granted, I was only listening to one side of the story, but I understood what was being said. I was in no position to question J-Loc's story, but there was one thing that had taken me by surprise.

'So what about the sexual abuse charge?'

'I didn't rape no child, man,' he said adamantly. 'She just said that so the jury would immediately hate me. As soon as the thought of a black man raping a child is raised, well, I'm done for whether I did it or not.'

My lack of knowledge of criminal law and procedures limited my ability to grasp all the ins and outs of the case, but I still didn't understand how something like that could just be argued without proof.

'They had a doctor check the child at the scene and there was no proof of penetration or anything else. Of the three charges, that's the one I fought first! I never raped no child!' J-Loc spoke like he had a point to prove.

'So what happened to the charge?' I asked cautiously.

'I beat it, and it got thrown out, man.'

I was relieved.

'She lied, man, but it worked, because the jury already hated me, so now I'm still fighting them other two charges.'

The more he spoke, the more it became clear that he had spent a lot of time defending his case. Times were precise, wording exact, and conviction flawless.

'But that's my saving grace, that's what keeps me going: my innocence. I stay strong, but at the same time if I have to die in here while proving my innocence, I'll do it. And if that in some way helps others who are wrongfully imprisoned too, well, I'm willing to die.'

J-Loc spoke with a calmness and assertiveness that captivated me. With nothing to do but think all day, I imagine that you could go one of two ways: crazy or empowered. J-Loc was certainly the latter. He had spent two stints in death row totalling eight years. In this time, he had studied many religions and had found a peace within. He spoke as if he was sitting on a park bench in the middle of suburbia, his temperament and attitude not befitting of a man who was scheduled to die.

'I don't believe in justice anymore. If that existed, I wouldn't be here. Instead I believe in one God. Prison guards here sell inmates stuff illegally just to make money and so how can I trust in a system that is run by these people?'

I couldn't help but feel enraged at the corruption that J-Loc was alluding to. Justice is an ideal based on fairness, but it seemed that in practice justice is only as strong as the honesty of the people administering it. J-Loc had a point.

I hardly said a word within the first hour. Instead I listened as J-Loc spoke nonstop; he had a lot to say. Usually confined to his cell for twenty-three and a half hours of the day, this meeting gave him an opportunity to escape it at least for a while. And, he told me, it would also give his cellmate a chance to 'read' a *Playboy* magazine that they had in private.

'There's nothing worse than being in the cell when you gotta go, you know, man! He's crazy, anyway!'

Again we found laughter in a place without humour, but this time I felt bad as I was afraid it might echo to other inmates within the jail who might not have the opportunity to laugh too often.

Whilst chatting to J-Loc, the bubbly Dutch woman whom I'd met in the reception area sat down at window number one to my left.

In a place of much darkness, her chirpy attitude as she'd prepared to see her husband had startled me.

'How often do you come and visit?' I'd asked her earlier.

'Every day now.'

I was impressed; that was commitment.

'I've moved here for the last month,' she'd said. 'You see,

he's being executed on July 9th.' This was just two weeks away.

The sobering reality of death row hit me flush in the face. I couldn't even come close to comprehending the situation that she was in. I asked if she was all right, and she just smiled.

As I continued to speak to J-Loc, I could see that her meeting was very intimate, and very loving. J-Loc noticed that I kept looking over and whispered into the phone, 'That man's being killed soon.'

'What did he do?' I asked.

'Oh, man, he murdered someone. He's not an aggressive man, but he just snapped one time. Most people in here are like that.'

Again I just listened.

'She met him whilst he was in here; she found his profile on a database, started writing and soon they got married.'

'What? Really? Married like that?' I couldn't believe it.

J-Loc nodded.

I had heard of this type of thing happening but still couldn't understand it. I suppose some people get lonely on the inside and on the outside.

'You wanna see my girls?' J-Loc offered.

I wasn't too sure what he meant by this but I agreed. Excitedly, he placed the phone down on the ledge between him and the window and turned around. Then, attracting the attention of the prison warden by continuously knocking on the steel door behind him, he was let out of the small concrete room. I sat there imagining J-Loc returning with a group of girls hanging off him, but instead he returned with an A4-size yellow envelope.

Opening the envelope carefully, he peered in as if searching for a favourite lolly from a mixed lolly bag. It was full of photos.

One by one, J-Loc grabbed at photos and began to introduce the girls who were posing in each shot. Each girl had written to him since he had been on death row. He knew each one intimately.

'This is my Sunshine. She's from Germany. She writes once a week and sends me money when she can. This one here is Laura; she's from England. She is my baby. Very funny girl! This one here is from America; she's darn right crazy, man!'

Over the next five minutes, J-Loc must have shown me almost fifty girls! He carefully placed each girl's photo against the window so that I could see clearly and within minutes there was no more room on the ledge. It was an endless procession of women that left me feeling quite insecure.

'You know more ladies than I do!' I joked.

At this moment, the Dutch woman seated next to me stood up and left. J-Loc waited for her to leave the meeting room and then looked at me again.

'Some people in here just want the needle,' he said. 'Her husband wants to die. He told me. He's given up. He's guilty.'

I had trouble digesting this thought.

Once on death row, each prisoner is allowed six separate appeals of their charge. If these are all exhausted unsuccessfully, the prisoner is then given a date – a date to die. In this way, death row acts partly as a game of cat and mouse between the death penalty and the offender, sometimes lasting up to thirty years. Following his successful appeal of the sexual abuse charge, J-Loc still has six appeals left to fight the remaining two charges.

Again J-Loc reached for his face cloth and wiped the back of his neck before lifting the bottom of his T-shirt to wipe his face. As he did so, he revealed a huge tattoo on his stomach. In fact, for the first time I noticed he had tattoos everywhere!

'You like them tatts?' he asked, having caught me looking. Instantly, he took off his T-shirt. 'This one here is a picture of my daughter.' He pointed to a portrait of a child's face on his right forearm. He stroked it once and smiled.

J-Loc never wanted a child and his girlfriend swore that she would not fall pregnant, but she kept her pregnancy hidden from him. Shortly after they were both jailed, a little girl was born. She is now eight years old and is looked after by J-Loc's father who brings her in to visit on occasions.

Sitting in the depths of this maximum-security penitentiary, J-Loc has only memories of the things he speaks about with so much pride. Now he lives confined, three floors below ground level, allowed only to exercise in a yard for thirty minutes a day. Even the yard is three floors deep, with just a small skylight at the top allowing obstructed glimpses of daylight – sometimes with the right timing, sunlight – into his life.

'You know it's lunchtime now, homie, but I hate it. Boloney every day, man. Small portions. I eat the salad, but that's it.'

With that, J-Loc pointed through the window in the steel door at the back of the room. I stood up to get a better vantage point and peered through. Sure enough, as I did, a warden strolled past the door pushing a trolley of neatly stacked polystyrene lunch boxes. They looked tiny. J-Loc pulled out a piece of paper from the yellow envelope and pushed it against the glass. It was a list of items that inmates could purchase from within their cells.

Spices 15c
Salt and pepper 7c
Chicken stock 85c
Snack packs $3.43
Medical kits $7.35
Sweatshirts $10

The list was three pages long. Strangely, I noticed that each price had been crossed out in pencil and higher prices had been added. Salt and pepper had risen by six cents, snack packs by almost a dollar. All of the items had become more expensive.

'What's with the increases?' I asked.

'Global Financial Crisis, my man.'

I couldn't believe it. How could the world's economy have anything to do with a man held in a concrete hole three floors below ground in the small town of McAlester?

'So, with a little money from friends, we can make life in here slightly more bearable.'

Early on in our correspondence, J-Loc had mentioned that he wanted a TV. This cost around $200. I never sent the money. I didn't really know him at that stage, and I had been wary from the outset that perhaps some inmates, having been sent money from a stranger, would then stop writing. However, now sitting in front of this man, I could tell that he was genuine.

'I don't need no TV anymore, homie. My Sunshine bought me one.'

I felt terrible, yet relieved. Having now met J-Loc in person though, I made a decision that I would help him where possible.

'J-Loc, if given the chance to live one more day on the outside, what would you do?' J-Loc looked down at his feet and again wiped his head with his dripping rag. 'If I can, I'd like to try and do whatever it is you choose on your behalf. I'll even send you photos!' I continued.

'Oh, man, I just want to live and see the world. Kind of what you are doing right now,' he said.

'Well, I promise to keep you updated with my journey, but is there something more specific?'

J-Loc smiled and looked up at me.

'Man, I always wanted to be the best known gangster in the world.'

This, I thought, might prove quite difficult for me to achieve. By virtue of owning a scooter back in Sydney, I feared my street cred would be fighting an uphill battle from day one.

'Anything else?' I laughed.

'I want to buy my mum a car so she can come and visit me more often.'

This wasn't going as planned. I barely had any money myself and the last thing I could do was buy him a car.

'Tell me more about the gangster thing,' I joked.

'Let me think about it, and I'll write about it to you,' he said.

'Please do, mate. I'm serious about this.' And I was.

J-Loc and I had certainly connected over our talk. Regardless of whether he was guilty or not, it was clear that we enjoyed talking on a similar level, and I think that he appreciated the time we were spending together.

'Please keep writing, homie. I live through you and my girls. Each thing that you tell me about, I live that moment too. And every time I send a letter to Australia, France, Holland or England, a piece of me travels to that place. It keeps me living in this hell that I'm surrounded by. You know, I once heard someone say this thing that really gave me hope: "Our life is like a burning flame, and no matter how much darkness surrounds our flame, it can never extinguish our light. In the end our light will always win."'

Again I smiled.

'They won't keep me here, Sebastian.'

I believed him.

There was no clock in the room, but I knew we had been talking for a while. My numb backside told me so.

We had covered a lot of ground, and by the end of our talk,

I'd forgotten about the reinforced glass and the steel bars that separated us. I felt like I was chatting to a friend on that park bench in suburbia. If I could have stayed longer, I would have, but I had a two-hour drive ahead of me in order to catch a plane that evening.

'Mate, I can't begin to explain what this has meant to meet you here today,' I said.

'I know, homie. It's good to put a face to the letters.'

'I'll be back, man, and I promise that you'll hear everything that comes from my travels. Remember to let me know what I can do on the outside for you.'

'I will, homie. I will.'

We both stood up slowly and faced each other one last time. Again I placed my fist on the glass. J-Loc did the same. It was time to go. I turned around and escorted myself down the same corridor I had walked through earlier, automatic steel doors opening and then shutting loudly behind me as I went.

Reaching the entrance further down the corridor, I grabbed the sign-in book on the table in front of me. The clock on the wall gave me my official sign-out time: 1.30 pm. I had spent almost five and a half hours talking with J-Loc. I was drained.

'So, did you find out what you needed to find out?' asked the same prison guard who had walked me in earlier that day. Her tone suggested that I was slightly strange for wanting to visit death row.

'I didn't come here to find something out,' I snapped. 'I just came to talk with someone. Have you ever spoken to J-Loc?'

'No,' she said bluntly.

'Well, you should try it sometime. It'll make you think.'

With that, I pushed the entrance doors open and left.

I'm not sure what it was about the guard's comment that annoyed me so much but there was something very robotic about her. Her view of life was very black and white. I think she just wanted her pay cheque at the end of the week.

Outside, the day was still hot and the sun intense. I took my shirt off and drew in a deep breath. I looked at the clear blue sky high above me and truly appreciated my freedom. Thankfully for me, there was no darkness surrounding my flame. In that moment, I only hoped that justice would serve J-Loc fairly and that his darkness would be lifted as well.

The events of that day would take a long time to digest fully.

Is J-Loc guilty? I have my own view. This, of course, is based on one conversation only, and it is nothing more than my own opinion. All I hope is that whether it be through prayer, karma or justice, the right outcome eventuates, whatever that is.

Hopefully this means that one day, we can actually meet at a park bench in suburbia.

Chapter 6

TAL WAS A MAN whom I had only ever met once before leaving Australia. A jetsetting air steward, he was introduced to me by a mutual friend one day at Manly Beach while I was still studying at uni. Based in LA, Tal visited Sydney often and even though we only spoke for five minutes that day, he was nice enough to offer his couch to me at his place if I ever found myself on America's West Coast.

The funny thing about my trip was that having now visited J-Loc, I had absolutely no plans, and so I decided to email Tal to see first if he was around and second whether his offer was still open. As it happened, it was, and so after visiting J-Loc, I flew to LA. Whilst there, I could start thinking about my next move, whatever that might be.

Tal kindly picked me up from LAX and although we had only met once before, he treated me like a long-lost relative. He spent days showing me around LA; from the star-studded sidewalks of Sunset Boulevard to the Californian beaches of Venice, Santa Barbara and Manhattan, I saw everything. It was as if Tal had somehow sustained a heavy blow to his head and woke up believing that he was in fact a tour guide working on a performance-based salary. After a whirlwind few days, I had to ask Tal for a break. Other than getting my own star on Sunset Boulevard, there wasn't much left to do in LA. With a welcome rest, I then learned where his generosity came from.

A long time before I'd met Tal, he was diagnosed with liver cancer. The disease wasn't caught early and the doctors were not confident that Tal would survive; in fact, they only gave him six months to live.

At the prime of his life, Tal had two choices: to stop working, to take a back seat and wait for the inevitable, or to focus on the things that were important to him and live each day as if it were his last. Tal chose the latter and so when he wasn't confined to a hospital bed, he decided to travel as much as he could. With a great sense of fashion and style, Tal also spent days wandering in and out of designer clothes shops buying up everything and anything that he liked. With only six months to play with, Tal refused to see a price tag as a hurdle and so he added to his expansive wardrobe of designer clothes and accessories to the tune of $90,000!

More than twenty years on from being given six months to live, Tal has never been in better health. Of course there is the small issue of trying to repay the credit card debt, but this he doesn't worry about; instead he smiles proudly in the knowledge that he is most likely the best dressed air steward in the world. He has never been happier and has no regrets about spending the money.

Ask Tal now what he thinks about life, and he'll tell you, 'I've been a survivor for more than twenty years, and I've learned you only get one chance at life – so enjoy it!'

You often hear of those who have survived a near-death

experience, or those who are diagnosed with a terminal illness, reaching a state of enlightenment. This usually results in them discovering a new energy and focus that allows them to achieve things that they previously avoided. Time and again, I have wondered why it is that it often takes the dark moments in life to trigger such positive change. I guess it's only when life is uncertain that we can truly begin to recognise what it means to us.

Back in Sydney, the same friend who'd originally introduced me to Tal had sent an email to say that he wanted to put me in touch with another friend of his. Having read my blog, he thought he may be able to help with item Number 64: Challenge a World Champion. It just so happened that he knew a man named Ollie Lang, a world champion of sorts. I'll admit that I didn't know who Ollie Lang was, but following his instructions to 'google him', I discovered pages of images, videos and magazine articles, all talking about Ollie.

The first article I clicked on asked, 'Ollie Lang; is he the greatest player of all time?' After reading the article, I found out that the answer was a hands-down yes!

Was this my chance to challenge a world champion? All I needed to do was write to him and find out.

> Hey Ollie,
> My name is Sebastian and I've got a slightly cheeky question for you. Now I don't know if this is something that you would be interested in, but I'm wondering if there is any way whatsoever that I could challenge you to a one-on-one paintball match? You see I have a list of 100 things . . .

Ollie Lang was the world's best paintball player.

His reply was rapid. It simply said:

Sure. Come down to San Diego next Wednesday at midday.
Ollie

Despite having no plans at all, a very interesting prospect had popped up. I was suddenly one step closer to ticking off another item from my list and as a bonus there was even a slight chance of becoming a world champion in doing so!

My life was becoming quite strange.

Chapter 7

I'VE ALWAYS WONDERED WHAT it would be like to be a world champion. It wouldn't matter what it was that I was the best at, as long as for one moment I could say that I was the best. Imagine knowing that no matter where you were on the planet, you could beat anyone at your chosen discipline, whether it be running, chess, boxing or finger painting.

Sadly, I've never come anywhere near to being the best at anything. Instead what I've found is that I'm just *average* at most things. But what if I had an opportunity to challenge a proper world champion at their discipline, and even to beat them? Technically, this would make *me* a world champion, no? Me and my irrational thoughts sometimes get me into the oddest situations . . .

The sun was out and the sky was blue as I entered Velocity Paintball Park near San Diego. The sound of rapid-fire gunshots ricocheted loudly through the air, letting up only briefly as competitors reloaded their colourful ammunition.

As someone who had never seen a paintball arena, I was struck by an unexpected sensation of fear as I viewed it for the first time. Surrounded by tightly woven netting, the fifty-metre-by-fifty metre landscape was scattered with large inflatables acting as both obstacles to navigate around during a game as well as objects to hide behind as balls of paint flew towards your head in an attack. Covered in explosions of brightly coloured paint, the inflatables told a story of many a paint-riddled battle.

'Do you guys know an Ollie Lang here?' I asked a bunch of spectators as we looked out across the fully enclosed paintball arena. At the time there was an exciting game of five-on-five paintball taking place.

'Ollie Lang? Sure!' yelled one guy as he pointed to a man hiding behind a large inflatable cone on the far side of the playing arena. 'That man's famous, dude!'

With that, Ollie Lang, dressed from head to toe in army attire, leapt aggressively from behind the cone, firing a barrage of green and yellow paintballs ten metres through the air, each ball slamming into the head of his unsuspecting opponent. Ollie had found his man; in turn, I had found mine.

After Ollie had 'killed' all of his opponents, he made his way over and introduced himself.

'I'm glad you could make it, man!' He beamed as he walked me over to his team. 'We've been talking and we've decided that you'll take me on, one on one, full court. What do you think?'

Of course I was okay with it!

'Awesome, Ollie! Let's do it! If I beat you though, that makes me the best in the world, right?'

'Sure.'

OLLIE LANG VERSUS SEBASTIAN TERRY

The rules for our challenge were simple: first kill wins. A five-match series, the first man to win three matches would be declared the world's best paintballer. We would start from opposite ends of the arena, and a siren would declare the beginning of each match.

Game One

In the heat of a typical Californian summer's day, I took up position at one end of the arena. At my side I held a fully automatic paintball gun that fired approximately twenty paintballs per second whilst around my waist I had four canisters of extra paintball ammunition. Camouflage army clothes covered me from the neck down and a heavy-duty protective mask meant that my face was visible to no one. This was fortunate as by virtue of this, no one could see my petrified expression.

Across the battlefield, facing me, stood my opponent, Ollie Lang. He looked ready for business; after all, I had approached him with the idea of stealing his crown. Would his experience, skill and tactical genius triumph over my own misguided ambition, or would beginner's luck be on my side? Only time would tell.

Everyone present at the arena had by this stage heard that an Australian had challenged Ollie Lang to a game of one-on-one paintball. They were intrigued and so quite a crowd had gathered around the arena to watch our match. Among all the peculiar looks given to me by random spectators as I readjusted my goggles, one friendly soul offered me some insider knowledge by yelling through the netting, 'Whatever you do, don't ever lose sight of him. Know where he is!'

This seemed like crucial advice and so again I focused on Ollie who was now pre-emptively pointing his gun directly at me.

With that, the siren sounded. I immediately let rip on my trigger, unleashing a round of wayward paintballs into some trees positioned roughly twenty metres outside of the arena.

By the time I looked back down, Ollie was gone. I had already lost him.

With the sound of my own heavy breathing filling my ears, my eyes darted around in the hope of seeing him rushing between inflatable objects, but there was no sign of him. It was like a scene from *Jaws*, only it was me playing the part of the helpless swimmer, floating in what was soon to be blood-filled water. I was being circled.

I decided my best bet was to find shelter and so I sprinted behind a cone to hide. Surely here I would be safe. I tried to reduce my loud panting but I couldn't. Still there was no sign of Ollie; he was a silent assassin. Gathering myself whilst gripping my gun with fear, I hastily made a plan to be the aggressor by way of firing all of my ammunition. However, within moments of springing into action, it dawned on me that I didn't even know which direction to shoot in. Regardless, I fired some shots into a nearby cone, more so to alert the crowd that I was at least aware of how to use my gun. This was probably the worst thing I could have done; Ollie now knew where I was. Moments later, a barrage of paintballs, sent from God knows where, impaled my face at a pace that gave me no option but to fall down, rather ungracefully too. With goggles completely blacked out, I rolled on the ground wondering if perhaps there were other types of world champions in the crowd.

Ollie 1, Seb 0.

Game Two

Having been pelted to the point of blindness in game one, I had quickly acquired a dread of paint and therefore surmised that the best option for the second game would be to use the element of surprise. My thought process was that if I scared Ollie by running straight at him as the siren sounded, he would be struck with so much shock and fear that he would lose the ability to aim his gun accurately, hence allowing me to shoot him at close range. There is, of course, a thin line between bravery and stupidity and sadly I am yet to learn where this line is.

Immediately after the siren sounded, my premeditated kamikaze-style attack was off to a great start; Ollie was still in sight and I had not been hit. However, after only a few seconds, my explosive direct run towards Ollie had become a slow-moving amble. As paintballs whipped past my head, exploding on the ground next to me, I remained unscathed. I'd been lucky and so with the prescience of mind to dive behind the central X-shaped marker, I crawled stealthily to its right side to gauge how scared Ollie was. As I did so, a flurry of paintballs ricocheted into the base of the inflatable millimetres from my fingers, apparently a message from Ollie telling me that not only was he not scared, but he also knew where I was. Nevertheless, game two was going a lot better than game one and so I decided to continue with my plan. I took a deep breath and jumped out into the open before unloading the majority of my ammunition in Ollie's direction. Unfortunately for me, though, Ollie had again disappeared. If it wasn't for the sudden pain in the back of my head, I would have remained in the dark as to his whereabouts. Ollie was somehow now directly behind me and was nice enough to shoot me square in my cranium to let me know so. No wonder this man was the world's best paintballer; he had the ability to teleport!

Ollie 2, Seb 0.

Game Three

This was a game that many of the people present that day will never forget. Having wiped my face of both embarrassment and paint debris, I decided that I needed to channel past war heroes for tactical guidance. Mentally flicking through all of the war movies that I had ever watched, I soon remembered something about the Spartans using a flanking technique to defeat their rivals. If they could do it, so could I, even if there was just one of me.

The siren again sounded and off I dashed to my right, headed for the fence. Apparently having channelled the same war movie, Ollie mirrored my movements. We each fired plumes of ammunition as we sporadically caught sight of one another dashing between inflatables. With near misses occurring with every step, I once again decided to dive for cover, but as I did I felt a ball of paint strike the ankle of my trailing leg. Ollie had got me, again.

Popping back to my feet in order to reveal I had been hit, I saw that Ollie had already started to walk back to his end of the arena. I didn't understand why, as a win here would mean a clean 3–0 scoreline and ultimately a successful defence of his world title. A little confused, I watched him turn around as he walked away and point to the back of his right arm. Somehow I had hit the world's greatest paintball player moments before I myself had been hit!

I was ecstatic. With the scoreline of 2–1, all I needed to do was hit Ollie twice more to become the unofficial best paintballer in the world. It turned out that lifting my arms to the crowd in celebration of my success was the worst thing that I could have done. Whether this action infuriated Ollie, or whether he had now decided I was a genuine threat, I will never know but watching the man stare directly at me as we waited for the game four siren sent shivers down my spine.

Ollie 2, Seb 1.

Game Four

What happened next is still a blur. In short, within ten seconds of the siren sounding, Ollie had painted me as if I were a mobile art canvas. Quite literally my clothes were covered in splashes of red, blue, orange and pink while beneath, my skin was turning black and blue with bruising. I had no vision, no idea where Ollie was, and very little breath. I was a work of art, a product of the world's best paintball artist, Ollie Lang.

Ollie 3, Seb 1.

My chance of becoming a world champion – much like a paintball, really – had exploded in my face, but this didn't matter as I had successfully ticked off another item from my list.

Number 64: Challenge a World Champion – tick!

Chapter 8

WHEN PACKING MY BAGS in Sydney, I had decided that one item that simply had to come with me was my trusty map, the same one that lived on my wall back at home as I worked from my bedroom office. It still had 100 tags placed carefully across the continents and with mental and physical bruising from the world's best paintballer still fresh, I thought it was about time to have a look at it again.

Rolling out the map on the kitchen table at Tal's place, I put my finger on my current location in LA and simply looked at what was nearby. I gazed over Canada, the US and all the way down into Central and South America. There were plenty of tags but one that caught my eye was stuck on the island of Cuba. On it was pencilled 'Number 42: Cycle Through Cuba'.

For no other reason than the fact that it caught my attention, I decided this would be the next item I attempted.

Tal was the first person I told about my new plan and immediately he wanted to help.

'Seb, why don't I give you a few buddy passes on my work account?'

From the tone of Tal's voice, I could tell that he was offering me something nice, but embarrassingly I had no idea what a 'buddy pass' was. Noticing my dull expression, he then explained that as a perk of being a flight attendant, he could offer a certain number of discounted flights to friends and family. With a new understanding of what he was on about, I looked at him with a huge smile plastered across my face. He was a generous guy and I thanked him for the offer. Five minutes later, I booked a ridiculously cheap flight to Cuba.

By this stage I was updating my website as well as my Facebook page almost daily; I loved having a space to write and store photos. With a small group of people following my journey online, I excitedly declared that I was off to Cuba next and that if anyone wanted to join me they should email me. My Facebook status read:

Cycling through Cuba next week, anyone keen to join?

Within hours, I received an email from a bloke called Nic – someone I'd never met.

Mate, I'd be keen to come to Cuba if you're serious?

Never in a million years did I think that someone would actually say yes, but with a positive response from Nic, I was absolutely serious. I loved the idea and so I emailed Nic back saying so.

One day, cheap tickets; the next, the prospect of riding through Cuba with a stranger – things were getting interesting.

Within two days Nic had confirmed he was up for it by booking a flight to Central America and just two weeks later, we set out on one of the most culturally enriching experiences of our lives as we pedalled two calamitous bikes through Cuba. Somewhere between my bike pedal falling off on day one of our trip and giving our bikes away to two families with whom we had become very close on day twenty-one, I realised two things:

1. Money has nothing to do with happiness. If ever you need proof, just go to Cuba and watch the smiles on the locals' faces as they dance barefoot in the streets to the sound of salsa music each and every night of the week.
2. The July Sun in Cuba is just as hot, if not hotter, than the April Sun in Cuba. Either way, unless you're curious to see what sunstroke feels like, I would not recommend attempting cycling through Cuba during these months.

By the time Nic and I had finished our adventure together, we were the best of mates. (Incidentally I had also begun to grow a beard which was Number 88 on my list.) The trip had been incredible in so many ways, but underlying all of these was the refreshing thought that I'd been able to connect and share the experience with a virtual stranger.

Whilst I was in Cuba, two old friends had written to me offering help. The first, Pauly, was an old rugby mate from Australia. Now racing sailboats in and around the US, Pauly insisted that I meet up with one of his crew members by the name of Creature. According to Pauly, Creature was a good man to know and had a spare bed in Coronado, San Diego if I wanted to stay for a while. The second friend to email me was

Rugsy. Hailing from the UK, Rugsy now found himself living the high life in New York as a successful hedge fund manager.

With no idea what I was doing after Cuba, these two emails from Pauly and Rugsy instantly offered me an itinerary and before I knew it, I was knocking on Creature's front door in San Diego.

'Hello?'

'Hey, Creature, I'm Seb – Pauly's mate.' I couldn't think of a better way to phrase my first sentence to Creature after he opened the door.

'Dude, I've been expecting you! Come in. I've got a spare bed waiting for you.'

From the outset, Creature spoke with a friendliness that you'd usually associate with a close mate. He was laid-back, warm and typically Californian.

As he invited me into his house, he gave me a big hug and told me it was great to see me. He showed me to my room and told me that if I wanted anything, all I had to do was ask. When he made us dinner, he mentioned that his family was also excited to meet me and that in the morning we would be going stand-up paddleboarding. After this he'd organised to introduce me to some of his mates. Happy but confused, I couldn't help but wonder if he had mistaken me for his brother. (Funnily enough, I met him the next day too; his name was Pete.)

The next morning I woke up to find Creature standing at the end of my bed with two smoothies.

'So, Seb-Monkey,' he already had a nickname for me, 'I've seen your website, man. I like it.'

I was still half-asleep and grunted.

'What are your plans though, Seb-Monkey?'

I was stoked that he had already had a look at the site, but it was also strange to meet someone for the first time knowing that they already knew quite a bit about what I was up to. I thought about his question whilst sipping on what was quite possibly the best smoothie I'd ever tasted.

'Mate, I don't know. I'm going to visit a friend in New York after here, and then who knows?'

'Come on. You have no plans?' Creature probed for information. Although it didn't matter to him, he seemed to care.

'No, mate; no plans,' I confessed.

Creature sipped on his smoothie then blurted, 'You made of money, Seb-Monkey, or what?'

I certainly wasn't and just to make him laugh I showed him my latest bank balance. I was down to $3000, meaning that somehow I had already spent $6000 since leaving Australia just three months earlier.

'Well, I could get you some work with my dad if you like, Seb-Monkey.'

With no schedule, it's easy to say yes to things, and taking into account that I could probably have done with a few bucks, I agreed to his offer without knowing what Creature's dad actually did. Thankfully it was nothing to do with inflatable movie screens. Instead he just needed help with the upkeep of some of his properties.

For the next four weeks, I worked hard and enjoyed it. The job allowed me time not only to reflect on my recent journey but to brainstorm my next moves.

Sometime during the second week, I ventured into downtown San Diego and bought myself a ukulele. I'd always liked belting out a tune around friends but for the purpose of achieving Number 78: Write and Perform a Song, there seemed to be no better time to confront my fear of performing on stage. Two days later, having written three songs on some scrap paper, I went to a small bar in Pacific Beach and put my name down to perform as part of an open-mic night.

Until this point, my guitar playing had always been in the context of late-night bonfires with mates and if the truth be told, even this intimate environment caused me some degree of nerves. The mere thought of not only performing on stage, but opening up to a crowd of 200 people was a hugely confronting concept.

Worries of being judged, scorned or, even worse, laughed at, deprived me of sleep the night prior to performing. Forgetting the words and falling out of tune were not just nightmares but real possibilities. My only saving grace was that I wasn't doing this for acceptance or recognition; I just wanted to get out of my comfort zone and prove to myself that I could do it. This was my challenge.

On the night of my performance I'd like to say that among a crowd of a few hundred people, my songs made people reflect, laugh and cry, but in reality I have no idea – my eyes barely left the ukulele; I was too nervous to look. Instead I just concentrated on playing the right chords. After the first line of the first song, sweat began to drip from my forehead and by the first chorus it looked as though someone had thrown a glass of water in my face. I was petrified! Somewhere in the middle of the song, my left leg had found its own rhythm and began to shake uncontrollably; I was a wreck.

Luckily I got through the first song unscathed and the crowd started clapping. Although my performance was shabby at best, the fact that they recognised that the song had finished gave me confidence. This in turn somehow helped my overexcited shaky leg to settle down a little as well. With this new-found confidence, I began my second song which sure enough spilled into my third and final song. At some stage, I even managed a quick look up at the crowd and noticed that people were actually listening. It was a great feeling.

As yet Sony BMG has not made a formal approach to sign me up as a solo artist, but I did see one drunken man on his stool try to sing the chorus with me, which – I'm sure you'll agree – was a fantastic effort, for a song that he had never heard before!

When I finally put down my ukulele and walked offstage, the feeling I had within was one of sheer ecstasy; I had teased the boundaries of my comfort zone and had definitely stretched them a little further. My only regret was that I didn't have any more songs to sing. I had loved it!

Number 78: Write and Perform a Song – tick!

Chapter 9

THREE MONTHS HAD PASSED since I'd left Sydney and although I appreciated every little bit of this amazing city, I knew that my immediate future lay elsewhere. I wanted to explore the unknown and for this reason I tried to keep contact with family and friends to a minimum. It wasn't that I was being selfish; I just felt like I needed to be alone, devoid of others' influence. This trip was about me developing as an individual through new experiences and, having always been surrounded by close friends and a wonderful family, I now wanted to find out what life was like without these comforts. By myself, I felt that I could truly see who I was, and this was what I needed.

As I moved around the West Coast of America, so too did word of my journey. The trip was causing quite a stir with friends and strangers alike. I met people from all walks of life who each found a certain aspect of my trip intriguing. 'What have you done so far?' 'What happens when you complete all 100 items?' 'How are you financing this?' The questions were endless and to be honest, I didn't know how to answer most of them. I just did what I did because I could; plans and expectations didn't seem important to me, and as such I had none. Simple.

Considering I had only completed about ten items up to now, I had never anticipated this level of interest and was often amused by the varying reactions that people gave as I explained to them exactly what I was doing. Fellow travellers would high-five me; friends of friends would parade me and others seemed baffled by me.

Something unexpected was developing; I could feel it. I just had no idea what it was! There was something about the journey that excited people.

One morning I received an email from a Brazilian school student in his final year of studies. Somehow he had found my website.

I had received plenty of supportive emails to date but this young man's email was different. It read:

Sebastian,
I am finishing school at the end of the year and I want to know what you think I should do when I finish.
Hugs,
Kahu

Kahu, for some reason, wanted advice from me. I was flattered but ultimately I wasn't sure that *I* was the right person to ask.

I've never claimed to be a source of knowledge or wisdom but when I read Kahu's email I felt a responsibility to answer him. Previously I had always told people that if they were asking *me* for advice, they'd be better off flipping a coin, but this young man had taken the time to reach out at an important time in his life. I remembered feeling the same confusion when I was about to leave school.

I'd like to say that the advice I eventually gave Kahu directly resulted in him becoming President of Brazil whilst also single-handedly winning Brazil their sixth football World Cup title as their inspirational captain, but perhaps that's a little far-fetched. All I said was this:

> Mate,
> Thanks so much for taking the time to email me. I remember when I was at school, weighing up my options of what I should do next, I felt very lost. It was a confusing time. My only advice for you is not to rush into anything that you don't feel is important to you. I have only recently done this myself and I'm twenty-eight years old!
> Just make sure you take a moment to think about the things that are important in your life and make sure that you don't forget this as you move forward. Whatever you do, there will be ups and downs but embrace them all, mate, as they'll combine to make up your memories and experience in life. Let me know if I can be of any help.
> Seb ☺

As I pressed send, by chance, my mum rang from Australia. We hadn't spoken in a while and so after saying hello, I excitedly began to tell her about J-Loc, challenging a world champion and performing songs that I'd written all by myself, but her responses were short and unsupportive. It was clear there was something on her mind.

Then she said, 'Sebastian, don't you think it's time you thought about your future and came home to get a career?'

Instantly I was angry. We had spoken at length about my journey before I had left and although what I was doing was admittedly abstract, I thought I at least had the support of my family.

'Mum, I thought you understood what I was doing. Do you really want me to come home right now?'

It's amazing how the only people able to annoy me so quickly are members of my family.

Her reply was a simple yes.

'I'm so happy at the moment though, Mum. I feel like I'm doing the right thing here. Surely you're happy for me?'

My point, I thought, had been conveyed brilliantly.

'Come home and get a job, Sebastian,' came the reply.

The conversation finished shortly thereafter.

I didn't blame my mum for not understanding my thinking; I think that most mothers would be concerned if their firstborn decided to embark on a journey that included such goals as Skydiving Naked, but with every day that passed I knew I was exactly where I needed to be. With every item that I completed from the list and with each encouraging email that I received from a stranger, I felt enriched with a new appreciation for life. I'd never felt more satisfied.

With Kahu's initial email staring at me on my computer screen, I decided that I would forward it on to my mum; by doing so, I thought that she may see the positive effect that the trip seemed to be having on others. After I pressed send, I decided that I'd go one step further and forward *every* supportive email that I received from then on. Strangely I didn't hear from my mum for a while, probably a result of her inability to turn on a computer let alone send an email, but after a week or so my sister, Pascale, got in touch with me. As always, she asked how I was doing – she loved the idea of travel – but this was not why she was ringing; she wanted to tell me something.

'Seb, do you know that Mum keeps asking me to print out your emails, so she can stick them on the fridge at home?'

Immediately any frustration that remained in my body

disappeared. The fridge, not for the first time in my life, had satisfied a hole within. I never quite realised until that day how important my family's support was to me. I would have continued my journey regardless, but now armed with the knowledge that those closest to me understood me, I felt lighter on my feet.

I was ready to move on.

Chapter 10

DURING MY TIME IN San Diego, I became very close to Creature's family. The warmth they showed me was something that made me feel right at home and when I wasn't working with Creature's brother Pete, I'd be having dinner with their parents, Peggy and Dutch. In fact, in what was becoming something of a daily occurrence, I was making good friends with most people I met. One such group of people to whom I was introduced were friends of Ollie Lang, the paintballer. So tight was this colourful bunch of friends that you'd often find them in the same room, no matter what time of day or how small the room.

From barmen and hairdressers to DJs and jewellery makers, personalities from all kinds of professions came together in one amazing melting pot when these guys met up. Part bohemian, part alternative, part corporate; it was like watching an episode of *Friends* on steroids.

Robbie, a hipster of immense street cred, was one man within this group whom I got to know quite well. The front man of locally known hip-hop group Vokab Kompany, Robbie was a great bloke and before long mentioned that I should consider attending an upcoming festival that they were playing at called Burning Man. In what I believe was more than just a case of coincidence, it just so happened that attending this very event was Number 14 on my list.

Burning Man was a gathering of sorts that took place in the middle of the Nevada desert every year. Themed around self-expression and sustainability, this unique festival was known for its eclectic assortment of individuals and had always seemed to me like an event where any traces of normality were dispensed with along with dress codes, rules and any need for a watch. I was intrigued.

'We've all been to "The Man" for the past eight years, man!' said Robbie. I should have known. 'Why don't you join our camp this year? We call it Camp Pep.'

'I'd love to,' I said, and that was that.

Meeting people was seemingly the way in which my journey now took shape – something that reminded me of surfing. When you surf, the power of your board is reliant on the size of the wave and the momentum you have. A wave is made of many parts, called sections, and the more sections you're able to link up, the further you'll go. Whether I had stumbled upon an amazing wave break or somehow created a wave of my own, sections within my own journey just kept linking up. I had no plan or expectation that they would do so, but I simply knew that there were many more sections to come. I was enjoying this wave.

Another interesting character within this group was known only as Killer. Killer didn't give much away, but with a flowing ponytail, good looks and a certain aura that would lead you to believe that he was a time traveller from the future, he seemed to have it all sorted out. I actually had no idea what Killer did with himself for a living but could only hope that his nickname was not a reflection of any of his pastimes. He was a mysterious but seemingly very grounded bloke and with this came my respect.

Whilst at a house party that the group had invited me to one night, Killer and I spoke about things in life that meant a lot to us and casually he mentioned the time that he married two friends at their wedding.

'One of the most amazing moments ever, dude. Got to help two of my best friends reach a place together where they connected on a higher level,' he said, his calm voice enforcing that he meant what he was saying. I thought this sounded amazing.

'So you're a priest?' I guessed.

'No, man. I just became ordained so I could be their celebrant.' His expression never changed. I was thoroughly confused.

'I don't understand, Killer – so you just became a celebrant for one day? How can you even do that?'

'Online, man; it's easy. You should do it.'

The expression 'only in America' is sometimes misused but in this context I thought it was perfect. How could anyone simply become a wedding minister by applying online? Whatever the answer, at that moment in my life I couldn't see anything more important.

'It's all official too, man, full-on ordination,' he added.

'But how much does it cost?' I asked.

'It's free, dude!'

And by the powers vested in me as a free thinker, I pronounced that I had filled in one of the vacant items on my list, Number 27: TBA, was now Minister a Wedding.

That evening, on my laptop, I found the website offering free ordination and began filling in the online application form. One minute later, I had completed it. All I needed was a name and an address, both of which I had.

From that moment on, I was Reverend Sebastian Terry; my friends called me Rev Seb.

I left California a few days later to join Camp Pep in Nevada for the Burning Man Festival.

Chapter 11

HEAD EAST OF RENO for two hours and you'll find yourself in the middle of the desert, quite literally. The Black Rock Desert.

Barren desert spans for kilometres, with mountain ranges peering down from afar. A vast sky hangs high above while a slow-passing sun scorches all that rests below. There is nowhere to hide out here. The only frequent visitor is a wind that creates a huge duststorm across the playa. As it builds, mini dust-tornadoes chase each other like kids at play, before zero visibility sets in. This place is desolate, dry and uninhabitable. That is, until 50,000 people from around the globe throw a party here for one week every year. This is the Burning Man Festival.

If you've ever wondered where the world's most bizarre, unique or eccentric people hang out, here is your answer.

For seven days at the beginning of September each year, a huge tent city, in a circular formation, is created. In the middle of this circle stands an enormous wooden effigy, the Burning

Man – he is why everyone has come. On the seventh night this man will be set alight as a sign of freedom.

The Burning Man Festival embraces the free spirit through radical self-expression. People come here to escape life's normal constraints. No power is used, no whitegoods, nothing. There is no money used at the festival, either; instead you live in a temporary society that is founded on a strong sense of community and free trade.

Burning Man answers a very interesting question: If you took away all the rules, regulations and societal expectations that exist in our world, what would you be left with?

For two hours we crawled in a long procession of cars to the entrance, a fascinating vision in the middle of a desert. As we got closer to the actual gate, strangely dressed officials darted between cars checking tickets and also that each person had enough water, food and shelter for the seven days. Camp Pep had all these bases covered.

Finally when we reached the front of the queue, a naked man thrust his head through the window and welcomed us to the desert.

'Welcome, my brothers. Are there any Burning Man virgins in the car?'

The answer was yes, and out of the car I was dragged, with Mek Mek, Flip and Robbie all laughing at my expense.

Before I could yell 'Help!', the sweaty naked man grabbed me and hugged me tightly. The initiation was awkward yet friendly.

'Welcome, my brother. Now get down on the earth, my brother, and roll around!' he ordered.

The earth was, of course, dusty, and unlike this naked man, I had clothes on, clean ones at that, but I had already decided that for the next seven days I was going to embrace anything that came my way. I jumped to the ground accordingly.

After rolling around and filling my nostrils with dust, I was asked to stand before being handed a hammer. With this hammer I would complete the initiation by striking a large bell that sat just beyond the festival entrance. The guys started cheering as I swung the hammer wholeheartedly, creating a chime that travelled across the desert.

We had arrived.

Camp Pep knew exactly what to do when it came to Burning Man. They had food rations, tent set-up and bicycle distribution covered. With tens of thousands of people pitching their tents across a three-kilometre diameter, we needed bikes as walking would become too exhausting.

The Burning Man Festival is bizarre to describe but let me start with its physical appearance. Picture a watch face and for a moment imagine that this watch face is actually a bird's-eye view of the festival. Centrally on the face, where the hands of the watch are joined, sits the wooden effigy of the Man whilst on the outer perimeter of the watch face are the second markers; these represent the first of many rows of tents which stretch way out beyond the edge of the watch face. There are literally tens of thousands of tents which, starting from the two o'clock mark and stretching around to the ten o'clock mark, encircle the Man. The space between the Man and the first tent row is left bare for an array of objects and activities that take place during the festival.

People of all sorts had come to the festival and everyone knew that once through the gate, all links to things considered as normal on the outside should be forgotten. Doctors, lawyers and business owners mingled with artists, hippies, spiritual healers. There were no differences here.

As part of Camp Pep, I was given a nice little two-man tent that held all my belongings perfectly. After setting it up and neatly packing all my possessions at one end, while leaving

space for my sleeping-bag and pillow at the other, Robbie
came over and told me not to worry about zipping it up. When
I asked why, he just laughed and told me that the playa dust is
so fine that no matter what you do, it blows right through the
fabric. He wasn't wrong; the next morning I woke up covered
in a thick film of grey dust.

In any other circumstances this would have prompted a
shower and a change of clothes, but it just seemed to be part
of the deal here in the middle of the desert. Lucky that; there
weren't any showers anyway.

Waking each morning to a blistering sun beating down on
your tent, the first move out of bed was always the hardest. It
was a matter of gaining enough energy to get up, get dressed
and get excited.

'Have a look in this, Oz, and take what you need for the
day,' said Robbie.

Apparently I now had my own Burning Man name, Oz. With
that, he threw me a massive bag full of fancy-dress clothes.
From Arabic headwear and strange leather items, to feathers
and G-strings, this bag had fun written all over it. I took what
I thought would look most ridiculous and quickly transformed
myself into a bandana-wearing pirate with no dress sense. The
beard that I'd been growing since cycling through Cuba with
Nic would only now find its true calling and it took next to
no time for a random girl to paint it orange. In a place where
facial hair of all types was not only accepted but encouraged,
I, like many others, fitted right in.

Proud of my outfit of choice, I went to find the rest of the
guys who had gathered at the front of our camp. As I turned
the corner to see them all together for the first time, I suddenly
realised how overdressed I was. Some wore nothing but see-
through plastic, others wore only body paint, whilst those who
simply couldn't bother getting dressed stood around casually in

the nude. From that moment on, I resorted mainly to Speedos, a mankini and for one afternoon, my birthday suit.

My first excursion in and around the playa was like a scene from *Star Wars*. On every corner, people were playing music, meditating or making crafts. A makeshift rollerskating rink sat next to a twenty-four-hour free-hug parlour. As we cycled around, I felt an intangible energy that came from liberation and self-expression, and the longer we pedalled into the tent city, the clearer it became that we were only a small part of something so much larger.

With no showers available, the only way for those desperate to wash during the week was to follow the water trucks around. These trucks, employed to wet the sandy roads so that bikes could ride freely on them, would release a spray of water from their rear as they drove slowly around the city for a few hours each day. The first time one passed me, I saw ten or so naked women and men chasing after it trying to get sprayed. However weird I thought this was at the time, within days I found myself doing the same thing. (That water was refreshing!)

Next, a group dressed in tinfoil stopped us on a dusty road, insisting that they hug every one of us before wishing us a 'Good Burn' and moving on in a direction that quite honestly I don't think mattered to them. We were all just *there* – it didn't matter what we did.

T-Bop, one of the larger-than-life characters at Camp Pep, noticed that I had a ukulele and approached me with his 'keytar'. Slung around his neck like an electric guitar, this child-sized keyboard played a wicked demo tune and perfectly complemented the tiger-print hotpants that T-Bop wore proudly. Striking up an amazing rapport based on the fact that we both owned tiny instruments (so to speak) and shared a love of kid-sized fancy dress, we decided to walk around the city stopping at themed camps that offered free drinks or free use of hammocks and checking out the incredible art pieces that would pop up overnight. A giant spaceship that sat alone in the playa on day one would be clad with a climbing frame, just as tall, by sunrise on day two.

Seconds melted into minutes and hours fused into days. Before long any comprehension of time was lost. On one occasion I decided to wander out into the desert for a break from every-one. As I walked towards the horizon, the playa dust whipping off the ground in the wind and limiting my vision, I glimpsed a man in the distance sitting alone on a chair. In front of the man was what appeared to be a tall wooden lemonade stand and on the other side of that was a vacant chair facing him. Looking around, confused as to what this guy was doing all by himself in the desert, I decided to approach him. As I got closer, his image became clearer and I realised that he was not there to give away soft drink; instead, written in chalk on the headboard above the stand was the word 'Advice'. I was intrigued. I sat down oppos-ite the man without saying a word.

After an awkward silence the man finally inquired, 'How can I help you?' He wore a scarf around his head and goggles over his eyes, effectively hiding his whole face. A colourful Hawaiian shirt protected his body from the sun. I, on the other hand, wore a pair of Speedos and a surf-lifesaving cap.

'I'd like some advice, please,' I replied, unsure of what else to say.

'Tell me about yourself,' he said, his hands resting lightly on the ledge in front of him.

I went on to explain my journey to the man. No matter how bizarre my explanation may have sounded to the many people I had met on my trip so far, I took solace in the thought that this guy was 100 per cent more peculiar than me.

'. . . and so that's how I ended up here in this chair talking to you,' I concluded.

By this stage, the man had leaned in as if to hear more clearly and his arms were now crossed, propping himself up on the ledge. He didn't respond immediately; he just sat there motionless.

'I haven't said this before to anyone at this stall, but I can't give you any advice,' he said at last. 'You're doing just what you need to be doing.'

With that, he rocked back into his chair assuming his original position and looked up to the sky, dismissing me. He was done. All I could do was say thank you.

I rose from my chair and continued walking into the desert, looking back over my shoulder once or twice wondering what on earth had just happened. Then I burst out laughing, at myself more than anything else.

Other than bikes, the only vehicles allowed on the playa were 'art cars', which belonged to individuals or camps. If you picture a standard vehicle such as a car, van or bus being cross-bred with a sea monster, a pirate ship or even a dragon before then being dipped in a barrel of mixed paints, you'll have a perfect image of what these art cars looked like. Confused? Well, so am I, and I've seen them from close up. They were huge and, cruising slowly around the desert like dinosaurs, they would host a party for all who cared.

For someone with very little cash, the concept of a money-free society was highly convenient. It was clear that no one at Burning Man looked at anything from a monetary point of view and so there was no concept of gain or loss, there was just community. Occasionally head massages would be exchanged for drinks, or hair braiding for the loan of a bike, but I never once saw, let alone used, money; it simply had no value.

After a hot, dry day in the sun, the biggest transformation of all, however, was saved for dusk.

'You wait till you see it at night, bro!' said Mek Mek on my first day at The Man. 'It's my favourite thing about this place; it looks like Vegas, man!'

Sure enough, as the sun set over the mountainous horizon to the west, this alternative-looking shantytown would come alive and change pace from walk to sprint. Lights appeared from nowhere and music began to pump. Art cars would glow in the dark and emit lasers that pierced the sky as they turned into mega party vehicles. The larger domes that sat unnoticed during the day now shone brightly, like beacons in the night, drawing in groups of people. By midnight our city of tents was one huge thriving organism. People partied in tents in the playa and in the art cars. It was a different type of energy, more emphatic than during the daytime, and it spread like wildfire.

Day attire was swapped for shocking yet stylish nightwear; glowsticks flickered in unison as music exploded across the desert. The feeling was unparalleled to anything I had ever experienced, a shared state of euphoria fuelled by a rare kind of openness.

Now, I'm fully aware that I probably sound like a 1960s flower-wearing hippie right now (which is interesting as I had never up until this moment considered myself particularly spiritual), but without doubt, that day, that night, and that week, there was an energy or presence that I had never felt before, a product of a shared mindset. We were in the middle of a desert, yet it was the greatest place on earth to be. We were one. It was a fleeting glance at Utopia.

On my final night, the after-dark activities revolved around the Man being set alight and burnt, symbolising freedom but in slightly different ways for everyone there. By midnight every art car, every person and every other type of being there (I'm convinced there were others!) had gathered at the centre of the camp, surrounding the Man. As whispers that the Man was about to light up spread among the crowd of 50,000 people, a hush slowly set in. Around me was everyone from Camp Pep – these guys I now considered the best of friends – and just as we wrapped our arms around the person next to us, there was an enormous explosion followed by a chorus of noise; the Man was alight! Fire lit up the desert and engulfed the Man within seconds. Everyone went wild; the true party had begun.

As the night sky became paler in the early morning, the crowd thinned out and soon I found myself with my old partner in crime, T-Bop. We had somehow scaled one of the larger climbing frames and were looking out across the desert towards the mountains to the east. T-Bop, wearing a top hat and vest, stared out into the distance while, next to him wearing eye make-up, a bandana and ripped clothes, I did the same. We didn't speak, but we each knew what the other was thinking; we wanted to see the sun rise and so in an act which made sense only at the time, we stretched our arms out with our palms facing up, urging it to rise from behind the mountains. In any other setting, we would have been looked upon as crazy, but at that moment it just seemed like the right thing to do and soon enough the first streak of light shot out across the desert as the sun slowly began to reveal itself.

This was the beginning of a new day – the day that sadly I would leave Burning Man.

It's been said that trying to explain Burning Man to someone who has never been is like trying to explain colour to a blind person. Only now, having been there, can I grasp what this means.

Is Burning Man a festival, an event or even a party? I don't think it's any of these things; it's a way of life.

Chapter 12

COURTESY OF TAL'S BUDDY passes, I enjoyed a business-class flight to New York. Having only ever flown in economy, I couldn't believe the discrepancy between the two classes and to be honest, I felt like a stowaway for most of the journey. Among fully reclining seats, endless supplies of food and drink and flight attendants rushing to your every need, I was embarrassingly still trying to pick flakes of orange paint from my messy beard.

It was time to meet up with my old mate, Rugsy. With a belief that having no plan was in fact the best plan, I met him smack bang in the middle of a city that I had a feeling would offer plenty of surprises.

'Seb, mate, you look about forty years old!'

'Cheers, Rugsy, good to see you too!'

Apparently my beard, which by this stage was sixty days old itself, did nothing for my appearance, and after years of not seeing each other, Rugsy probably thought that this was my usual get-up.

'Mate, is that orange paint in there as well?'

That afternoon, as we walked slowly towards Rugsy's office, we got to catch up on each other's lives. It had been a long time between drinks for us.

Previously a lone ranger, Rugsy had met a girl in England and moved to Switzerland with her shortly after we had said goodbye six years earlier. Not long after this, they had a baby girl, Annabelle. An avid sportsman, he then started to play rugby in the local competition, through which he made a new group of friends who helped him land a job in Geneva's illustrious finance industry. Soon after realising that he had a gift for making money, Rugsy's mother sadly passed away, prompting him to re-evaluate his life. This was the catalyst that Rugsy needed, and after much thought he decided that it was time to take on a challenge that he'd always known he'd wanted to attempt. This was to start his own business. Setting aside his fears and other things that had held him back, he began his own company and within a very short period, his Geneva-based business had spread successfully to New York and also to Brazil. Just like me, Rugsy had acted on his moment of clarity and achieved something that he had always wanted to do.

'And it all took off for me here in New York, Seb,' he told me.

We had found our way onto Wall Street and were standing in front of a bronze statue of a charging bull.

'If you kiss it on the head, it's meant to bring you money,' Rugsy explained. 'It was the first thing I did when I came to New York and it worked! Give it a go, mate.'

I was intrigued, but evidently so too were many other tourists in the area who I noticed had formed a long line towards the front of the bull. Although I wanted to kiss the bull too, I didn't want to wait in line. However, with an almost-empty wallet and a bank account to match, I knew a kiss wouldn't go astray and so I quickly ran to the back end of the bull and kissed him square on the buttocks. Now it was just a matter of waiting, no?

With a metallic taste still in my mouth, we headed for Rugsy's office which overlooked Lexington Avenue. In a corporate world that I had no experience with, I kind of felt like a teenage nephew that Rugsy had decided to show around his workplace for the day. As we walked into his office, he introduced me to a group of six people who worked for him. They all swivelled around from their computers and phones to see who had entered. Feeling like I'd disturbed a group of important adults from working, I put down my backpack and waved awkwardly. With that, the girl closest to me threw me offguard with a question.

'Hey, Seb, how long has it been with the beard now?'

Who was this person? I was pretty certain I'd never met her but she seemed to know me. To cover any surprise, I just laughed and quickly replied, 'It's been sixty days now, actually.'

'I've been following your site since Rugsy first mentioned it,' she explained. 'Well done – it's inspirational.'

Among a room that saw millions of dollars traded on a daily basis, I found it bizarre that these people even took an interest in what I was doing.

'Did you really marry a stranger in Vegas?' came another question from a man who had poked his head out from his private office to say hello.

'Yeah, I did,' I replied, laughing with the rest of the guys as the man leaned over in disbelief.

'You're crazy, man, but I wish I could do some of the stuff you've done.'

I've never been comfortable with accepting compliments – I don't know why, but for some reason they make me feel awkward – and even on this occasion I think I blushed. It just all seemed so surreal.

'Mate, you could do what I do,' I replied. 'Just fly to Vegas and find someone to marry!'

To me, it was as easy as this, but again the room filled with laughter.

Then he walked over to me and handed me a fifty-dollar note. 'That's for your charity, man! Good job and keep it up!'

Rugsy then took me into his office. He could tell that I was surprised at the warm welcome.

'Mate, we've been following you for a while now; it's great! In fact, if you don't mind, I'd love to help you tick off one of your items while you're out here. What have you got planned?'

As it happened, whilst being served grapes by attractive female flight attendants at 10,000 metres that morning, I had actually come up with a few ideas of things to do in New York.

'Well, mate, there is something I'm thinking about doing here, actually. All I need is a guitar,' I said.

Chapter 13

I'VE ALWAYS BEEN FASCINATED by street performers. Does someone choose to perform on a footpath because they love singing, juggling or posing as a statue? Or is it purely because they need money? If so, how much could a person make? Now in New York, a city virtually overrun with incredible street performers, it was time to find out by tackling Number 16: Street Performance.

My goal was simple. I was going to play guitar and sing until I made $100 – even if it took a week – and then I would donate it all to Camp Quality.

DAY ONE
Central Park

In theory, a street performance seemed easy. Find a spot, sit down and sing, right? Wrong. First I had to expand on the three songs that I knew by heart. The solution: print out song lyrics.

Armed with a guitar, its case and a wad of song lyrics, I ventured nervously into Central Park at 10 am on day one. An overcast day meant fewer park visitors, but regardless there was music in the air. My first destination was the popular Sheep Meadow, a large field within Central Park, where people often hung out.

A three-piece band had beaten me to the area. They were already entertaining a big group of generous onlookers with a fantastic mix of blues and funk. I would have enjoyed their performance but for the fact that today we were competing for the public's loose change and sadly, for me, they were far more talented than I. They even had their own CDs for sale. A guitar case full of notes, placed in front of their performing area, acted as a sign for other street performers to stay away and so onwards I walked. I could take a hint.

Navigating past violinists and saxophonists alike, I eventually found a quiet spot under a small bridge with no other performers nearby. I entered the dark, rarely frequented space and looked around, feeling a little bit like a troll. It was time to perform.

Nervously I got my guitar out of its case and placed my song sheets beside me. A narrow ledge offered a place to sit down and the dim light under the bridge hid my nerves. The act of placing an empty guitar case on the ground was something I never thought would be so hard – a desperate plea to the public that I wanted their money – but I did so then took a deep breath and readied myself to play my first note to the world. 'Save Tonight' by Eagle-Eye Cherry was first up and although I knew how to play the song, it certainly didn't sound that way as I forgot the first line.

Coincidentally, as soon as I started playing, a procession of people walked through the tunnel. I am adamant that this was pure coincidence and not because of my singing, but either way I managed to get a few early donations which settled my jittery stomach. In fact with every passer-by that looked my way, my confidence grew. I even took the mindless clapping from the occasional toddler being pushed past me in their pram as applause. My confidence was building, and with about fifteen dollars in donations within the first hour I decided to move to my next stop, Grand Central Station.

Grand Central Station

Grand Central Station, the second busiest train station in New York after Times Square–42nd Street, was a haven for street performers. A central transfer point for most stops in Manhattan, my mediocre music repertoire would be heard by thousands of people in the labyrinth of commuter tunnels, platforms and walkways. It was perfect.

The tricky task of finding a convenient singing spot resulted in me taking a position on the same platform on which I arrived, platform four. When the next train arrived and busy office workers and tourists burst out of the open carriage doors, I grabbed my guitar and began to strum. Everything was going so well until the doors of the next train opened. As the exiting passengers spilled onto the platform, a four-piece Mexican mariachi band stepped out of the train in full song. Adorned in traditional costume and holding guitars, they were brilliant and unfortunately for me, the crowd loved them. They had the X factor and managed to transform the platform into a vibrant street in Mexico City. With my head bowed, I left the Mexicans to wow the crowd while I again headed off in search of a quieter area to play.

By late afternoon I had become highly efficient at setting up camp at a moment's notice. Leaning against pillars, sitting on empty milk crates or even balancing on gates, I witnessed an array of reactions as people walked past; some turned their noses up at me while others smiled or stopped to listen. I felt dirty, disrespected and happy all at the same time. Regardless, it wasn't long before I was belting out high notes with no apprehension. By the time I left Grand Central Station and headed for Union Square, I had over forty dollars!

Union Square

A creative hub for youths on Manhattan Island, Union Square is filled with breakdancers, clowns, celebrity impersonators and any other type of performer you could care to name. Not needing the competition, I reluctantly gathered my thoughts as I set up my virtually empty guitar case under a big arch structure and began the playlist.

Now, I'd be lying if I said I made good money that afternoon; in fact, I think I only made about two dollars courtesy of a little child whose mum encouraged him to donate, but I did get some invaluable advice from a talented saxophonist who was playing just across from me.

'It always good to stand out when performing to a crowd, man.'

Standing at almost two metres himself, his movie star looks and dreadlocked hair certainly made him stand out. Eyeing the hat full of money that he also had sitting at his feet, I began to think about this piece of advice.

At the end of day one, I had just less than fifty dollars in the case, meaning that I needed more than double that to raise my target of $100.

DAY TWO

That night I brainstormed ways to stand out whilst performing and as I drifted off to sleep, an idea struck me. A phone call to Rugsy to discuss my idea confirmed that it was ridiculous enough perhaps to work and so we hatched a plan on the spot. It was time to start a boy band.

With the addition of Rugsy and also Jack, a friend of

Rugsy's who was apparently always up for a laugh, the next morning we were three. After a quick wardrobe check at a nearby fancy-dress shop, our tone-deaf trio entered the streets of New York not as mere mortals, but as superheroes.

Courtesy of three kids-size costumes, we were Superman, Batman and Robin. I wore a retro-style Batman suit (including face mask), Rugsy fitted surprisingly well into a Robin outfit while Jack filled his Superman suit somewhat graphically. We were comical. Although armed with a ukulele, bongos and a rusty harmonica, neither Superman nor Robin had any musical talent, leaving us to rely on Batman's – that is, my – very limited ability.

It was a Saturday in New York and the streets were packed. Within seconds of setting foot in public, it was clear that we stood out. Cars tooted, children pointed and parents laughed. One group of ladies immediately ran over to us and asked if they could have their photo taken with us. Of course we said yes and in return they decided to give us five dollars. Next, a father who had been watching from a distance with his child asked for another photo before donating a further two dollars. Without playing a single note on our instruments, we had made seven dollars in just a few minutes and a growing crowd suggested that any plan to play a song would have to be put on hold. Quite literally we were being mobbed.

Two hours later, with a guitar case brimming with money, we decided to change location but only a block away we were dragged into a pub to play a song to a bemused bunch of inebriated locals. This soon led us to play in a variety of spots, including one restaurant where we were invited to stand on the tables and perform to lunchtime diners.

Before long, nothing seemed weird anymore and interestingly we had also proved two important points:

1. Talent is not a necessity to becoming a successful boy band.
2. Although able to fly faster than a speeding bullet, Superman lacks any form of musical ability including rhythm. Jack was ape-like on the bongos.

By the time we made it to busy Union Square late in the afternoon, we were having too much fun for our own good. I'd almost go as far as to say that we'd all got a little too into character; we thought we were invincible. After posing for photos with police officers, singing to a bridal party and entertaining a crowd of toddlers, an attractive nanny approached us and mentioned that her child had twenty dollars to donate if we agreed to the little one's request. Wanting to impress both the nanny and the child equally, we all leapt at the opportunity.

'So, what would you like us to do, buddy?' I asked the innocent-looking child.

'A song?' asked Superman.

'Maybe a photo?' chipped in Rugsy.

'No, I want you to swim in the fountain,' came the demand from the troublesome kid.

'Oh,' we all sighed.

Seconds later, we were in the middle of the large fountain, soaking wet. It's funny how a day of street busking can end up.

The day had been a roaring success. In total, our trio had made more than $300 and the next morning I donated the money online to Camp Quality.

Number 16: Street Performance – tick!

Chapter 14

EVERYTHING SEEMED TO BE falling into place for me in New York.

Having not worked for six months, I was down to my last dollar, but with Rugsy's need to tidy up some basic admin duties in the office came an opportunity for me to earn some money as an office assistant. Suddenly with a flexible work schedule that provided me with at least some money to survive, I found that I could quite easily continue to tick off items in New York.

Sometimes these two things, work and my list, combined to offer several of the strangest experiences of my life. One day I even turned up to work with a strip of duct tape across my mouth. You see, Number 29 on the list was to stay silent for one week and since I was living in one of the world's busiest cities, I thought it was an excellent setting to attempt this ridiculous challenge.

The rules were simple:

1. No oral communication of any sort. (This includes whistling or humming.)
2. Sneezing, coughing and burping are allowed (but only naturally).
3. Laughing is not permitted.
4. Written communication is fine.
5. If any of the above rules are broken, the seven-day time period will immediately reset.

The severity of this challenge was something I only realised once I started the seven-day timer and walked straight into a juice shop to order my favourite smoothie. Without words, I felt helpless; my jaw tightened and my mind raced. A mental set of handcuffs formed and my inner voice became immensely louder. I felt like I was in a bubble.

It wasn't only the fact that I couldn't speak to others that proved to be tricky; it became clear early on that people would find it hard to communicate with me! With all my pointing, motioning and writing down words on a whiteboard that I equipped myself with, many people assumed I was deaf or intellectually impaired. On one occasion, a lovely old lady grabbed my hand on the subway and led me to an exit as if I was a lost child. Not having the ability to explain that I wasn't looking for the exit, I simply had to go with her. Consequently I missed my train.

I'm not sure I've ever had to concentrate so hard to achieve something seemingly so effortless and after only one day of silence I stuffed up while meeting a friend called Liz.

'How was your day, Seb?' she asked.

'Good, thanks!' I replied.

My head immediately dropped as I realised I had just broken my silence that, up until that point, just twenty hours into the challenge, had exhausted me of all of my energy.

'Does this mean you can talk now?' Liz asked.

I just shook my head from side to side. The clock had been reset.

After attending various social functions, at which I was introduced to a room full of people as 'The Australian who can't talk', I couldn't believe how much attention my whiteboard and I would command. People would surround me as I gestured and wrote things down.

Humour was something that I also had to forget about for seven days as I learned that witty one-liners have a somewhat limited impact when written down on paper and delivered minutes after a conversation has finished. Ironically it was this inability to make a joke that made my blind date on day four so humorous.

In what was proving to be a bizarre social experiment, I soon discovered that by not talking I was able to offer something that many women feel they can't find very easily: a man who listens. After six days of silence, rumours had spread around the office that Rugsy had employed a sensitive New-Age guy from Australia who listened. As a result, female members of staff (some of whom I knew and some of whom I didn't) would come into my office and vent their feelings on either a business or personal level. I couldn't help but feel that I'd turned into a verbal boxing bag for frustrated women who were unable to talk to their male colleagues.

One girl who felt particularly frustrated was Hayley, a girl I knew from school whom I ran into on the street one day. You can imagine our surprise when we bumped into one another on Manhattan's busy 14th Street, having not seen each other for almost ten years.

'Seb! Is that you? Oh my God, how are you?'

I was, of course, quite literally speechless; all I could do in response was wave. Unfortunately I'd headed out for the day without my whiteboard and pen and knew that no matter how hard I tried, Hayley would not understand why I couldn't talk to her. I felt useless. Catching up on ten years would have to wait. After realising I couldn't speak, and then wishing me luck for what she thought was a meditation-related silence exercise, she walked off with a confused and slightly disappointed face. Without her details to contact her later, I could only hope she eventually found out the real reason why I had nothing to say to her.

Over the period of a week, I also realised just how many words people waste. With no verbal feedback to offer someone talking directly to me, I found that they would choose their words more carefully, constantly double-checking what they were about to say so as not to sound silly. Similarly for me, the silence which at first scared me so much was something I came to appreciate and once my mind learned to relax, I found I processed things with more ease and was so much more aware of my surroundings. I was more receptive on every level. I held people's attention with a simple smile and I learned the difference between hearing and listening.

Number 29: One Week's Silence was an item that made me re-evaluate the way I presented myself. Maybe I did talk too much?

Chapter 15

DURING THE WEEK OF silence, my old mate Pauly, who had put me in touch with Creature in San Diego, emailed to tell me that he and some of his sailing crew were in New York for a few days. This would be our first catch-up in years and was also a chance to meet some more of his crew. The only difficult thing would be that I wouldn't actually be able to talk to them. I apologised in advance.

'Here he is! Rev Seb, you idiot, how are ya?' Pauly's familiar voice boomed across the hotel lobby where we'd arranged to meet.

Pauly and his four crew members had taken up position on a long couch at the back of the room.

'Waitress, we need a pen and paper for this boofhead!' yelled Pauly again.

Pauly and his sailing crew all laughed loudly as I walked over and after shaking hands with everyone, they all stared at me waiting to see if I was legitimate about my silence. I was. Without a word, I just smiled cheekily. I was then introduced to the crew members: Lex Luther, Cocko, the owner of Team Bliksem, Piet, and his business partner, Thijs.

Sympathetic to my vow of silence, the guys were patient with me as we had a few drinks and before long they even began using my pen and paper that the waitress had brought over as a way of communicating between one another. They were good value and all top blokes.

Pauly, a lovely guy, took it upon himself to tell the boys why it was that I was silent. Mimicking the role of PR agent, he spoke of my list of 100 things, sharing a few of the items that I'd done and also mentioning Camp Quality.

'Then after the bloody idiot got smashed in a one-on-one game of paintball against the world's best player, he went online and became a proper reverend – Rev Seb!'

Until that moment I hadn't realised how closely Pauly had followed my adventures and as he talked about the items that I had completed, he became more and more animated. Once again, it was incredible to see that someone knew so much about my journey without me ever speaking to them about it.

As he spoke, the others started firing questions at me. Sadly for me, not being able to speak meant that I had to write down all my answers and soon my wrist was sore.

With every story told by Pauly came slightly more intrigue and even more laughter. Thijs, a tall Dutchman like Piet, seemed to be loving it but he also just kept shaking his head in disbelief at me. He was astounded that someone would voluntarily impose a week's ban of talking upon themselves, among the variety of other things I'd done. The more he laughed, the more he leaned forwards.

'Do you have a website, man?' he asked.

I nodded and wrote down the address on our communal piece of paper that by now looked as though a bunch of infants had been practising their handwriting on it; it was a mess.

Thijs told me he'd look it up. He appeared genuinely interested.

Unfortunately by the time we'd all got used to communicating via the written word, Pauly had to leave. Our catch-up, although possibly a little thin on information exchanged, was awesome, and it made me happy to see Pauly enjoying himself.

As we said goodbye, a sense of complete satisfaction ran through my body; despite standing in the lobby of a random hotel in New York with little to my name other than a back-pack full of clothes, I felt I was just where I needed to be – surrounded by great people and an awareness of opportunity. I was loving life.

The last two people to whom I said goodbye were Piet and Thijs. As I shook Piet's hand, he gave me a big smile and offered his house at nearby Scarsdale if I ever needed to crash somewhere. I smiled and awkwardly half-bowed in an attempt to gesture thank you. Thijs then approached me and stretched out his arm to shake my hand as he smiled from ear to ear.

'Seb, man, I think you're a crazy guy but I want to talk to you when you're able to speak. What you're doing is great, man, and I think I might be able to help you out!'

As I had done all day, I nodded my head and smiled. I had no idea what Thijs had in mind but the thought of someone showing support, especially a stranger, was always a good feeling.

Little did I know just how much Thijs wanted to help me.

Chapter 16

WITH ANOTHER ITEM TICKED from the list and a few more planned for the coming weeks, a friend emailed me one day and suggested I meet up with some of her contacts in New York if I had the time. Time was certainly something I did have and that same evening I headed into town to meet a couple of strangers whom I was told I'd love. With the ability to speak once more, I couldn't wait! This led me to meeting Ailie.

Living and working in New York had been a dream of Ailie's for a while and now that she was accomplishing it, it was quite clear she was enjoying every minute she was there. She loved the vibe of the city and slotted in comfortably with its fun social scene. Over the course of the evening, we got around to talking about what I was doing, which – as it tended to do – led to a lot of questions that seemed to leave others either questioning my sanity or applauding my spirit. Interestingly though, after an hour or so of laughing mainly at my expense, Ailie excused herself for a moment and, when she came back, sat down and made a confession.

'You're a little intimidating, you know.'

This took me by surprise; I had never been told I was intimidating before and so I asked her why she thought that. Her
reply was short and to the point.

'You make other people feel boring.'

I didn't know what to say. I never meant to come across this
way and even the suggestion that this might be the case made
me feel terrible.

'Really? I'm just doing what I need to be doing. Everyone
should be able to do that, right?'

'But we don't all have a list, do we?'

My list was the simplest way for me to gather all my goals
in one place and also happened to be the easiest way to explain
to people what I was doing.

'Well,' I said, 'I think everyone has at least one thing they
want to do before they die, no matter how big or small, and
if you happen to have more than one thing, then by definition
that's a list, no?'

Ailie nodded as she considered my explanation. Her brow
tensed as she began thinking.

'Well, I've always wanted to learn how to play guitar.' As
she said this, her brow returned to its original position. 'And
I've always wanted to see if I could live off twenty dollars for a
whole week in New York!' It seemed like I wasn't the only one
with a list, after all. 'That's it,' she continued without me saying
a thing. 'I'm going to write down my own list and send it to
you when I'm done!'

And sure enough a few days later, I received an email from
Ailie with an attachment titled 'My List'.

Ailie's list was awesome. From naming just two things
in the bar, she managed to send me a full list of precisely
100 things. To see that she had taken the time to think about
what she wanted to do made me feel great. She too was

overjoyed and by virtue of us both having lists, we became good friends.

Ailie began concentrating on her goals and very soon she became the proud owner of a guitar. Not only this, but she started to learn how to play it; she literally couldn't stop talking about it. She had developed a refreshing focus and her enthusiasm for her goals was huge. I was so moved by what I saw that I wrote a little blog about her and her new guitar on my site, but this didn't seem enough. I wanted to do more and so I created a separate page dedicated to Ailie where I posted her list and even a little picture of her that she'd sent me; it was basically a personalised profile page where all her goals, like mine, were listed. She wanted to ride a horse through a busy town, host a murder mystery party, ride a Segway in a pack and even milk a cow. No longer was she intimidated; she was empowered.

Although I didn't know it then, Ailie had become my first campaigner. It had taken some time, but slowly it was dawning on me that there were people out there, like me, who needed a tangible list to use as a driver in their lives. Ailie was just the beginning.

Everyone has a list, right?

Chapter 17

THE WEEK AFTER MY meeting with Pauly and Team Bliksem in the hotel foyer, I received an email from Thijs. The email was short and simply read:

> Seb,
> I checked out your site and man I'm blown away. I want to help you in any way I can and so please let me know if you need any money. Just give me an amount that you think will allow you to complete all your items and consider it done. Really love your attitude to life.
> Thijs

Even though I was now allowed to talk, I just sat there in silence. As far as emails go, this one made me lean in closer and I re-read it, to make sure it was saying what I thought it was. Was Thijs actually offering me a blank cheque, just so I could complete my list? It certainly seemed that way. If so, how would I even begin to calculate the amount? This was quite an offer from a man to whom I'd never said a word. It seemed that kissing the Wall Street bull on the arse was working out, after all!

Thijs was a very successful man. Although I didn't know him well, and of course he never told me so (he was gracefully modest), it was just implied. I mean, who owns a sailboat team? From our one and only meeting though, I also got the impression that he was a really nice guy and so his offer was certainly one I saw as genuine and altruistic. He just wanted to help me complete all 100 items on my list.

The email I sent back to Thijs was a tricky one to write. I was flattered that my journey had affected him to the extent that he wanted to help in such a way, but with this came a feeling of awkwardness from my end. If I accepted, I felt like I might owe him something far greater than a simple thank you. I needed some thinking time before I could make a decision and replied telling him so. I needed a taxi ride.

I'd found that whilst overseas I'd developed a love of travelling in taxis. Once seated in a cab, I was able to set aside life's qualms and reflect as the world passed me by. Call me naive but forgetting the money, I always saw taxi drivers as selfless Samaritans; complete strangers who, after inviting you into their car, would take you to your destination no matter where it was. Not only this but they were streetwise; they knew the local area and they knew people. With time to sit and think as they drove for hours each day, I also found that they knew about life too.

My taxi driver that day was driving me through Greenwich Village.

After chatting for five minutes about why I was in New York and what I had been doing with my life in the last six months, the driver, a big African-American man who was saving money to stay afloat in the aftermath of the Global Financial Crisis, stopped the car at a set of lights, undid his seatbelt and swivelled around in his seat 180 degrees to face me directly.

'What is it you do that allows you to do what you do?' he asked in a curious, animated tone.

This immediately shot to the top of my all-time favourite questions asked of me by taxi drivers. Like many others, he needed to know how I was able to do what I do. The only problem was that I hadn't ever put much thought into it myself and so to be honest I didn't quite know how to answer him. What was it that allowed me to do what I did?

'Mate, I just put my mind towards something I want to do and then I make it happen. That's all I do.'

'You have a rich daddy?' he asked, not satisfied with my reply.

'No, mate,' I laughed. He looked disappointed that his first guess was wrong.

'So, where d'you get the cash? You need money to do this all, son. You know this, right?'

Although I understood why the driver thought I needed lots of money to finance my lifestyle, I was beginning to think that this wasn't so true. I had got pretty far with only minimal funds to that point and the challenge of continuing the list in the same vein was starting to grow on me. If I had money, the challenge was gone.

As I began to think of how best to answer his question, he shot another theory into the back of the cab.

'So, you're the rich one, huh?'

Again I laughed. 'Nope, I've got less than $500 to my name, mate!'

He thought about this for a moment and looked at me with curiosity. He appeared to be confused as to why I seemed so blasé about something that he admitted was pivotal to his own life.

'Okay, so what are you going to do when you run out of that? This is New York, man. You won't have a dime to your name by Friday.'

This was a valid point – what was I going to do? I shrugged my shoulders.

'Well, I don't know how you do it, but I like it; hats off to you, son! I thought you were just some rich kid running around with your head up your ass.'

With that, he turned around, adjusted his rear-vision mirror so that he could see me and started singing to himself as we drove off.

A few blocks later, we had reached the destination. Of all the taxi rides I had ever taken, this was one of the most important. Things seemed clearer in my head and I thanked him for the ride.

'What's on this street for you, man?' he asked just before I shut the door.

'Oh, I'm here to tick off item Number 59: Attend an Extreme Religious Ceremony.'

As I paid the fare, he laughed before calling me crazy. He then pulled away.

Chapter 18

I'VE NEVER BEEN A devout follower of any religion. As a child I was ceremoniously dragged to church every Christmas by my parents, but since then I haven't spent too much time in any religious setting. This is why I thought I'd give it another go and what could be more interesting than trying a Pentecostal church where there was a chance of witnessing God in his supernatural form?

The initiation began.

'Dear Lord, Sebastian has come to us today, so that he can connect with you and see your wondrous ways! Please speak to him and grace us with your presence!'

Pastor Lu, the head of the church, was a devout Pentecostal preacher. His supernatural work has spread worldwide and after a few emails back and forth he had kindly agreed to initiate me into this extreme religion. If successful, I would be allowed to attend an official Sunday service with the congregation.

'Dear Lord, we can feel you in the room. Please bless Sebastian and allow him to feel your voice!'

Not knowing what on earth I was getting myself into, I knelt down on a mat with my arms resting on a chair in front of me. This was the ideal position, I was told, and once there I was instructed to begin chanting the name 'Jesus' repeatedly.

Pastor Lu knelt next to me channelling God on my behalf as I continued to chant Jesus's name. His voice became louder then he slowly began to speak in tongues.

Speaking in tongues, Pastor Lu had explained, is the product of God's spirit being successfully instilled within your body. It is believed that God uses your voice and body as a vessel to communicate with his followers. *His* voice is the gift of tongues.

'Jesus, Jesus, Jesus, Jesus, Jesus.' My eyes were shut but my mind was open. My quick chanting became more of a slur after just ten minutes and every so often Pastor Lu would interject with an elated *yes!* before again continuing his appeals to God.

'That's it, Sebastian! Feel God. Allow Him to bypass your brain, Sebastian, and reach your inner man! Reconstruct your inner man and that will point you in the right direction! God is in the room – I can feel Him!'

The two other church leaders, who were female, were also on hand to help initiate me and had made their way directly behind me. They too were speaking in tongues. With their hands placed on my shoulders, an indecipherable murmur filled the room of which I was quite clearly the centre of attention.

'Sebastian, God is accepting you; if you feel compelled to use your tongue, just do so!'

With that, Pastor Lu began clapping his hands frantically together, increasing the intensity. It was as if we were working towards an almighty crescendo. My chanting kicked up a gear as a result and in return Pastor Lu decided to start patting my head at speed.

'Use your tongue, Sebastian! Use your tongue!'

As ordered, I took a breath and began flailing my tongue around my mouth in an attempt to copy the noises of the others. Admittedly, it sounded spot on.

'That's it! Yes! That's it!' The pastor was amazingly supportive, as were the two female church leaders who also began encouraging me with remarks of 'Well done!' and 'That's it!'

It seemed as if the head tapping was working and I think that's why it again increased in ferocity. By now my tongue was lashing around my mouth like the tail of an excited dog as I tried to replicate the gibberish that the others made. I felt like a baby experimenting for the first time with the concept of noise.

After thirty minutes of chanting, I was genuinely tired. Although I couldn't feel a direct connection with any super-natural being at this stage, I could certainly say that the voice of Pastor Lu was echoing in my head. The controlled form of hysteria that had developed among the three leaders was almost deafening. With beads of sweat dotted on my forehead, my awkward kneeling position had become fairly uncomfortable. I needed a rest. I feared that opening my eyes might cause insult, so instead I slowly raised my head and let out an exaggerated sigh, hoping that they noticed my discomfort. Sadly this didn't work.

'Sebastian, if you feel the Lord is trying to get you to say something, please tell us! I can feel He is trying to communicate through your vessel.'

This I couldn't feel. I wished that I did, but all I could think was that I didn't sigh loudly enough.

'Sebastian, transform those tongues into words. The Lord has messages for us, and He wants to communicate through you!'

Again feeling pressured to perform, I half-heartedly added a mixture of vowels and consonants into my repertoire of infantile noises.

'That's it, Sebastian! More, more, more!'

This triggered a chorus of *hallelujahs* and *thank you, Lords* from the two leaders behind me who, by this stage, were firmly gripping my arms and shoulders.

'Oh yes, Lord! That's it!'

Seemingly we had reached our climax and accordingly the chanting diminished. When I opened my eyes and turned around I half-expected Pastor Lu to be smoking a cigarette, but instead he was just smiling intensely at the ceiling.

My initiation was a success. I know this because one of the two female leaders told me that she had received a message from God during the chanting. It turned out that *I* was a messenger; God told her so. God also took the time to share with her that He would teach me very quickly and that I would tell many people of His supernatural ways.

How exciting!

SUNDAY SESSION

With an open invitation to attend the more serious Sunday evening service, my curiosity was rivalled only by nerves as I walked once again up the stairs leading to the room of worship. Located on the fourth floor of a small and dingy office block, a peculiar mixture of shouting and music echoed through the stairwell as I got closer to the door. Sounding like an argument had broken out midway through primary-school band practice, I tentatively pushed the door open to reveal a scene that took me by surprise. On a small stage at the back of the room was Pastor Lu. Armed with a micro-phone, the charismatic lead man was running around chant-ing wildly and patting the heads of a crowd of ten or so devout followers, all of whom were on their feet mesmerised by the sound of his voice.

In each of their hands was an instrument; one man chimed a triangle, another clashed the cymbals. With the addition of drums, maracas, a xylophone and a tambourine, the resulting noise – much like the feeling when watching someone walk into a lamppost – was violent and uncomfortable, albeit just enough to make you smirk. One smaller woman, without the aid of an instrument, had decided just to jump up and down whilst occasionally mimicking the sound of an alarm clock.

I tiptoed further into the room and stood silently against a side wall, conscious not to interrupt whatever it was they were doing. In truth, though, they weren't even aware I was there; most had their eyes shut. With absolutely no idea what was going on, a woman banging on drums on the stage gestured to me that I should pick up an instrument from a nearby box. This I did with a great amount of unease and after grasping at the first thing my hands reached, I found I was clutching two bits of wood which I guessed I needed to bang together. This I could handle.

It took a further forty-five minutes for the erratic noise to subside. At last everyone sat down and opened their eyes.

Pastor Lu, now standing at the front of the room, gazed silently at the crowd and cleared his throat; the stage was set for a speech, it seemed. He didn't talk, though; instead he laughed hysterically. As he did so, he pointed upwards as if responding to a joke that God had chosen to share with him from up above. Then he decided to tell us (via the impressive sound system that had already proved to be far too powerful for this small room) the story of his life.

It turned out that Pastor Lu's first sighting of God came in the form of a black cloud that seeped from the mouth of a man who was lying unconscious on the ground. (I apologise if this seems slightly vague but this is as much detail as was given.) After that moment, Pastor Lu spoke of his progression towards religion, encouraged largely by a series of conversations that he had with God. He began to preach to people all over the world and with an overwhelming sense of purpose being introduced to his life, he made Pentecostalism his main focus. His account of feeling God enter his spiritual body for the first time was eerie to say the least, but his sporadic laughter in between sentences suggested that their relationship had since progressed into mainly joke telling.

Pastor Lu warmed the room with tales of miracles, divine intervention and personal beliefs. The crowd responded with applause and yells of 'hallelujah'. After a short period of normality, the pastor told us all to start talking in tongues. The transition, although seemingly forced, was immediate and within a few seconds everyone was on their feet again making strange sounds with their mouths. I found it hard to jump into character but, keeping an open mind, I managed to lower my inhibitions enough so that I could start to make the same sound.

Although somewhat reserved, I tried my best but couldn't quite duplicate the noises that everyone else seemed to be making so effortlessly. This time without instruments, followers displayed varying behaviours: some people stood up with arms outstretched, while others placed their hands on their heads and vibrated their lips together. One girl screamed then sprinted up and down the aisles whilst replicating the war cry of a native American Indian.

Sprinting up and down the aisles himself, Pastor Lu worked up a healthy sweat and again made sounds like no others I've ever heard. So animated were his movements that it was hard not to watch without questioning what he'd put in his coffee that morning. Just as he claimed, he quite possibly was a man possessed. At this point, he encouraged those who could feel God in the room to take the microphone and speak. The theory, as explained to me at the initiation, was that any words that were voiced by a person speaking in tongues were in fact those of the Lord. Miraculously it seemed that God was indeed in the room at this very moment as a heavy-set African-American woman announced that the Lord was inside her. I saw no evidence that He was outside of her, so I just took her word for it and stared with squinted eyes. With that, she walked to the front of the room and took up a position next to Pastor Lu. We were ready to hear what God had to say.

With sweat covering this woman's whole face, she began by flinging her arms about frantically whilst pivoting on one foot as she completed small spins on the spot. But this was just the teaser of what was to come. After thirty seconds of incoherent rambling, she announced to the room that she *was* God.

'I am God. Yeah! Yeah! Yeah! I do not do what you think you want me to do; I do what I want to do!'

Who was I to argue with that? Fifteen minutes later, when her energy had diminished, another woman walked to the front of the room and grabbed the microphone. She too began chanting; I presumed that God must have somehow skipped over into her body. The excited pastor was by now jumping up and down as well as laughing hysterically. The second woman also began making bold statements. On this occasion God's words weren't quite as clear, but that wasn't important as midway through a sentence the possessed woman walked into the crowd and plucked a man from his seat. Forcing him to stand up, she began pointing at him whilst speaking in tongues. It seemed as if God wanted to pass on a message to him and so the man responded by placing his hands out in front of him as if getting ready to receive a gift. A few seconds later, God spoke to him.

'You're going to see it with your own eyes. Breakthrough – in your life. Breakthrough – in humility. Breakthrough – yeah! God sees in your heart. You desire good things!'

I would never have guessed until this point that God would refer to himself in the third person.

The woman then started to slap the man's hands as she spoke. With every sentence came a harder slap. This, we were told, was some form of blessing. I'd probably just call it a beating, though.

Meanwhile, still unable to connect with any form of spirit, I stood there quietly taking it all in. I certainly wasn't there to judge; I just wanted to experience this unique ceremony. The emotion, the passion and the commitment were incredible and whatever it was that these people were doing seemed to at least be making them happy and somewhat fulfilled. In that alone, I saw this as a good thing.

My only fear was that I too might be plucked from the crowd, so I avoided eye contact with anyone holding a microphone. Just as I thought my plan was working, the woman who had been slapping the poor man's hands began to stare at me as she chanted loudly to the room. I immediately looked down at my feet but of course it was too late; it seemed that God wanted to have a quick chat with me as well.

'Come here, my child!' she cried, her outstretched arm beckoning me to walk into the aisle. I did as I was ordered and stood facing her to receive my message.

'You will pick it up quickly. I will do it for you. God will do it for you! You will be blessed. You will bless others. I see you!'

Confused as to who was actually talking to me, I just stood there like a schoolboy being reprimanded for something he didn't do. The intensity on her face was immense. It was soon explained that I'd been recognised as a worthy messenger of God and that this was the beginning of my time. Feeling awkward and not knowing what to do with my dangling arms, I decided that like the man before I would place my hands out in front of me with my palms facing up. Of course, this led to them being 'blessed'; I should have known better. These slaps heralded the end of my time in the spotlight and the end of the speaking in tongues. The pandemonium was coming to a finish.

Similar to wrapping up a night at the circus, the process of calming everyone down, so that they could walk the streets of New York in a normal manner, took quite a while. Even I felt like I needed a moment to rest and I hadn't even been possessed by God!

Pastor Lu, who was a friendly guy, approached me at the conclusion of the service and asked how I was. I told him I'd have to let him know in a few days. What I'd just been through would take some time to digest. With that, he laughed hysterically and pointed at the ceiling once more. I hate not being let in on a joke.

Regardless of what I did or didn't feel, I think it's good to believe in something, no matter what it is, and although Pastor Lu did invite me to the next Sunday evening service, I thought it best to decline. I needed time for my hands to recover from the slapping.

Number 59: Attend an Extreme Religious Ceremony – tick!

Chapter 19

By mid November, some five months after leaving Sydney, I was having a ball in New York, meeting new people and learning about life. A farewell dinner for Pauly in Uptown Manhattan provided me with my next lesson.

Around a table full of expensive wines and hearty Italian food sat good friends. Some were sailors; others, like me, weren't. As it happened, I was sitting next to Thijs and his lovely wife. It was only the second occasion that I'd ever met him and the first time that I could actually use my voice.

With a fresh story to share about talking in tongues, the conversation went from religion to boat racing, and everything in between. We even spoke about the possibility of Team Bliksem one day attempting a transatlantic crossing simply so that they could help tick off Number 40 on the list: Sail the Seas. It was a great night.

When we got ready to leave, Thijs approached me quietly and asked if I had thought any more about his offer to fund the remainder of my trip. A fun-loving person himself, Thijs seemed always to be smiling and his laid-back and friendly demeanour made me even more comfortable with my decision.

'Thijs, as much as I appreciate your offer, I can't accept it. I'm sorry.'

I felt terrible. Not for me, but for him. He genuinely just wanted to help me and I worried that I'd disappointed, or even offended, him.

'That's a shame, man. You know I'm jealous of what you're doing. Look at me, for example; I have a house, a business, a wife. I'm living vicariously through you, man! I want to be part of your journey and as I can't come with you, I want to help you get it done by giving you the finances and then I can read about it when I'm at work.'

Annoyingly, this made sense. Thijs was so genuine that I wanted to say yes, but I just couldn't. I'd been thinking about it ever since reading his email and no matter how I looked at it, it didn't feel right.

By accepting a blank cheque, I would be changing the essence of my whole journey. Sure, with money I would be able to tick off all 100 items on my list with a lot more ease, but I was beginning to see that this trip wasn't just about ticking items on a list; it was about something less tangible: stripping back life to its rawest form and trying to see how it all worked.

I felt like I was in the middle of one of the most important lessons of my life – that of life itself – and I wanted to learn everything. Money was not going to help me do this.

Without having thought about it much up to this stage, my trip had taken me on a spontaneous path that seemed to link up effortlessly from section to section. I enjoyed this momentum and believed that it came from a positive mindset and the necessity to float having thrown myself into the deep end of life.

One thing that I had realised was that since physically writing down my goals on a piece of paper, my thoughts had focused on nothing but my list and things related to the journey simply happened as needed. Echoing something that had been said to me in the middle of Nevada's Black Rock Desert, I felt that by opening myself up to the universe, the universe had done the same to me. By accepting Thijs's money, I thought that this relationship would cease.

'Well, the offer's always there, Seb.'

Although I still felt that I'd let Thijs down, his selfless generosity based solely on the desire to help out a stranger filled me with a sense of confidence in the trip; people were truly willing to help.

I went to sleep that night with a little smile on my face. I had done the right thing and I felt that I was growing. It was now time to take on the next chapter of the journey; I just didn't know what that was yet.

With the sense that a fresh start was just around the corner, I also decided that there was no better time to shave my beard off. Eighty-eight days of growth had resulted in me resembling a pirate. Ticking an item from my list has never felt cleaner.

Number 88: Grow a Beard – tick!

Chapter 20

HAVING MET A LOT of people in various capacities in New York, a few items on my list that I hadn't previously planned on achieving there now seemed possible. After meeting a highly esteemed artist known for his brilliance in life-art drawing, I suddenly had an opportunity, by way of invitation, to tick off Number 75: Pose Nude.

I'd always liked this item simply because it would put me way outside my own comfort zone, a place that I was learning I liked to be. I was beginning to recognise that I grew in that space. At Burning Man, for the first time ever, I felt a loss of inhibition when I paraded around in my birthday suit for an afternoon. But that wasn't so challenging, as I was surrounded by other naked people. Like most people, the mere thought of standing nude in a room full of clothed people was one that made my heart race.

For this reason I had to do it.

'Ten minutes starts now!'

Thirty artists eagerly committed charcoal to paper as

I stood naked in front of them in a contemporary art gallery on the Upper East Side of Manhattan. I tried to remain composed, but sure enough all I could hear was my heart beating loudly from within.

My body, although still, squirmed in awkwardness as my eyes darted around the room taking in the busy artists who seemed to stare at my flesh with a vacant yet judging glare. Lacking any imagination, my stance was horrible: feet planted shoulder-width apart with my arms dangling at my sides as I looked straight over the heads of the artists in front of me. Too nervous to try anything else, I resembled a shop mannequin.

A bead of sweat squeezed its way out of my armpit and began to meander down the side of my torso. Agonisingly, I couldn't do anything to stop it tickling me as it slithered along.

Nine and a half minutes remained in my first pose.

Hidden behind the numerous easels surrounding the stage were gathered some of America's best known artists including Will Cotton, who somewhat intimidatingly kept popping his head over the top of his easel every few seconds to view me. Shaping a pistol with his hand, he'd pointed directly at my body before closing his left eye and staring down the barrel past his extended thumb. Moments later, after gaining perspective and scale, he'd pulled the trigger and begun to sketch. Exaggerated strokes on his paper suggested he was starting with my torso, but who knew?

Seven minutes remained.

Next to me sat another naked model, an attractive girl far more comfortable without clothes on than I. I asked under my breath whether talking during the pose was deemed okay, but a slight shake of her head in reply told me that it wasn't. All I could do instead was stare at the far wall, wondering if someone had left a window open – it was cold!

Five minutes remained.

As I listened to the sounds of charcoal scraping paper and the ticking of a distant wall clock, I realised there was barely another sound in the room. A veil of concentration had been cast over everyone. With what could've only been a few minutes left until the end of the pose, my legs suddenly felt heavy as my thigh muscles began to spasm. A second later I'd lost my balance, causing me to sway like a tall tree in a stiff wind. This, of course, only encouraged my bead of sweat to gain momentum and a tickling sensation on my hip let me know its exact whereabouts. I'd all but lost my ability to focus.

'Okay, guys, that's ten minutes, but I love the pose! Can you hold it for another ten?'

If I was allowed to talk, I would have said no, but as it was I had to endure another ten minutes of stillness. I could have sworn that I heard my bead of sweat laugh at me as it rolled past my foot and onto the floor. This was turning out to be a lot harder than I imagined and with that thought I felt a second bead of sweat leave my armpit. Dammit!

Previously, I presumed that I'd only be doing one pose on the night but as it turned out there were about seven poses planned for me, all differing in times. One twenty-minute pose, two ten- and five-minute poses and even a few thirty-minute poses. I'm not joking either when I say that each one, no matter how basic the position, tested my body physically. Whether I was sitting, kneeling, lying or standing, the concentration and awareness of each muscle in my body that was required was incredible. This, I think, is why I found myself lightly sweating in a room that was actually quite cold; that and the fact that I was naked in front of a room full of strangers!

One benefit of being a nude model was that the champagne was free; as such, after a few different poses, my guard dropped a little. I could tell this because I kept forgetting to put my complimentary towel around my waist as I moved around the room in between poses! By the end of the night, I even found myself stopping for conversations with people while wearing nothing but a smile.

This behaviour did seem to please one particular middle-aged woman who I noticed was paying close attention to my nether regions during both the drawing sessions and also the conversation afterwards.

As the night moved on, so too did the level of noise in the room and with this came a sense of comfort. I could feel myself gaining confidence on stage and my whole body became less rigid. Now, for those of you smirking at the last sentence, I suppose it would be naive of me not to answer a question that many of you are probably wondering about regarding the issue of rigidity. The answer, quite simply, is no. I was lucky. Having said this, there was a brief moment midway through a certain pose when I thought my statue-like stillness may be compromised, but thankfully my excitement, like my nerves, quickly dispelled. Phew!

I can't say that by the end of the night I had entirely overcome my awkwardness at being nude in a public forum, but I can tell you that I was happy I did it. I think it had something to do with the fact that underneath the outfits of everyone in the room was a naked body and in that sense we were all the same; I just took it one step further to see what it was like.

As I slipped back into my clothes, Will approached me with an unlabelled envelope and handed it to me.

'Sebastian, this is your payment for the night. Thanks so much.'

I had no idea until that moment that I was actually getting paid to pose nude, and so when I opened the envelope and looked inside to find $200, I joked whether I was worth this much.

Whether I was or not, however, I decided immediately that I would donate the money to Camp Quality. Why not? After all it was an item on my list. This was becoming a habit.

Number 75: Pose Nude – tick!

Chapter 21

IT'S TRUE WHAT THEY say: New York really is the city that never sleeps. Having spent almost three months there, I'd had an amazing time but I realised I felt almost too comfortable now. I needed to move on.

Over a lunch with Superman and Rugsy one afternoon in the Meatpacking District, I told them that I was planning to leave. It was a sad moment as it meant I would be saying goodbye to two good friends.

'So, where are you off to then, mate?' asked Rugsy.

'Not sure,' I said, 'I guess I'll keep going in the same direction and head to Europe.'

Although there were still items that I could have ticked off in the US, I felt like I needed a big change of scenery and with some exciting items transpiring across the Atlantic, it just felt like the right thing to do. I knew I'd be back in the US at some later point.

'Well, I was looking at your list the other day, actually, Seb,' said Superman, 'and I saw that at some stage you want to learn French.'

Superman was correct; Number 46 on my list was indeed to Learn French, the reason being that my mum is Mauritian so her native tongue is French. As a child I remember her trying to teach my sister and me French, but sadly, stubborn kids that we were, we refused to learn. Only in the last few years did I realise how utterly ridiculous it was that I couldn't speak my mum's first language, and so on the list it went; I wanted to speak French with my mum.

Next Superman said, 'I can't remember if I told you but I'm part owner of a small sports bar in Geneva.' Superman had never told me this. 'It's where I met Rugsy, in fact. If you like, I could get you a job there behind the bar so that you could earn some spending money and also learn some French, old boy. What do you think?'

There was nothing in the world that made more sense to me at that moment and with a big grin I said yes! Just like that, I was heading to Switzerland and yet again the next opportunity had presented itself at the right time. Just as I was about to let go of one swinging vine, Superman had literally put the next one in my hand. Funnily enough I'd always thought the Swiss only spoke German but apparently not.

With my next destination decided, all I had to do now was to figure out how I'd get there. Keen to somehow incorporate an item from my list in the journey, extravagant thoughts of donning a pirate hat and sailing from the US to mainland Europe, and hence ticking off Number 40: Sail the Seas, immediately filled my head. Disappointingly, due to the seasonal nature of ocean hurricanes, my research suggested that this would be impossible at this time of year and so the only option was to fly. Thankfully Tal, who had just arrived back in LA after a trip to Sydney, had been in touch and after updating him on my recent adventures, he'd mentioned that he had more buddy passes should I need them again.

'The only condition of taking a pass is that you have to come and say goodbye to me first, here in LA!'

Visiting Tal before I left was the least I could do and so with a cheap flight to Europe sorted, my mind turned to ways of getting across the States, from New York to LA. Again running my finger down the list in an attempt to incorporate one of the items in the trip, my finger stopped at Number 82: Hitchhike. Without a second thought, I had chosen my next item – I was going to hitchhike across America from East Coast to West Coast, before then flying to Europe.

Chapter 22

NUMBER 82: HITCHHIKE. Potentially dangerous but undeniably intriguing, this challenge had everything that I yearned for; placing myself in the hands of complete strangers would put me in a position beyond my control. My thinking was this: if the risk was so large, imagine how big the reward must be! Not only that but it was all qualified by an oh-so-practical consideration: I needed to get across America. It was perfect.

Standing on the side of the road with 2260 miles of bitumen between me and the West Coast of America, the feeling of opportunity was huge. Of course, I had realistic concerns of being left standing all day long without a lift, but these were overcome by the fact that once I jumped in the first stranger's car, the journey would begin and I'd be closer to the finish line. The simplicity of that logic kept my mind clear.

It's always seemed to me that when in a situation involving strangers, people feel most comfortable when they're able to connect with someone. With this in mind, I decided that instead of simply sticking out a thumb to ask for a ride, I'd approach parked vehicles at service stations and make contact with potential drivers by smiling and saying a big g'day. Working from this strategy alone, I was amazed to be picked up after only thirty minutes of trying; the driver's name was Sarah and she was beautiful. My journey had begun.

By the end of that four-hour ride, I'd exhausted all of my jokes, had been invited to a wedding in Florida, and I'd developed a schoolboy-like crush on the generous driver. It was a draining ride and one that, as I exited the car in a busy truck stop, made me question whether I could maintain this type of pace all the way to the other side of America. Before I could lay down my bags and ponder this question, however, a man sporting a long white ponytail and a stained white T-shirt pulled over into the truck stop and offered me a ride further up the road. How could I say no? One minute I was sitting next to the lovely Sarah and the next I was beside Skip, a kooky Vietnam War veteran. Hitchhiking was quickly becoming addictive.

When Tony and Suzanne, a fervently religious couple, picked me up from a lonely service station towards the end of the first day, I was beginning to learn there was a lot more to hitchhiking than met the eye. For example, once inside a car, there was an inherent need to settle everyone's nerves by making conversation. Silence of any sort was clearly bad and so it was avoided at all costs, at times even forcing me to make things up simply to keep the flow of conversation going. At one point I found myself speaking to someone about Australian architecture for hours! I also realised that sleeping in the passenger seat was perhaps one of the greatest of all hitchhiking faux pas and therefore any thoughts of hitchhiking at night were quickly replaced by the need to find a motel on the side of an interstate highway.

Sleep, as I soon found, was crucial to keep me in the right state of mind to make critical decisions such as who to ask for a ride. On the second day, after a good night's rest in a road-side motel, I brushed the sleep from my eyes and approached a proud-looking man sitting in his car readying himself for the next leg of his journey.

'G'day! Are you guys heading west?'

'Sure are,' he said.

'Any chance there's room for a friendly Australian in your back seat?'

The man, who was travelling with a woman in the passenger seat, seemed open to the idea and with a quick glance over to her, he got out of the car, walked towards me and looked me up and down slowly. This man, as it turned out, was a sheriff. I could tell because he had a shiny star hanging off his belt with the word 'SHERIFF' written across it.

'You can ride with us but first empty your bags on the ground. I wanna see you don't have a gun on you.'

Feeling like I should've asked the same of him, I tipped the entire contents of my bags on the ground, after which I was then ordered to produce two forms of ID to prove to him that I was who I claimed to be. This guy was no ordinary sheriff; he was a super sheriff who would leave nothing to chance. With my identity confirmed, all I had to do was submit to a final pat-down at the side of the road. Once he was done, the sheriff gave me one last piece of advice.

'Just so you know, buddy, my wife is in the car and if you so much as look like you're going to cause any trouble, I'll shoot you.'

My reaction of forced laughter, as if dismissing a bad joke, was immediately silenced as he lifted up his shirt to expose a pistol that was casually nestled next to his shiny sheriff badge on his belt. This was no joke and for the first time in my life I'd been threatened with a gun. It was time to make a decision and as I saw it, there was only one thing to do: gather my toiletries and underwear from around my feet and jump in for the ride. It goes without saying that I avoided sleep on this journey and spoke without a breath for the next 200 miles. The funny thing was that I also found that I couldn't stop smiling the whole way; I was excited about my progress!

Before starting out, it hadn't occurred to me that some rides may in fact last an entire day, but I found myself on day two spending more time next to one complete stranger than I had spent with any loved one of late. Nick, a man who travelled the country in a big white van with his dog Millie at his side, picked me up from a secluded rest stop in Alabama and kindly drove me clean across the state of Mississippi and into Louisiana in a trip that ended well after the dark had forced him to switch his lights on.

It took roughly ten minutes after Nick had picked me up for us to rattle through our limited repertoire of small talk and we quickly found there was nothing left to do other than to relate personal stories, most typically reserved for those much closer to us. I guess in part our lack of inhibition was fuelled by a trust that we now both shared as car buddies, but then again who knows? Sometimes it's just nice to let it all out and in honesty it felt good being able to talk without reservation, knowing that once the ride ended, we were likely never to see each other again. As a result, by the time we'd crossed the Mississippi River, the van had turned into a mobile confession booth fostering secrets that provoked thought, laughter and even tears. This openness was a feature of every ride as I edged my way westwards across the states and often I found myself giving and receiving advice about things I never thought I would discuss with strangers.

Mario was a crazy Mexican man. Upon seeing me slowly shuffle through a service station in eastern Texas, he waved me over and invited me into his truck for a ride. A large man wearing a ten-gallon hat and a bright orange shirt that read 'Property of Texas Jail', he claimed that after driving nonstop for eleven hours he needed company to keep him awake at the wheel. As a hitchhiker, it seemed that this was as good an offer as any and so into his truck I jumped. If Mario's fatigue wasn't enough of a threat, his pistol, which he kept on his lap as he drove, certainly was. Incredibly though, his sense of humour seemed to click with my own and so I never once felt threatened. In fact, over the next 340 miles as we drove through the heart of Texas together, Mario and I sang songs, exchanged views on life and I learned of how as a child Mario had to find food for his family at landfill sites. Proudly showing me his latest pay cheque as a pipe welder as we pulled over for lunch, it was clear that times had changed for the better for Mario. I was happy for him.

Each time I was invited into a person's car, all worries of being stranded would disappear. But as soon as a ride had reached its conclusion and I was again alone on the side of the road, I would feel a slight pinch of anxiety. Luckily for me, though, I was discovering that a broad, and at times exaggerated, Australian accent coupled with a big smile was enough to get me out of trouble. Even when Mario's truck ran out of fuel only metres from a petrol station in the middle of nowhere, two nearby women who couldn't help but laugh as we pushed his vehicle towards the petrol bowser were the very same women who minutes later would offer me a ride all the way to the western border of Texas. At times I couldn't have organised the rides any better if I tried. I loved it.

By day five I'd travelled three-quarters of the way across America and had been picked up by charity workers, hippies, more war veterans and even the man who invented the machine that paints the white lines in the middle of the road. Everything had been perfect up until now.

The two women who had picked me up at the petrol station had managed to drop me at El Paso late that same night, close to the border of New Mexico. A strange little place, you could also make out the streetlights of Juarez, an infamously dangerous city just over the border to Mexico. For this reason when I woke up the next morning, I headed straight to the nearest petrol station, hoping to get out of town as quickly as possible.

Having had an unbelievable succession of quick pick-ups, the one place where I felt quite uneasy brought about my longest wait. However, after an hour of little traffic but many rejections, my opportunity for a lift came in the shape of a motorhome that slowly pulled into the isolated petrol station. As both doors opened, my knights in shining armour revealed themselves; they were in their seventies and dressed as if aboard a cruise ship.

'Are you guys heading west by any chance?' I inquired with a magnificently desperate smile.

'We sure are but if you're after a lift, let us have breakfast first and we'll think about it.'

Forty-five minutes later, after a nervous wait, the two elderly men emerged from the cafeteria and announced, 'Jump on board, son. I'm Bob and this is Vern.'

I was in!

Having both had successful careers in the US military, brothers Vern and Bob were retired. At the age of twenty-eight, Vern told himself that he would one day be a millionaire, and now, forty-nine years on, he sat back in his driving seat with a sense of accomplishment in having achieved this. Learning that I was also twenty-eight, he asked me what my goal was in life and after a moment I told him I just wanted to be happy.

As we marched westwards on the interstate, I couldn't help but feel guilty as I reclined on the large couch in the living room of their motorhome while Vern and Bob concentrated on the road ahead. It did give me a chance, however, to observe two brothers clearly grasping life by the horns and enjoying themselves together as they toured the open road. Laughter often filled the driving cab while hand gestures acted as signals to look out the windows at the unique Southern landscape. Cactus, dairy farms, cowboy ranches, oil refineries and mountain ranges fused together to create a picture I won't forget. Although everything was foreign to me, I couldn't have felt more comfortable anywhere else in the world.

By nightfall, we'd made our way through New Mexico and into Arizona, leaving just one more state between me and the West Coast of America: California. Relatively speaking, I was close to reaching my destination but not knowing how far the boys would take me, I was unsure if this would be my last ride or whether I'd be dropped off on the side of the road to fend for myself again. Then Vern turned around and looked at me with purpose.

'So, Sebastian, we're heading to California tomorrow and if you'd like, you can come with us.' Although I did answer the question, there was no need as the boys could tell from my instant smile that my answer was yes.

'That's amazing, of course I'll come!'

'There is one thing, though; we'll be staying in a RV park tonight,' said Bob. Failing to see the problem with this, I looked at Bob and Vern with a confused face and asked if I perhaps needed to find separate accommodation.

'No, you can stay with us, but there's one proviso,' said Vern. An air of seriousness filled the vehicle. 'You just can't fart loudly!'

Seriousness turned instantly to laughter. This I could manage. I was on the home straight!

The next morning, although still a few hundred miles away from the West Coast of the US, I felt like I'd done something special. My last ride through California was confirmed and that same day I would achieve my goal of hitchhiking across America.

Over the duration of the six days and thirteen rides that it took me to go from coast to coast, I saw that people could be giving, compassionate, open and selfless. Despite all the concerns and fears voiced by friends and family along the way, I saw nothing but the goodness of others. The journey wouldn't have happened without this and on the evening of the sixth day, after I'd said goodbye to Vern and Bob, when I dipped my toes in the Pacific Ocean signalling the completion of my journey across America, I was reinstilled with faith for my greater journey.

Number 82: Hitchhike – tick!

Chapter 23

GENEVA, SWITZERLAND IS ONE of the world's richest cities. A powerhouse in global finance and home to some of the world's largest NGOs; I'm still not sure why they let *me* in! I was by far the poorest person within 100 kilometres. Perhaps they knew that I would be able to serve them beers at Geneva's friendliest sports bar, The Clubhouse.

The lakeside pub, based in the Pacquis area, was a local watering hole for many English-speaking expats who had moved to Geneva for work opportunities. Here, bankers, traders and international delegates of one variety or another all rubbed shoulders over beers at the end of a workday. The atmosphere was lively at night with scores of rich kids who would party into the early hours using credit cards clearly not linked to their own accounts. Not too much French was spoken within the bar itself but this wasn't a huge issue; I had decided long before arriving in Geneva that I was going to learn French no matter what and tick off Number 46.

By the time I realised that thongs were not the most

appropriate footwear for a snowy winter in Switzerland, I had enrolled myself at a local language school that committed me to a five-week intensive French course. At the same time I also began playing rugby with The Clubhouse bosses, Iain and Geoff, at their local club, Hermance. Slowly but surely I was surrounding myself with French.

In my first month in Geneva, I began my day by watching a good hour of French kids' cartoons, followed by a walk in the streets as I attempted to translate shop signs or tram time-tables. I was fascinated with everything French. When I wasn't working at the pub, I trained for rugby and among mainly French and Swiss players, I started to pick up a brand of French that they certainly didn't teach in my debutant course (*merde* as it turns out also translates as good luck). The French rugby coach, Christophe, whose English was somehow worse than my French, would speak with as much passion and feroc-ity as you'd expect from, well, a French rugby coach and after poking players in the chest and nearing tears at what was only a Tuesday night practice, he would always look to me for my feedback.

'Good, Australian?'

'*Oui, monsieur!*' I would reply.

This was better than good; this was bloody brilliant. I had immersed myself in Geneva and felt I was exactly where I needed to be, even if I could barely understand a word that Christophe said. Just quietly, I don't think any of the French players could, either.

Heading back to school at the age of twenty-eight was something I had never previously conceived, but unlike my degree in Human Movement, I actually *wanted* to learn what was now in front of me; I was like a human sponge absorb-ing as much information as I could. Previously I had thought that I was too mature to learn anything new, but I realised that without learning new things I wasn't actually growing at all.

Excited by the French vocabulary that I learned at school each day, I would annoy everyone at work that same evening by practising my new words and phrases. Awkwardly though, since I was enrolled in a beginners class, my material was mainly limited to the topics of weather, clothing and musical instruments. Consequently, any patrons drinking at the bar, unaware that I was new to the language, could have been forgiven for thinking that Iain and Geoff had employed a twenty-eight-year-old with speaking difficulties. Over time, however, the locals found out why I kept stating that it was sunny outside and that I liked guitars, and soon they enjoyed testing my French. I've never felt as proud as the time a local Swiss man came in and ordered a drink from me in French. I had no idea what he said, but the fact that he assumed that I could speak French made me feel like I was progressing; at least I looked as though I could speak his language.

I'd be lying if I said that things weren't falling into place for me in Geneva and yet again it was largely due to the hospitality of others. Iain had not only offered me a generous rate of pay at the bar, but he also connected me with some of his mates who were kind enough to let me use their couches as beds on what was almost a weekly rotational basis. I remember waking up one morning at Vernon's, a local at the pub who had offered me his place for two weeks whilst he went on holiday, and having one of those reflective moments where you think to yourself, *Is it weird to feel so comfortable in a stranger's bed?* I chose not to answer this question and instead burst out laughing with no one around to hear.

On only my second night in Geneva, I met a girl called Jenny, a petite girl with a huge smile. Her smile was the first thing I noticed about her. The fact that she showed such warmth in a place where people's moods often mirrored the outside temperature made her stand out from everyone else in the depth of a cold Swiss winter. She was friendly, full of life and her laugh was contagious. Approaching her nervously, in my best French I introduced myself and told her that I was learning her language. She turned and laughed at me before verifying my worst fears.

'Sorry, I didn't understand that.'

Evidently my French needed improving. Luckily Jenny kept smiling before offering to teach me the next day. Our first date – *magnifique!*

After a few months, work, rugby and my social calendar had all fused together and again I found myself surrounded by new close friends. The reason I knew we had become so close was because we'd developed nicknames for each other and as any Australian will tell you, this is the defining factor in separating mates from acquaintances. Iain and Geoff were now known as Wizzo and Jiggles, and among a gang that consisted of Gravy Johnson, Fuzzy and Gluteus Maximus, we found it hard not have fun. Even Jenny, who by this stage I was seeing a lot of, had picked up the somewhat unflattering nickname of Penguin, which of course meant that we too were becoming closer. I think she saw me as some form of comic relief from her stressful internship at a law firm, and she soon invited me to stay at her place for the remainder of my time in Geneva.

Feeling settled and with a sense of efficiency and progress, before long I was eager to tick off another item from the list. Learning French was turning out to be an enjoyable but lengthy process and so I felt as though I needed something a little punchier to offset the hours I was putting in at school. One day, after a conversation about national sports in Switzerland, Wizzo said something that made me think.

'You should get yourself down to one of the local ice hockey games if you get a chance; it's a great night out!'

I had no idea until this moment that there was even a local ice hockey team in Geneva but Wizzo wasn't lying. After some research it turned out that the local team weren't just any old team either; Genève-Servette, as they were known, were in fact the current national champions. Playing in front of thousands at each home game, they were the pride of the city. But best of all they had two team mascots, both giant eagles, Calvin and Calvina. I convinced myself that it was no coincidence that sitting at Number 77 on the list was Be a Team Mascot for a Day. The wheels had started to turn once again.

Chapter 24

CALL ME IMMATURE, BUT the idea of running through a sporting arena wearing a giant animal costume is something that I'd dreamed about for a while.

With such a clear goal, I decided a simple phone call would work best.

'I was wondering if I could be one of your mascots at an upcoming home game. It's part of a to-do list that I'm currently trying to complete.'

The man on the other end of the phone line, Henda, paused for a moment as if considering whether this was some kind of prank phone call before replying.

'Well, Sebastian, I can't promise anything because our mascots are very, very good at what they do, and also a lot of mascots now actually study a specific mascot course at university, but I will ask and get back to you. It's not just a matter of putting on a suit, you see.'

A university course to be a mascot? Was this man joking? The image of a university professor lecturing an auditorium full of students in costume made me smile.

Luckily for me, it turned out that the current team mascots must have had a sense of humour as a few days later I received a call from Henda to say that they would overlook my under-qualification in Mascot Behaviour and give me an opportunity as a team mascot.

'The only thing, Sebastian, is that you must realise how personal these suits are to the mascots. They sweat a lot in these costumes and care for them greatly.'

This I understood. I felt the same way about my Batman outfit.

'I promise I'll show the suit the respect it deserves,' I replied.

'Great, well, the next home game is this Saturday so turn up around 6 pm and we'll get you on your way.'

I was over the moon!

GAME DAY

Apart from a few devoted supporters who were busy applying face paint and unrolling flags in the car park as I arrived at the stadium on game day, the scene was still fairly quiet.

Henda met me at the VIP entrance at the rear of the stadium and escorted me inside. After chuckling at a few of the antics that he had read about on my website, he handed me a white envelope explaining that it was a small gift on behalf of the club.

'This is for you. Keep up the good work and good luck with your list!'

As Henda led me on a tour of the stadium, officials darted around like bees busy at work while the arriving teams stood casually around the ice in preparation for the big game. TV cameras lined the outskirts of the rink ready to transmit the game across Europe while overhead hung a huge triangular scoreboard positioned over the middle of the rink. It was becoming clear that this was the real deal; media presence, security, sponsored vehicles and even a mini indoor hot-air balloon covered in logos all added to the feel. I was nervous.

The tour finished in a quiet dressing room where Henda told me to wait until Calvin and Calvina arrived. At that point, they would show me the ropes.

'Now there is a small complication, Sebastian.'

This took me by surprise as it seemed that everything was in place. 'Basically Calvin and Calvina have had a last-minute change of mind and they would prefer that you didn't wear either of their costumes. They're very personal to them, you see.'

My heart sank.

'But don't worry – we do have a solution.'

I waited anxiously, unsure what it could be. Had my dream of being a mascot been dashed? What could possibly remedy the situation?

'We've found you a tiger costume instead!' Henda announced.

'A tiger?'

Henda again chuckled. 'That's right.'

I'm sure that a university degree in Mascot Behaviour would have helped me deal with a last-minute change of character from 'Appropriate Eagle' to 'Misfit Tiger' better, but as it stood, I remained confused.

Henda must have noticed my disappointment.

'It will be fine, Sebastian. We actually have a name for you!'

At that very moment, a man and a woman walked into the dressing room and laid a brand-new Genève-Servette jersey on the table in front of me.

'This is yours!' said Henda, smiling.

I got up and looked at the jersey. On the back was the number 77, with the name 'TERRY' printed underneath.

It took me a second to realise that it was no coincidence that this was my last name and that being a club mascot was item Number 77 on my list. Henda had gone above and beyond the call of duty.

'For tonight, you'll be "Terry le Tigre"!'

In less than a minute I had gone from the heights of an eagle, to the lows of nothingness, and back again.

I stood up with purpose. Terry le Tigre it was! I was excited.

The two people who had entered the room were introduced to me as Calvin and Calvina, the usual mascots. Still dressed as humans at this stage, it was made very clear that their identities were to remain secret. In fact it wasn't long before the ground rules of being a mascot were explained to me:

1. A mascot remains silent once out in public.
2. A mascot must NEVER remove his or her headdress while out in public.
3. A mascot must respect and be courteous to the public.
4. A mascot must not assault anyone.

The last point was fairly obvious even for someone who had not completed Mascot Behaviour, but again I nodded.

A fourth person then entered the room holding an enormous suitcase. As if a large exchange of money was about to take place, he put it carefully on the physiotherapy table that sat in the middle of the room and undid the latches. Calvin, Calvina and I crowded around the case as the man revealed the goods. Inside was a glorious tiger outfit!

It was time to get changed.

I would liken the experience of trying to get into a giant tiger outfit as being similar to the act of wrestling an actual tiger. It was hard, at times dangerous, and best done with the help of four people.

Once inside the suit, I noticed that the heat alone was enough to cook meat. Without the aid of a mirror I could only assume that I looked the part, although with severely obstructed eyesight a mirror would not have helped too much, anyway. So bad was my vision that I needed someone to hold my hand at first to walk in a straight line! The problem was that the only eye holes were located where the eyes of the actual tiger were and these were spaced about 30 centimetres apart. This meant that I had to focus both of my eyes through one of the tiger's. Not only this, but a thick mesh material concealing the tiger's eyes further impaired my vision.

As Calvin and Calvina routinely changed into costume, I walked around the room bumping into every object possible. Being a mascot was not as easy as I thought.

Suddenly, the stadium MC grabbed me by the paw and escorted me to the beginning of the tunnel that led to the centre of the ice rink.

'Just wave or do whatever you feel like and I'll talk to the crowd about your 100 things and explain that we are helping you tick off Number 77 tonight,' the MC said. With two big paws aloft, I attempted to give him a thumbs up, without realising that tigers don't have thumbs. It must have looked like I was getting ready to punch him in the head.

Standing in the darkness, metres from the rink itself, I saw a spotlight circling the ice in an effort to find me. Terry le Tigre, the never-before-seen team mascot, was about to be introduced to the crowd. Images of kids bursting into tears yelling at their parents, *'But that's not Calvin!'* cluttered my head.

With that, the MC gave me the signal to walk forwards as he began his pre-game spiel to the crowd.

This was my moment. Exhaling a deep nervous breath, I stepped onto the ice. I managed a quick glimpse up at the triangular scoreboard overhead and noticed the Camp Quality logo shining brightly. It was great.

Everything was going perfectly until the second step when my leather shoes, which were hidden beneath my tiger feet, failed to offer any grip. I half-slipped, causing me to stick my arms out like the wings of a plane. Luckily I managed to keep upright, but only to find the same problem occur at the third and fourth steps. Thankfully I avoided completely falling over in front of 8000 people by shuffling my feet along quickly. Tigers aren't comfortable on ice.

With the costume playing havoc with my spatial awareness, I stopped walking after twelve or so paces. This, I assumed, was the middle of the ring. Although I couldn't see any of the crowd, there was a mighty roar as I started to wave blindly at the air. It must have looked as though I was trying to swat a plague of flies. Regardless, it seemed as if the crowd had accepted Terry le Tigre, after all. I smiled from within the costume. I was centrestage and loving it.

The MC soon joined me on the ice, along with Calvin and Calvina. Calvina now stood directly behind me; this I found out when I walked straight into her. Not wanting to appear flustered, I simply began to pump my fist in the air and to my surprise the crowd began to cheer as I did so.

Once the game started, Calvin and I moved to the top of stand A. It was now time to interact with the fans. Having conceded an early goal, the home crowd needed something to cheer about and we were it!

Calvin had explained on the way up that we were to make our way to the far side of the stand whilst cuddling people, sitting in vacant seats, and basically making idiots of ourselves. With only ten per cent vision and giant tiger feet that severely impeded my natural walking gait, I figured this would not be hard.

Immediately, a couple of kids ran at us and jumped up to give us huge hugs. Terry le Tigre had well and truly been accepted. I picked up the larger of the two kids and placed him on my lap as I sat in a nearby vacant seat. The game was being played at a rapid pace and so fist pumping and clapping were musts. With the kid now on my lap, I could not actually see him, and so when he fell off my knees, I had no idea he had done so until I kicked him with my foot as he lay on the ground. Luckily he was okay but it was certainly time to move on.

Calvin was brilliant with the crowd, and whenever I managed to find him, he would be flirting with girls, tapping kids on the head and generally creating laughter. This was impressive for someone who couldn't talk.

Before long Genève-Servette scored two amazing goals. The score was 2–1 and to celebrate our revival I decided to cuddle a group of middle-aged men who were more than happy to show me some love. By the time we'd added another two goals, I'd patted a bald man on the head, cheekily stolen popcorn from an unsuspecting female fan and even found the time to make a half-time appearance on the triangular screen above the rink for all to see. It's amazing what you can get away with as a cuddly tiger.

Soon the game was over. The final score was 4–1 – our team had won!

Now, I don't want to make an outrageous claim and say that the team took inspiration from Terry le Tigre, but I think the maths speaks for itself!

The high of being among the crowd was quickly followed by exhaustion and so by the time I'd made it back into the dressing room, I learned that getting out of a giant tiger costume is even harder than getting into one. Eventually though, I succeeded, and with Calvin and Calvina still running errands on the other side of the stadium, I sat alone in the dressing room for a while contemplating my time as a mascot.

With the tiger outfit and my new jersey both hanging on the peg next to me, I reached into my pocket and got out the white envelope that Henda had given me earlier. I opened it up to find a little card that read:

The GSHC wishes you all the best! Good luck!

Inside the card was 150 Swiss francs – a donation to Camp Quality. Awesome!

Number 77: Be a Team Mascot for a Day – tick!

Chapter 25

BEFORE LONG, WORD HAD started to spread around town that The Clubhouse had a crazy Australian with a bucket list working behind the bar. The mascot stunt quickly became a favourite story among patrons and that naturally led to us talking about many of my other recent experiences. Whether I was meeting new people or talking to people who were already aware of the list, slowly but surely the list became the only thing I spoke about, at and outside of work. Wizzo and Jiggles, being the good mates that they were, joked that I needed to come up with a different story of why I was in town, if for no other reason than to save them from hearing the same thing every shift. In my defence, I didn't know how else to answer the standard question, 'So, how did you find yourself working behind a bar in Geneva?'

One night whilst working, I began chatting to a bloke called Nat who ordered a beer from me. Nat, another Australian working in Geneva, was a friendly guy and a real straight shooter. After asking me what I was doing in Geneva, we got stuck into a conversation about my chosen charity, Camp Quality. After a further five minutes, Nat, who by this stage had consumed enough alcohol to drown a small horse, looked at me and in a very matter-of-fact way declared, 'Mate, I'll double whatever you've already made for Camp Quality.'

At some point in our lives I think we've all said something with a beer in our hand that perhaps we only realised was a mistake the next day and so even though I thanked Nat for his offer, I didn't expect to see any development from it. After all, we had only known each other for the better part of ten minutes and within the hour he had left the bar without saying another word about it.

The very next day, however, Nat returned to the bar and, not bothering to say hello, approached me and asked to use the office computer.

'You're back, mate!' I said with genuine surprise.

'Well, I said I'd double your donations and so I'll do it. An Aussie never goes back on his word!'

As emotionless as Nat had made it sound, there was in fact a very meaningful reason for his generosity which he had told me the night before: Nat had experienced someone close to him losing a battle with cancer. He wasn't there simply because he wanted to follow through on his word; he was there because he truly wanted to help with the cause of Camp Quality. I respected him immediately.

Funnily enough, I didn't actually know the exact amount I had raised up to that point, so neither Nat nor I had any idea of how much he was about to donate. I joked that at last count it was about $20,000 but a quick check on the office computer told us it was actually $2500. Two minutes later, after producing his credit card and following the online prompts, Nat had doubled this figure. I had now raised $5000 in total and was halfway towards ticking off Number 4 on the list:

Raise $10,000 for Camp Quality. It was awesome. Nat's only proviso was that I didn't tell anyone that he had made a donation. I then said jokingly, 'What if I write a book one day?' to which he replied, 'Okay then, but that's the only reason.'

Since being in Geneva, everything had been ticking along nicely. Not only was I making good headway with the list but on top of this I'd created a simple lifestyle revolving around a great bunch of people. Sadly it was this group that was about to be rocked by some terrible news. One cold but sunny spring morning I received a phone call from Andrea, a good mate from the rugby team, who had some news to share. I shook my head in disbelief as Andrea spoke. Alesandro, our much-loved number 8, had died that morning. I couldn't believe it.

As the news circulated throughout the day, each of the team members gathered down at the bar to try and make sense of this unexpected loss. A pillar of our team, Alesandro was a top bloke. Originally from Argentina, he had moved to Geneva as a progression in what was a great career and whilst there he had renewed his passion for life. His death, from a scooter crash, was nothing short of tragic.

In what ended up being a horrendous week in Geneva, we also found out that two days earlier, we'd lost another friend called Chris. Chris was a young Scottish guy living and working in Geneva, and like Alesandro, he also died in a freak accident. A friendly regular at the pub, his loss again affected everyone. I still remember walking into The Clubhouse to join everyone on that grim Monday afternoon and noticing that at each end of the bar was a group of people: one grieving for Alesandro and the other for Chris. Many of us knew both of them very well and as such walked in between the groups offering our condolences. It was horrible.

At a time of such lows, the last people who you would expect to show so much strength were the families of Alesandro and Chris, but this is exactly what happened. Chris's mum, who flew to Geneva as soon as she heard the news, dealt with the situation with a level head and a firm belief that although her son's time on earth had ended, he was now part of a bigger picture that would see his journey continue elsewhere. Although tragically short, a greater force had decided that his time with her was over and with this belief she found comfort, as we all did.

By chance Alesandro's wife and baby boy, who both still lived in Argentina, were visiting Geneva at the same time as his death. Sadly his son was too young to know what a great man his dad was, but his brother Pato, who flew out from Argentina the next day, certainly did. Together they'd played rugby as kids and had grown up side by side.

Whilst grieving at the bar, we decided that the following day's training – although attendance was optional – would go ahead in remembrance of Alesandro. (We all knew that he'd accuse us of being *soft* if we didn't!) In a statement of solidarity, the next evening every single player turned up and with a full team present we began our warm-up lap. After a few minutes, however, another two people appeared at the side of the field. Together they simply watched us as we warmed up; one of them held a pair of rugby boots in one hand, while the other just stood there in support. It was Alesandro's brother Pato and his best mate. Although we knew they were in town, no one had actually met them yet and so we gathered under the goalposts as they walked over to us. Clearly emotional, the quietly spoken Pato composed himself before breaking what was a very sombre silence within the semicircle of players that had formed in front of him. He introduced himself then continued, 'Although I do not know any of you, I know that my brother always spoke about this rugby team as if you were brothers. Because of that, I feel the same way about you. Alesandro felt more comfortable here on the rugby field with his friends than he did anywhere else and so I am here to see the place that he spoke of so fondly and to experience what he felt. I have come over here to train with you tonight, if that's okay, as a mark of respect to my brother.'

Silence again fell over us, broken only by sniffing and sobbing. After a moment, the player closest to Pato walked up to him and gave him a long embrace, before then hugging his friend. We all followed suit and welcomed them to our team. Pato had found his peace.

The loss that was incurred that week undoubtedly cast a shadow of sadness over everyone but through this darkness emerged something of great importance: we all found strength in each other. On an individual basis it may have been religion, spirituality or perhaps something entirely different that we turned to, but combined it was the sense of community that enabled us to cope.

The legacy that both Alesandro and Chris had left was made of only positive memories. We remembered the things that they enjoyed and the things that they had chosen to do with their lives. We smiled when they did.

Not for the first time recently, I had felt the effects of loss, and once again, it caused me to take a step back from my reality and assess where I was in my life. Was I heading in a good direction? It'd been just eight months since I'd left Australia and without knowing it I'd managed to tick off almost thirty items altogether. This satisfied me but beyond this was a feeling of exploration; I began to sense that there was something underlying my journey, something of a positive nature that I knew I wanted to uncover some more. Life, after all, is an opportunity and I just wanted to get on with it. I wanted to dig deeper.

Chapter 26

JUST BEFORE MOVING TO Switzerland, I received an email from a guy by the name of Will, who'd been following my site for a while. Having been on various adventures of his own, Will suggested that I should consider speaking at a London-based travel show. Not only did Will think that others would find the talk inspirational, but he went one step further and actually put me in touch with the organiser.

Although speaking at a travel show wasn't on my list, the idea of being able to encourage others in a positive way was something I valued highly and so I wrote back saying that it was something that I'd certainly consider.

This seminar was England's largest free travel show and attracted tens of thousands of people over three days, most of whom were looking to score travel deals in and around Europe. It's amazing how many people turn up to an event offering an escape from England.

Sure enough, months later and now living in Geneva, I received an email from Hazel, the event organiser. I was delighted to read that she loved my website and wanted to invite me to talk on the main stage of the travel show about my journey of 100 things. 'Seb, people would love to hear a story as inspirational and motivational as yours!' she wrote.

I was flattered, elated and a little confused. I'd always thought that motivational speakers completed some form of training, so via Hazel's offer I felt like I'd accidentally found my way onto the stage. If it wasn't so exciting, I'd probably have been scared. Regardless, I wrote back and said yes! Now all I had to do was work out what I was going to talk about.

Back in the pub in Geneva, I had struck up a great friendship with Edgar, a Bolivian chef working in the kitchen. Edgar had a wicked sense of humour but was also a hard worker; he was saving money so that one day he could buy a house for his family back in Bolivia. Aside from laughing at my attempts to improve my French, Edgar would occasionally pull me aside during a work shift and ask about my trip. Interestingly, although he'd sometimes ask about specific items from the list, he was far more intrigued by my reasoning for the journey and how I was able to afford it. He couldn't understand that I was able to survive solely from money I earned from working at the pub. I would explain that I had no other commitments in my life, so it was quite easy, but he would then demand to know why I didn't care about things like buying a house or starting a family.

'What would happen, Sebass, if you met the girl of your dreams and all you had to show her was your pay packet from that week's work?'

I would explain that these things weren't important to me at this stage of my life as I felt I needed to explore the world and develop on a personal level first. Ultimately though, no matter what I said, Edgar would end with, 'Well, I think you have a rich family.'

At the end of the day, we'd both be laughing.

Echoing the sentiments of Edgar – and the taxi driver in New York – were emails from strangers everywhere; people wanted to know *how* I was doing what I was doing. The presumption, of course, was that I was a lucky person. This I disagreed with, as it suggested that luck was the driving factor, implying that those without luck were unable to achieve their own dreams. When leaving Australia, I had made a decision to drop everything in my life to pursue something I felt I needed to do. This was not luck; this was a big sacrifice. Essentially I had to walk away from friends, family and the opportunity to develop a career, to name a few things. It wasn't luck people needed; it was perspective and application.

This point I found myself explaining on a daily basis and soon I began to see that the main difference between myself and those who questioned me was mindset; nothing more, nothing less. The reason I was able to do what I did was because of a mental attitude. I felt this was the key to my trip and as such, I made it the focus of my talk at the TNT Travel Show. The only thing I knew I needed to be mindful of was claiming to know the answers to life. I had to make it clear that I was just a young bloke still trying to work it all out. All I could do was tell my own story and hope people took something from that.

One day with pen in hand, devising ways to connect with the audience, an idea struck me that made complete sense: the best way to show people what I did would be by ticking off an item live on stage in front of them. This would be the finale to my talk; actions would certainly speak louder than words. I just had to choose an item that would suit an indoor event involving the public.

Given the setting, I was forced to rule out Numbers 10: Chase a Tornado and 37: Be a Horse Jockey for safety reasons (well, that and logistics) and as interesting as ticking off Number 23: Deliver a Baby might have been, you could say that it slightly overstepped the thin line separating edgy and grossly inappropriate for a travel show. As I continued to browse my list, I stopped at Number 19: Guinness World Record. I immediately knew that this was the perfect item for the occasion; I would attempt to become a Guinness World Record Holder live on stage. All I needed to do was find a Guinness World Record that I could possibly break.

Number 2: Marry a Stranger. Luckily for me, Chevali *(right)* had a great sense of humour!

Number 12: Visit a Death Row Inmate. Standing outside Oklahoma State Penitentiary, death row, moments after meeting my penpal inmate, J-Loc.

Number 42: Cycle Through Cuba. A culture that proves that you don't need money to be happy.

Number 14: Burning Man Festival. T-Bop *(right)* and me, discovering that the door is always open in the middle of the desert.

Footwear is crucial in these parts!

Number 16: Street Performance. *(From left to right)* Superman, me and Rugsy, proving that musical talent is not essential to make money on the streets of New York.

Number 29: One Week's Silence. My whiteboard captures a typical day without speech.

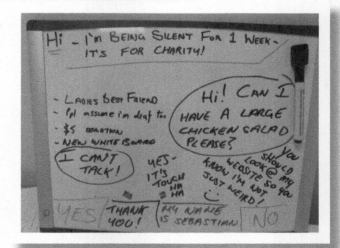

Number 88: Grow a Beard. Every man should try this; just don't be surprised if girls stop talking to you.

Number 77: Be a Team Mascot for a Day. Me, dressed as 'Terry le Tigre',
making my way through Genève-Servette's ice hockey stadium.

Thankfully Calvin *(left)* and Calvina *(right)*, the official team
mascots, took me under their wings.

This cheesy promo shot appeared on the front page of a Swiss newspaper just days before I embarked on Number 85: Go on an Adventure.

Number 85: Go on an Adventure. It's as simple as getting on a board and paddling. Dave Cornthwaite *(left)* and I paddled for two and a half days over one of Europe's largest freshwater lakes, Lake Geneva.

Bittersweet; you'd never guess that the night before this beautiful photo was taken, I slept under a rat-infested boat jetty in the quaint village of Yvoire, France.

Number 19: Guinness World Record. The art of egg crushing is a messy endeavour. This day also doubled as the first motivational talk I ever gave. A big thanks to Dave *(right)* for his 'expert egg placing' skills.

On 13 March 2010, I became the official world record holder for 'The most eggs crushed with the toes in 30 seconds'. I've yet to meet someone who keeps a straight face when I tell them this.

Number 98: Crash a Red Carpet. A moment of desperation at the Cannes Film Festival; this would go down as one of the greatest days of my life!

After pretending to be a security guard, I somehow made it onto the red carpet and even spent some time signing autographs in my hired tuxedo.

Number 30: Join a Protest. May Day protests in London. I had no idea what we were protesting until I turned up on the day.

Number 18: Hit a Hole in One. I've hit almost 4800 golf balls, but this item is still incomplete!

Number 63: Get a Tattoo. My tattoo says '*On ne voit bien qu'avec le coeur. L'essential est invisible pour les yeux.*' (*Le Petit Prince/The Little Prince*, Antoine de Saint-Exupéry) Translated, it reads: 'One can only see truly with the heart. The essential things are invisible to the eyes.'

Number 58:
Skydive Naked.
Complete
liberation
coupled
with extreme
embarrassment.
I felt sorry for
everyone else in
the plane.

The hardest thing about
skydiving naked was not
finding a place that'd allow
me to jump naked, but
finding an instructor willing
to have me strapped to
them naked.
Thanks, Jorge!

The Live Every
Litre crew got
a lot more than
they bargained
for when they
decided to
follow me
around for one
month through
Europe.

Number 36: Walk Across a Country. During the sixteen days it took us to walk from east to west across France, Big Matty (left) and I adopted a travel companion – a shopping trolley that we named 'Trojan'.

Along freeways and country roads, Matty and I walked from dawn till dusk.

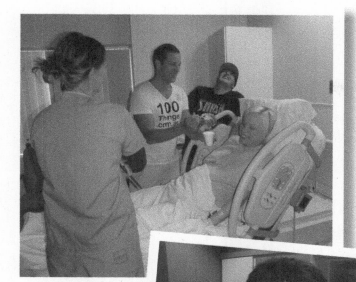

Number 23: Deliver a Baby. Here I am feeding ice chips to Carmen, the expectant mother. The funny thing was that I only met Carmen and Dane (*laughing in the background*) for the first time the night before the birth.

28 August 2010. Welcome to the world, Oakley Sanguin.

Number 80: Have Something Named After Me. My Canadian family: (*clockwise from top left*) Roddy, Janita, Isla, Jack and (*middle*) a recent arrival, James Malcolm Sebastian Macleod.

Number 27: Minister a Wedding. Only in America. After a free one-minute online application form, I became Reverend Sebastian Terry. Shortly after this photo was taken, I announced Pete and Osamu as husband and wife at their San Diego wedding.

Number 73: Get Shot. Playing with firearms at the Miguel Caballero bulletproof clothing factory in Colombia.

The moment of impact as Miguel fires a 9 mm bullet at my torso. This was the turning point in my journey.

Number 41: Buy a Stranger Lunch. Of all the people in the Sydney CBD, there were only two, Chris and Emily, who seemed open to chatting. As it happened, they were homeless.

Number 26: Help a Stranger. All smiles with Billie and her mum Sian after being asked to talk to Billie's school about my journey.

Motivational speaking, something that I never dreamed of doing, has now become a great vehicle to spread a positive message. Just quietly, I love it.

Number 4: Raise $100,000 for Camp Quality. It's great to see Camp Quality putting smiles on the faces of kids and families affected by cancer. Here, I got to meet 'Giggle', the robotic puppet who roams hospital wards looking to crack jokes and talk with the kids.

Campaigners. Helping others complete items from their own lists is something I now value highly and so when Kylie asked me to join her for Number 22 on her list, Be a Human Billboard for One Day, I happily obliged!

17 July 2011. 'That was special.' These were the words Mark whispered to me after I helped to push him for the duration of the Run Melbourne Half-Marathon.

Number 67: Live on a Desert Island for One Week. Absolute solitude. Stranded some fifty-five kilometres out to sea on a deserted island with not much more than a bunch of coconuts, a hammock and a ukulele, I'll never forget this week.

My favourite time of the day, sunset. I counted seven shark fins at one time on this evening.

Chapter 27

FROM A YOUNG AGE, my Christmas stocking would always contain the latest copy of the *Guinness Book of World Records*. I would spend hours poring over it and the tallest man in the world, the fastest human on the planet and the world's biggest dog all became childhood heroes of mine.

Quite tragically, my height is average (185 centimetres), I don't own a dog, and I run the 100 metres in about the same time it takes to roast a chicken. With a strong desire to make it onto the pages of the record book, it was clear that to realise my childhood dream of breaking a Guinness World Record, I had to find another skill, one that no one else in the world would be able to beat me at. I had to do some research.

After a long day of flicking through the pages of recent editions of the *Guinness Book of World Records*, I had created a short list of records that I thought I had half a chance of beating:

- The most custard pies received to the face in one minute

- The most spiders on the body at one time
- The most Ferrero Rocher chocolates eaten in one minute

United by extreme obscurity and a lack of skills, these records not only mirrored my own qualities but would also offer my best chance of success.

So which record would I throw myself at? Well, let's just say that sometimes in life you come across opportunities that seem too perfect to be true; some call this fate while others call it fortune. Either way, as soon as I laid eyes on this record, I knew I had found my calling:

Most eggs crushed with the toes in 30 seconds

All I had to do to realise my dream was to beat the current record of twenty-three eggs.

Although the act of crushing eggs may seem simple, further research showed that there were in fact many rules to adhere to in order to make the attempt official. The science of egg crushing was involved. Eggs were only allowed to be crushed with the big toes, and each egg had to be of a medium size (6 centimetres minimum!). On top of this, eggs had to be crushed from the side (not the top) and should the challenger wish, they were allowed to employ an assistant to help place the eggs in between their toes for increased efficiency and speed. In fact, the egg placer could extend his or her role to feet cleaning and eggshell debris removal at any stage during the attempt if he or she felt like it!

Amused by the meticulous attention to detail for something so ridiculous, it immediately became clear that it was crucial I found myself an Expert Egg Placer. For this I needed someone who was not only experienced in the obscure area of world record attempts, but also a little bit mad. Luckily I knew just the man.

Now, if you've ever wondered whether it's possible to skateboard across the entire width of Australia, the answer is yes. A man named Dave Cornthwaite rode 5823 kilometres from Perth to Brisbane on a longboard called Elsa in 2007 as part of a world record attempt. As it happened, I had read his book *BoardFree* back in Australia. At the time I used his account of his journey as a form of research for Number 54: Scooter Across Australia and after finishing the book, I sent Dave an email with a few questions and my congratulations. Although our brief email conversation was now a distant memory, I knew that a man willing to push a skateboard for five and a half months would at least consider placing twenty-four eggs in between my toes. I only hoped he still lived in England. After sending a hopeful email from Geneva, I received a reply a day later.

> Seb,
> I'm in. Sounds brilliant! If you need a place to stay, why don't you come to my house? We can train for a day and then go and get you a record the day after!

The man spoke my language. Without ever having crushed an egg with my toes, I was confident that this record was attainable. I flew to England a day later, the day before the TNT Travel Show.

'Welcome, fella,' said Dave as he greeted me with a hug outside his local bus station in North London.

It was a cold day and so he was dressed warmly with a big smile to boot. I, on the other hand, was wearing a pair of shorts and thongs while holding a shopping bag containing ten dozen medium-sized eggs that I had just bought at the supermarket. In terms of first meetings, this was certainly a strange one and it was made no less peculiar when, after only thirty minutes of talking, Dave and I found ourselves in his bathtub surrounded by egg yolks and the shards of eggshells. I, standing excitedly at one end of the bath, cut an awkward figure while Dave, positioned somewhat disturbingly on his knees in front of me, probably felt very similar. This is what it took to perfect the ideal egg-crushing technique and after an hour we'd come up with a great system.

I had to sit down on a chair with my feet strapped together by a length of material (a T-shirt) tied around the balls of my feet (the rules stated that this was okay). My feet would be resting on their outside edges, creating a pair of pincers with my big toes. As Dave placed the eggs dutifully between them, I was able to squeeze the eggs powerfully with my big toes. We were pushing the sport of egg crushing to a new level and just quietly were also feeling confident about the next day's world record attempt.

The day of the attempt I woke up nervous but focused on what had to be done. Dave cooked up a breakfast before we headed off to the show. Whilst sitting on the packed tube on the way there, Dave picked up a copy of *Metro*, a well-distributed free newspaper in London, and began laughing.

'Look at this, bro!' He giggled as he pointed at one of the pages within.

I peered over wondering what had made him laugh so much, then I too burst out laughing. I couldn't help it; I mean, what else would you do if you saw a photo of yourself plastered across a page of a foreign newspaper with the heading 'I'm here to smash a record'?

Unbeknown to me, Hazel had been promoting my TNT talk and as a result news of my record attempt had circulated widely. Somehow I had made it into the newspaper!

Thousands upon thousands of people lined the streets

waiting to enter the exhibition hall when we arrived. With attractive travel discounts and packages being offered, the event was huge. My nerves since breakfast had certainly increased but I wasn't quite sure what I was more nervous about: presenting my first-ever motivational talk or attempting my first-ever Guinness World Record!

'G'day, my name is Sebastian and to be standing in front of you today is the latest turn in what has been an incredible journey for me so far. I call this journey 100 Things.'

This is how I started my speech to a full room of interested onlookers and media.

Wearing only a pair of board shorts and a T-shirt with the words '100 Things' that had become my favourite item of clothing since beginning the trip, my bare toes gripped the soft carpet with a mixture of nerves and anticipation. This feeling, however, I quickly grew to enjoy and by the end of this first line, I'd fallen in love with the art of public speaking. I remember feeling the same way when I ticked off Number 15: Stand-Up Comedy Routine, back in Sydney before I left.

As my speech went on, every time the crowd laughed or asked a question, I felt more alive and more enthusiastic, almost as if I'd consumed multiple energy drinks before stepping on stage. Soon I noticed a room of faces looking up at the photos and videos on the projection screen, all with big smiles, and I sensed that they were not only enjoying the talk but also taking something from it. Contrary to my time spent at university where I gave presentations on topics such as biomechanics and the implications of overtraining, I truly cared about the subject of this talk. It was an amazing feeling.

'And so on the piece of paper that I left on your seats before the talk, you should have written at least one thing that you have always dreamed of doing. It could be travel-based, or it might not be, but whatever it is, I hope that by seeing that an average bloke like me can achieve his goals, you now know that so can you.'

The important point that I tried to convey was that everyone's list is different and while my items tended to place me out of my comfort zone, someone else's goals might in fact be the complete opposite. Having read through many of my campaigners' lists that I'd added to my website since creating Ailie's profile page back in New York, I'd seen a huge variety of items, some driven by emotional or spiritual reasoning to those more financially or physically focused. Everyone's list is different.

'And just to show how easy it is to tick an item on your list, I am going to try and tick off an item on my list in front of you all right now.'

With that, Dave approached the stage holding the bag of eggs and announced to the crowd that I was about to try and break the Guinness World Record for crushing the most eggs with my toes in thirty seconds. As he read out the rules, the crowd gathered around the front of the stage in full view of forty-eight medium-sized eggs (leftovers from training) which sat contentedly on a large plastic mat used as a protective layer for the carpet beneath. In front of the eggs sat a chair, and as I walked over and sat down, my nerves, along with the crowd's, began to peak.

Once again, my Expert Egg Placer Dave was on his knees in front of me, hands hovering above the eggs. My feet were bound by material and we were ready to go. Behind the stage stood two official timekeepers and on either side of my feet were two cameras, there to capture evidence of the event.

'Five, four, three, two . . .' the crowd counted down to the start of my record attempt, 'one!'

The first egg took three separate thrusts from my toes to crush. This was worrying as in practice each egg only took one thrust. Only then, a few seconds into the attempt, did I realise that we had made a huge mistake; we had not taken into consideration that unlike in the bathtub, we were now crushing on a soft carpet which would have more give. This was problematic.

As the seconds ticked by, adrenaline had set in and one egg crushed led to more and more. Plumes of yolk and eggwhite shot up from between my feet, spurting directly onto Dave's forehead. He was a mess, yet still he continued to place the eggs robotically between my toes which by this stage had crushed ten eggs in good time. At the halfway mark of twelve eggs, we seemed to be on schedule but with eggshells collecting between my toes Dave had to sacrifice valuable seconds to scoop out the debris before placing the next egg.

The crowd by now had begun counting loudly the number of eggs crushed with every crack, and my toes responded with excitement and determination. I had no idea how much time we had left as the timekeepers kept silent. As yolks and eggwhite continued to explode – in what must have been one of the strangest spectacles that anyone present had ever seen – we destroyed another three eggs at pace before Dave lost control. Literally, eggs began to spill everywhere as they slipped between his fingers and rolled around the mat. I joked later that bad ball skills were to be expected from an Englishman, but in reality the amount of slime now festering everywhere within a one-metre radius of us was almost certainly to blame. We battled on.

With the egg count shooting up to twenty, I knew I needed to crush just four more eggs to reach the record but still I didn't know how much time I had left; the only option was to keep crushing. At that moment, like a racehorse hitting its straps down the home straight, Dave regrouped and placed a succession of four eggs perfectly between my feet as my tiring toes crushed each one emphatically.

A split second after I had crushed the twenty-fourth egg, a timekeeper yelled, 'Time!'

We had done it! The crowd erupted as Dave and I high-fived each other. As we stood up to face the crowd, I felt like a hero, beaming with a smile that no one could take away. Dave, on the other hand, covered head to toe in egg, resembled a villain from *Scooby Doo*.

I had smashed the previous record of twenty-three eggs by one and in doing so had ticked off yet another item from my list.

I have no idea who had more fun, the crowd or me and Dave.

I had become an official Guinness World Record Holder (if you want proof, check me out on the official Guinness website!), somehow being celebrated for an act so farcical that people could only laugh at the mere mention of it. Not just this, but I'd successfully delivered my first public talk.

Number 19: Guinness World Record – tick!

Chapter 28

ON A JOURNEY WITHOUT plans, guidebooks or checkpoints, it's sometimes hard to calibrate how it's all going. Up to this point I felt that my journey was heading in the right direction but other than this feeling, I just moved forwards without measure. The idea of brainstorming with someone who was on a similar path to me was certainly appealing, if for no other reason than to compare notes, but it wasn't every day I bumped into such a person. Never did I think that when I finally met that person, they'd also happen to be an Expert Egg Placer.

The life of a professional adventurer, as Dave explained to me, is based on a love of challenges. He enjoyed stepping outside of what he called 'herd mentality' to see what else lay out there. We were very similar in this regard.

After we cleaned ourselves of egg, that afternoon Dave introduced me to a few of his friends at a bar in the area.

I don't think I'd ever been so impressed by a group of strangers. The first guy I was introduced to had recently walked the length of Iran, while the second person had only just returned from cycling around the world for the second time. (I forgot to ask whether he went in the opposite direction on the second ride to combat dizziness.) As the introductions continued, so too did the trend that everyone at the table had achieved an incredible expedition of one sort or another. If I wasn't speaking to a girl who had rowed across an ocean, I was hearing from a guy who had run across a continent; it was deadset as if I had walked into a bar full of superheroes. If they had suddenly stopped after a minute and told me they were joking and that I was being filmed, it would all have made sense, but this never happened; they were serious.

After a few hours of sharing tales, it dawned on me that even though we had different goals, we all had one thing in common: the way in which we achieved our goals. Whether it was to be the first person to circumnavigate the globe under their own steam or indeed to crush twenty-four eggs with their toes in thirty seconds, we all prioritised our own goals and went through a similar process to achieve them.

This process started with realising what the goal was – goal setting. With something to strive for, it was then a matter of researching that goal for the first time: what, when, why and how. Armed with the knowledge of what was needed to achieve the goal, it was then a matter of applying ourselves or manoeuvring into a position where we could line up the goal in our sights. Then the only thing left to do was to commit, or pull the trigger; once you throw yourself at something in a measured and confident way, the fifth step of achieving the goal is hard to miss.

I hadn't ever consciously thought about this process before, so with some kind of model forming in my head, I wrote it down on a piece of paper as soon as I got home. No matter what the goal, this simple five-step process seemed to apply.

Our success was based on this mentality – combining vision, determination and commitment.

Funnily enough, I learned that most of the group had also spoken at the TNT Travel Show at one stage or another. From there they had all gone on to write books, make documentaries and speak at large events, hence forging careers as professional adventurers. They had turned their passions into careers. Of all the job titles I'd ever heard of, this was a pretty decent one to have on a business card, but even so I knew I didn't want to label myself as such; for now I was happy exploring.

By the time I made it back to Geneva, just one day after breaking the Guinness World Record, I found that my email inbox was full. Unsure of what to expect, I opened it and was blown away by hundreds, if not thousands, of emails offering support and congratulations. It appeared that word of the world record had gone global overnight and suddenly my adventure had been featured in media spanning five continents! It was overwhelming. In one instance I replied to an email from a guy living in Hong Kong, simply asking how he had heard of the journey. He wrote back to me with an attachment of a newspaper clipping from his local Chinese newspaper. In the middle of the front page was a photo of me riding a bike through Cuba. I would love to tell you what the article said but it was written in Cantonese. I could only hope that it was complimentary.

Not only were people sending their wishes and on occasions sharing their lists as part of my slowly growing Campaigners Page, but also for the first time I had now to deal with emails titled 'Media Inquiry' as radio stations, TV shows and magazines from England, Switzerland, Australia and beyond asked for interviews. I'd be lying if I said it wasn't exciting. As I sat at the office computer at The Clubhouse trying my best to sound professional in answering these requests, Jiggles and Wizzo would come in and laugh at me.

Of all the interviews that I gave within that week-long period, my favourite one was with a morning TV show on Australia's Channel Ten network called *The Circle*.

The Circle was comprised of four female hosts who, seated around a table, would discuss certain topics whilst sipping on cups of coffee. The show had huge ratings and so when they asked if I wanted to do a live Skype interview from Switzerland I jumped at the chance; I loved the idea of connecting with an Australian audience and I could even say hello to my mum! The only downside was that due to the time difference between Switzerland and Australia, I had to wake up at 2 am to give the interview.

'Live from Europe, via Skype, please welcome the world record holder for Most eggs crushed with the toes in 30 seconds, Seb Terry.'

The introduction, although accurate, was just ridiculous and after waving hello and giving a brief explanation of what it was I was doing with my life, they then showed the actual footage of the record attempt. Although I couldn't see the girls on my computer, I could tell they liked it as their laughter filled my lonely room; admittedly my record was one that seemed to make people laugh more than applaud. The most surprising thing, however, was to hear a live studio audience in the background join in the laughter. It was a strange feeling to have a studio full of strangers laughing at me whilst I sat in a dark room in Switzerland wearing nothing but a pair of undies and a T-shirt.

After we said goodbye and the live feed ended, I sat there on the couch buzzing with energy. It was almost 2.30 am and I didn't know what to do with myself; I certainly couldn't sleep. I never imagined my journey would attract interest, let alone that of the media, but suddenly I could feel a huge surge of momentum. This was confirmed as I checked my Facebook page, which only minutes after the interview had finished, showed even more activity from people throughout Australia who must have just seen the footage. Even better than this, I had received an influx of donations for Camp Quality. Once again I began to see the relationship between the media and my journey as a good one.

With donations nearing $9000, just $1000 shy of the $10,000 target, I realised this item would soon be ticked off but that once I'd reached the total, I'd still have over fifty items to complete. Raising money for Camp Quality had become something I loved doing and it made no sense to me to stop doing so at $10,000. There was only one solution: to raise the total.

Over dinner with a few mates in town that night, I brought up the topic of raising the total and by the time our plates were cleared it was decided; the fourth item on the list now read: Number 4: Raise $100,000 for Camp Quality.

Why not? To celebrate, Fabio, one of the nicest guys in town, donated 1000 Swiss francs on the spot. I was now just $90,000 short of ticking off item Number 4.

If there was ever encouragement for me to turn things up a notch, this was it.

Chapter 29

NESTLED PERFECTLY BETWEEN THE French and Swiss Alps, Geneva is an ideal spot for keen skiers looking for a weekend getaway. I certainly wasn't in Geneva to ski, but since Number 8 on my list was to attempt an Olympic Ski Jump, one day I decided to join a kids' ski class in Chamonix to learn the basics of ski-jumping. Having never skied before, it was a very unflattering experience to have six-year-old kids laugh at me as I floundered on the cold snow. But the experience was so funny that I wrote about it on my blog declaring that it didn't matter that I couldn't actually ski; all I needed to know was how to fly.

My very loose plan, as I went on to explain, was to simply turn up to a ski slope, walk to the top of a jump and throw myself down it with nothing but a pair of skis and a borrowed Lycra ski suit to cushion what would no doubt be a spectacular landing.

To support such wishful thinking, I placed a phone call to my private health insurance company in Australia in order to double-check that I was actually insured for ski-related injuries. After browsing my details, the lovely woman on the other end of the line confirmed that I was covered for the act of skiing, but then went on to specify that I was not covered for the actual stunt of ski-jumping. This last comment stumped me as I had made no mention of attempting an actual ski jump, and so I fell silent for a moment.

'Did I say that I was going to do a ski jump?' I asked sheepishly.

'No, Seb, but we all follow your website in the office and so we read it on your blog yesterday!'

Apparently there was a downside to media exposure, and didn't it make me feel stupid!

I postponed the ski jump for the time being and thanked the woman for the interest. I needed more training.

My policy of replying to all emails and messages that I received had meant that since returning to Geneva from London, I had spent most of my days at my computer. I didn't mind this at all, though; as I saw it, if someone had taken the time to write to me, the least I could do was write back.

Following a mini media blitz, many of the emails were from people offering help with items on my list. From offers of spare beds and dinners to contacts and discounted activities, I couldn't believe the support.

The only limitation, it seemed, was my own admin skills, or lack thereof, should I say. After all, I wasn't the most efficient person in regard to sorting out my own affairs. Drawing on recesses of my brain that I hadn't used since school, I often woke up in the middle of the night remembering that I'd misplaced an important email or forgotten to ring someone back.

One such email that I had neglected was from a girl called Nike (pronounced *Ny-kee*) who, after hearing of my antics, had written a short email asking if I was interested in being involved in a documentary of some sort. Now obviously the prospect of being part of a documentary was immense, but without much detail of what the documentary was about, I got the impression Nike was glorifying what was in fact some kind of mid-term university project. Nonetheless, I replied with my phone number then swiftly forgot about it.

It was only when my phone rang a few days later, minutes before I was due to start an afternoon shift at the pub, that my thoughts returned to the documentary.

On the phone was Nike; she was calling to see if I had thought more about the idea. I lied and said yes, but in honesty, due to the many emails I'd received in the past week, I couldn't quite remember her exact message.

Thankfully Nike was nice enough to jog my memory before then going on to describe in lots more detail why she had contacted me. It turned out that Nike was not a university student after all; she was actually from one of England's largest advertising agencies and was contacting me on behalf of one of her biggest clients, Honda. Basically Honda were releasing a new hybrid car, the CRZ, and as part of the marketing campaign they wanted to film a documentary that told the stories of people travelling around Europe as they endeavoured to follow their dreams. Called 'Live Every Litre', the underlying message of the campaign was that life is not about the destination but instead, the journey. 100 Things, she told me, fitted the mould perfectly.

After dismissing the possibility that a friend was playing a prank on me, I digested what Nike had said and asked the first question that popped into my head.

'Do you mean Honda as in the car manufacturer?'

'Yes,' Nike laughed.

All of a sudden my mind raced with possibilities. I

remembered feeling the same way in Year Six when my teacher sat the class down in preparation for our first sex education lesson. Similar to that occasion, I giggled to hide my excitement. Visions of driving a car around Europe whilst ticking off items from my list were already filling my head. I couldn't help it!

It all just seemed so strange to me that Honda, a leading car manufacturer, would be even slightly interested in a guy who wanted to achieve such things as Feature in a Bollywood Movie (Number 7) or Live with a Tribe for One Week (Number 79), but apparently they were.

'So, we'd like to invite you to enter our online competition and put yourself in the running to be chosen,' continued Nike.

Competition? My excitement died down immediately as I realised that I was not actually being offered a role in the documentary; I was just being offered the *chance* to be in it. I swallowed my misplaced joy and, minutes later, after agreeing to submit an entry form, thanked Nike for the call. Shortly after, I began my work shift; I was twenty minutes late.

Wizzo was the first person I saw at the pub. He asked me why I was late to my shift, so I told him about the phone call I had just received.

'It's all happening, Sebbo. Well done, mate,' he replied in the exaggerated Australian accent that he now practised on me whenever we spoke.

Admittedly I was stoked to have been asked to submit my story, but at the same time I was subdued by the thought that perhaps I wouldn't hear from Nike again. 'Cheers, Wizzo, but like I said, I didn't actually get the part; it's more of a competition.'

Thankfully I didn't have to wait long to find out. A week later, I learned that I'd been selected.

With images of driving a Honda CRZ through Europe once again entering my head, the realisation that the next section of my trip had arrived was an exhilarating thought. The funny thing was, I had no idea what a CRZ looked like. Regardless, mine was red.

Chapter 30

'So, Sebastian, I'd like to start by introducing everyone on this conference call.'

Until now, I'd never actually experienced a conference call; I thought they only existed in movies involving Tom Cruise, and so as Nike introduced me to the Live Every Litre (LEL) production team, all in their London office, I felt slightly awkward that I only had myself to introduce to them from the small office of The Clubhouse. I considered grabbing Edgar from the kitchen, but as always he looked busy.

After saying a brief hello to the team – Laura, Sarah, Paul, Rob, Jeremy, Fey, Gareth, Tamsin and Giles – I was introduced to the final piece of the puzzle: the project director.

'Hi, Sebastian. My name is Claudio von Planta. I'm the director of *Live Every Litre* and we're excited to have you on board.'

Now if you've ever seen the documentary series *Long Way Round*, which follows Ewan McGregor and Charley Boorman as they ride motorbikes around the world, you've probably

also laid your eyes on Claudio; he was the guy filming everything who featured quite a bit in the show when he at one
point fell off his bike.

As the conference call progressed, I soon learned just how
big this project was. The documentary would feature a total
of about ten people who, like me, had been picked because of
an interesting journey that they were on. Among us was a girl
who dreamed of performing a burlesque show in Paris; a mad
Metallica fan who aimed to attend every one of their shows
in Europe; and even a bunch of blokes from England who
wanted to sail a bouncing castle across Lake Garda in Italy.
Each of these adventures was impressive in its own way but
one thing that struck me was the amount of planning it would
take to capture them all on film. Hotels, flights, cameras, crew,
activities and a few Honda cars were just some of the things
that the team at Live Every Litre had to organise. It was epic.
I felt guilty for being so excited about it.

'We also agree that your journey has a lot of substance to
it and so we want to use 100 Things as a thread that links the
whole documentary together. In this way we will be helping
you complete about five separate items from your list around
all of Europe. From our end, we just need to know that you
are up for all the work.'

From my end, I still failed to see what the catch, or for
that matter the work, was, but in my most corporate-sounding
voice I declared that I was ready to commit. I feared that if I
screamed with excitement, as I honestly felt like doing, they
might be put off. Thankfully, minutes later, we had a deal.

The next few weeks of planning for the documentary were
awesome. We started with the task of picking five appropriate
items. Not wanting to seem too crazy at first, my initial suggestions were fairly timid, but it turned out Numbers 31: Build
Something, 45: Sumo Wrestling and 48: Act in a Play were all

passed up by the team. Instead, to my delight, they asked if I'd be up for attempting a few of the more risqué items that involved nudity, protests and giant needles. Of course I was.

The fact that the Live Every Litre crew wanted to support these types of items was incredible. The only issue was the legalities but with Nike on my side, I had no doubt it was all possible – you see, I'd argue that Nike is probably one of the most capable workers on the planet.

When she rang me to say that everyone had agreed that they'd like me to tick off Number 52: Sports Streak at an upcoming French sporting event, I couldn't stop laughing.

'Why not, hey? Which event are you thinking of, Nike?' I asked.

My first thought was that there might be an obscure sporting event happening in a remote country town where security, and public interest, would be minimal. It turned out I couldn't have been more wrong.

'The French Open,' replied Nike.

I couldn't believe it; Nike had suggested that I streak at one of the major drawcards not just of the tennis calendar but also the international sporting calendar. Was it possible? Yes. Would it put me out of my comfort zone? Yes. Was it possibly something that I would go to jail for? There was a trend in the answers that made this last question slightly worrying.

As it happened, Honda's legal team got back to us a few days later, telling us that there was no way Number 52 on my list would be able to go ahead as part of the documentary and only then did my heart rate drop. The French Open would have to stick to balls of the furry yellow variety.

Soon enough though, we agreed on five items from my list:

- Number 18: Hit a Hole in One
- Number 30: Join a Protest

- Number 58: Skydive Naked
- Number 63: Get a Tattoo
- Number 98: Crash a Red Carpet

In what was shaping up to be an incredible month, I also received another email from the girls on *The Circle* back in Australia. They wanted to do a follow-up Skype interview after what they said was a great first segment. Somehow they'd heard the news of the upcoming documentary. In fact, it looked as though they wanted to continue following my journey, labelling me as their own Aussie adventurer.

Things were about to get exciting.

Chapter 31

AS THE LEL TEAM worked behind the scenes in readiness for the five list items we had agreed upon, I continued to work towards other items outside of the documentary. My list made me far more productive as a person and as a result I found that I was always busy planning, scheming or doing. Consequently by the time I flew to London to film the first of the five items with LEL, I'd managed to tick off Number 85 on my list: Go on an Adventure, as Dave Cornthwaite and I completed a world first by travelling across Lake Geneva, one of Europe's largest freshwater lakes, on stand-up paddleboards. With blistered hands, an aching body and memories of sleeping under a jetty fresh in my mind, the contrast of getting picked up by a chauffeur at Heathrow Airport was strange to say the least.

In fact, this was just the beginning of what was an amazing weekend in London. My goal was simple: to tick off item Number 30: Join a Protest.

After a great night's sleep in a lavish hotel, I met with the director, Claudio, at reception bright and early the next morning. Having been talking with the team over the best part of a month about ideas and logistics, I had assumed there might be an itinerary for the day; however, Claudio told me, 'We're just following you around, Seb. Pretend I'm not here; you're the one who wants to join a protest!'

This was the best answer I could have got; I had free rein to do whatever it took to complete this item. The bonus was that it would all be captured on camera, just in case no one believed me.

So why did I want to join a protest? Well, as a kid, I played rugby with a boy called Hugo. He was a nice guy but often couldn't make weekend matches because he and his family were out protesting. This always fascinated me and so when I asked Hugo what it was that he and his folks protested about, he simply said, 'Everything.' It turned out that they just loved the right to protest. This struck me as being slightly strange but at the same time, having never participated in a protest before, I was intrigued to see what all the fuss was about.

Now in London, with Claudio following my every move, I was about to join the infamous May Day protests. The only issue was that I had no idea *what* I would be protesting!

On the first day of May, every year throughout Europe, protesters take to the streets to relay various messages of unrest and change. This day has over the years been labelled the May Day protests. I was going to be part of the 'UK Election Meltdown' protest which Nike had kindly researched for me.

My only real insight into the protest was that it had something to do with British politicians; this and the fact that it would take the form of a march. Starting at a quiet muster point at a secret location, the protest would then wind through London before ending in front of the Houses of Parliament at Parliament Square. Seemingly quite a straightforward plan, the only hiccup in our preparation was that we arrived at the muster point so early that we were the first ones there!

As I waited for my fellow protesters, I decided to pick the brains of one of the many policemen who were waiting in anticipation at the side of the road. A friendly chap, he spoke with a wry grin as he explained that traditionally these types of protests avoided violence. After a while a few more protesters joined me. Carrying rolled-up banners, a two-piece horse outfit and a tied-up mannequin depicting the then Conservative Party leader, now the UK Prime Minister, David Cameron, they certainly looked prepared.

I walked straight up to the newcomers to offer my services.

'I've come to protest. Can I help?' My opening line was sincere.

'Well, you can be the front part of the horse if you like,' said one of the protesters. Funnily enough, their opening line was sincere too.

Immediately I'd found my place for the day. I was going to be the front part of a horse. A horse with no idea of what we were protesting about!

One of the female protesters explained that the protest was about the lack of decent options the British people had in terms of candidates for the upcoming elections. She rattled off a list of names, none of whom I recognised, declaring that they were all *rubbish*. I thanked her for the info before scuffing my feet; matters such as politics don't interest a horse.

As more and more people turned up, the time to start marching was upon us and with a motley crew of about 200 disgruntled-looking anti-capitalists, we set off. I, now hiding beneath the front half of the makeshift horse, led the protest. Directly behind me was a bored university student who played the part of the horse's arse effortlessly. Behind him rallied the remainder of the group who, on foot, flew flags, sounded horns and chanted along with a fierce woman who commanded respect with her megaphone.

The next thirty minutes of marching took us along the River Thames towards the heart of Parliament Square. Claudio, whom I had forgotten about up to that point, jogged around the scene capturing everything on camera from angry protesters to concerned policemen. Photojournalists swarmed around our group mainly taking pictures of the horse. Beneath the horse's head, all I could do was laugh to myself. This was going very well indeed.

When we reached Parliament Square, you could have been forgiven for thinking the circus was in town. Despite sporting face paint, ridiculous outfits and misspelt banners, the group's ultimate goal was to be taken seriously. I seem to recall we even had a bearded woman among our group.

As it turned out, the square was a meeting spot for various protests and we were just one of four election-focused protest groups. Each group represented one politician who would then face the People's Court, designed to put each politician on trial. If the politician received an unfavourable sentence, the penalty was death by hanging or even beheading in the theatrical forecourt. Listening to the most recent chant that our group had sung, I felt that our politician's fate was already decided:

Build a bonfire,
Build a bonfire,
Put the bankers on the top,
Put Cameron in the middle,
And burn the bloody lot!

It took almost an hour of more photos and interviews with national press outlets before the trials began. At this stage I had managed to convince someone to take my place as the front part of the horse, allowing me to get near to the gallows which would host the last moments of our mannequins' lives. A portly executioner, dressed in full black attire (including mask and axe), stood at the front of the stage calling the politicians to the gallows one by one. His commitment to the role was so impressive that I would hazard a guess that this man had actually executed real men in his time.

Once strung up, the executioner would yell at the crowd something to the effect of, 'Shall we kill this scumbag politician?', to which the bloodthirsty crowd would respond with a flurry of fist pumps and shouts. The executioner would then hoist the body up and let it hang in the air for a moment.

By sheer luck, I was perfectly positioned next to the stage so that when the politicians were passed through the crowd and on to the executioner, I was the last person in the line and had to bring the body onto the stage. As if this wasn't good enough, the role soon developed into actually having to help the executioner apply the noose around the necks of these poor politicians. In front of hundreds of people, I had not only become an accomplice to murder, but also a welcomed member of what would surely be a well-known protest group in the papers the next morning.

As I stood gazing up at a cheap mannequin dangling from a rope, I grimaced as I wondered what my mum would think if she was there. As this thought crossed my mind, the executioner dropped the body into my arms and asked me to throw it to the crowd. There was nothing I could do – I had to play the part – and so I held the body in my arms and yelled at the crowd in a strong cockney accent, 'Who wants 'im?'

Apparently everyone wanted him, and so I launched the deceased politician to the third row of people who took to his body like a pack of sharks attacking a floating seal in the ocean.

The mayhem continued for hours. Finally Claudio stopped filming and removed the camera from his shoulder. He looked at me with a big grin and said, 'Brilliant, Seb. Brilliant!'

I had experienced a protest that I would never forget. Number 30: Join a Protest – tick!

Chapter 32

FOLLOWING THE PROTEST, THE LEL team and I hopped on a coach headed for Amsterdam, where my next item would take place. On a cold and grey London morning, for the first time I got to meet the whole team, including the lovely Nike.

'Well done yesterday, Seb!' Nike congratulated me with a warm hug. 'We saw some of the footage and it's hilarious!'

Things move quickly in the world of television, and it seemed that my work as the front part of a horse had been well received. I was in a good place.

I shook everyone's hand and introduced myself, but strangely I was met with familiar greetings similar to Nike's. The entire LEL team had thoroughly researched my story in the selection process and as such they all knew me intimately – not a hard task considering my website had a photo gallery including recently added pictures from my nude posing in New York!

Although it was becoming more common to meet people for the first time who already knew a lot about me, I still found it odd. It was like there was some kind of expectation of how I would be, but I didn't mind this at all.

The coach ride into Holland took the better part of a day and in that time it became clear that among the young and creative LEL team, this trip would be fun.

As we crossed the English Channel and travelled through France and Belgium, we discussed the thirty-six-day filming schedule. I would be needed for five days with a few travel days on either side of these. The other twenty-nine days would be focused on filming the various other people who had been picked for the campaign. The documentary would then be edited before premiering at a secret London location three months later. I felt privileged just to be a part of the documentary, but after hours of bonding, Tamsin, the caring motherly figure of the group dropped a bombshell.

'You know, Seb, we debated for two straight weeks whether the documentary should be based solely on your journey.'

I was stunned.

'What do you mean?' I said, not quite sure how to react.

'We very nearly decided to base the whole campaign on your 100 Things; we could have ticked off loads of your items over thirty-six days!'

In one sentence, she had rocked my world. Being followed by a film crew for an entire month as I continued my list was something I could never have dreamed of.

'Don't tell me that, Tamsin. Do you know how awesome that would have been? Yesterday was just amazing; I'd love to do that every day for a month!'

Although I felt as though I had missed out, I quickly realised that it didn't matter. I was enjoying myself regardless.

'So why did you decide against it?' I asked, not sure if I wanted to know the answer.

'The only reason we didn't do it was because of your

accent.' I suddenly felt really self-conscious. 'You see, this is a European-based campaign and to have an Australian as the face of it didn't quite fit. We wanted to so badly but in the end we just couldn't.'

I was disappointed but joked that I could have put on my best cockney accent if only I'd known it would have helped. Clearly, though, it was too late for any pleas.

The annoying thing was that back in Australia I was often pulled up for sounding English!

Chapter 33

AMSTERDAM IS KNOWN FOR many things, and although the majority of these would not be appropriate for filming, there was one activity that we agreed could appear in the documentary without the risk of being incarcerated: Number 63: Get a Tattoo.

For some reason I've never been able to commit to the simplest of things, from deciding on my favourite colour as a child to a particular style of clothing. As such, making a long-term commitment to something was my way of challenging my indecisiveness.

Of all the different and interesting places in the world to get a tattoo, Amsterdam seemed like a great option. Having booked the appointment a week earlier, I decided I needed to start thinking about what tattoo I wanted. I'd heard that most people take longer than a week to decide on tattoo designs that will stay with them for life, but bearing in mind my indecisiveness, this was never going to happen. Suggestions of flaming skulls, piercing daggers and Roman numerals were all considered but ultimately passed on. My latest idea for a tattoo was to have a collection of numbered dots that seemingly made no sense tattooed on my arm. When someone asked what the tattoo meant, I could hand them a pen and tell them to join the dots numerically, revealing the hidden outline of, let's say, an elephant. But still I was unsure. Humour is important to me as a person, but was this the right thing to base a tattoo on? I wondered.

Chris, the manager of the tattoo studio, in the middle of Amsterdam's red-light district, had opened his shop early for us but his immediately cold attitude as he led us into the bizarrely decorated studio gave me the impression that he'd rather be in bed. We didn't take it personally though, once he explained that he was always a little moody after three nights of nonstop partying. Admittedly this made sense but the idea of getting a tattoo from a grumpy bloke coming off a three-day bender made me slightly hesitant. Perhaps there was someone else available to tattoo me?

It was at this precise time that a skinhead entered the studio. With tattoos creeping out of his shirtsleeves onto his hands like a fast-growing vine spreading across a garden fence, I guessed that this guy was either there to get a tattoo or to rob the place. Soon I realised I was wrong on both counts.

'So, are you my victim today?' he asked me in a thick Russian accent.

A nervous laugh covered up the realisation that this skinhead was actually there to tattoo me.

'Yes, I guess so.' I looked over to Chris and then back again at the Russian, wondering who would do a better job, but at this stage I had no choice; it would be the intimidating skinhead.

'I'm Yuri. What tattoo do you want?'

Yuri, it turned out, had also been partying for three days but by the look of him, I would have guessed longer. Even so, he showed me pictures of previous tattoos he'd designed and surprisingly they all looked quite promising, if you were after a demonic-looking tatt. There wasn't much else in his repertoire.

In terms of my tattoo, I had a few ideas but the one that kept coming back to me was a simple saying that derived from a revered French author and aviator who lived at the beginning of last century, Antoine de Saint-Exupéry.

Saint-Exupéry wrote many books but was well known for one in particular, *The Little Prince* (*Le Petit Prince*). As it happened, I'd been reading the book in Geneva to help with my French and loved this tale about a little prince who lived alone on a distant planet.

The story relates a journey of self-discovery as the little prince travels the universe to see what else is out there. Each of the planets he visits is inhabited by an adult character who displays a foolish trait. He meets a king, a drunkard and a conceited man, to name a few. The seventh, and last, planet that the little prince visits is Earth. Eventually he finds himself walking through the desert where he encounters a wise fox. Having met an array of people and seen many foreign lands, the prince feels slightly depressed; his planet, he explains, doesn't seem unique or special anymore. Seeing the prince's pain, the wise old fox decides to share with him a very important secret:

On ne voit bien qu'avec le coeur. L'essentiel est invisible pour les yeux.

Translated into English, the fox's wisdom reads: 'One can only see truly with the heart. The essential things are invisible to the eyes.'

Fuzzy, a mate from rugby, had always loved this quote and as soon as he'd recommended it to me, so did I. My own journey of 100 Things was based on this very mantra; since leaving Australia I had followed only my heart.

This was to be my tattoo of choice.

It turns out that when getting a tattoo, not only do you have to decide on a design, but you also need a location. Yuri said that my left shoulder was fine. This was good enough for me, and so onto a chair I hopped in anticipation of a lifelong marking. Yuri began playing with a large needle that sat in a nearby medical tray. If it wasn't worrying enough that he had turned up not having slept, the fact that Yuri started to breathe deeply with excitement as he set up his tattoo gun, was. After a moment he flicked the on switch.

'Stay still now,' he insisted as I felt a pinching sensation on my shoulder.

In the lead-up to my big moment, I'd asked people what the pain of a tattoo was like and I heard some great analogies. Getting slit with a razor blade was the particular one that I was thinking of at that point, but I think that was a little extreme. If the truth be told, the pain was not too bad. Regardless, the tattoo was now underway and there was no turning back.

As Yuri sketched away on my shoulder, we spoke some more and I absorbed as much as I could about the crazy world of tattooing. Yuri obviously had a passion for it and this settled me a little. The sensation of the needle also soon became very dull, almost meditative, and after forty-five minutes, my tattoo was complete – and without a spelling mistake.

Although I'm not sure how much of the experience Yuri would remember, I shook his hand and thanked him for helping me tick Number 63: Get a Tattoo on my list.

Will the tattoo help overcome my indecisiveness? I can't say for certain, but it certainly brings a smile to my face.

On ne voit bien qu'avec le coeur. L'essentiel est invisible pour les yeux.

Chapter 34

DAYS AFTER RECEIVING THE tattoo, it was still there. This, of course, was a good thing and allowed me to show everyone back in Geneva that I had gone through with what was probably my first-ever lifelong commitment. Even the girls from *The Circle*, who were now interviewing me each time I ticked off an item from my list, wanted a look. I'll always remember this as the first time I took off my shirt on national television!

I had a full week before my next LEL commitment and so I took the opportunity to return to Geneva and work a few pub shifts. I had no idea what I'd be doing after the documentary and so I needed to earn some cash to give me some options. Sometime in this process I met a bloke called Big Matty.

In retrospect, 'Big Matty' was a fairly uncreative name for someone who stood at more than two metres tall, but it stuck. An Aussie bloke straight out of the air force, Big Matty was backpacking through Europe and needed some work. I served him a beer one night and after having a good laugh together, I introduced him to Wizzo and Jiggles.

Luckily there were a few spare shifts going at The Clubhouse at the time and so he began pouring beers. Let it be said that Matty was quite possibly the worst barman you'd ever meet but what he lacked in bar skills, he certainly made up for in trash-talking abilities; he was a funny bloke and swore like a sailor. A genuinely decent guy, he fitted in perfectly.

With great people, casual income, rugby and the beautiful weather heading into summer, my lifestyle in Geneva was something I really valued. Aside from this my French was also getting a lot better and I was now able to communicate in French with Jenny, albeit in a very simple manner, which gave me a great feeling of progress. Some things take time; for me, learning French was one of these.

My next stop on the LEL program was Cannes, on the south coast of France, and I'd been given the responsibility of driving a brand-new Honda CRZ all the way there from Geneva. It took almost a day to get to Cannes but at no stage was I bored; I was too nervous. I was only one day away from attempting a challenge as outrageous as it was unlikely – Number 98: Crash a Red Carpet.

I saw my list as a true extension of myself and one that reflected my curiosity and exaggerated the quirkiness that I was becoming known for. I loved the idea of chancing my arm and getting into situations that would normally seem completely surreal and so for this reason I always liked the idea of somehow getting onto a red carpet at a big event. Any red carpet would have done but the fact that this was the Cannes red carpet was even better.

Quite simply, the Cannes Film Festival is big-time. It's so big, in fact, that it draws more media attention than any other red-carpet event in the world. With this comes money. Boats carrying helicopters glisten in the harbour as supercars run laps around the narrow streets of the French Riviera. People are beautiful, bronzed and Botoxed. Clearly I would have to produce some magic if I was to be successful in Cannes.

Arriving on the eve of the opening day, we were greeted by thousands of excited people in the streets. A small beachside town, Cannes is based around one main road that hugs the French coastline. On the water side of this road sits the Palais des Festivals, which is where the Cannes Film Festival is held. Sure enough, as we drove by at a snail's pace, we passed a luscious red carpet that adorned the entrance area. The carpet ran along a large runway before following steps up to a grand entrance to the building. On either side of the carpet stood temporary grandstands for paparazzi. A huge barrier surrounding the area kept the media and tourists at bay. In the middle of the road, directly in front of the carpet, sat a traffic island designed as a pedestrian refuge which was swamped with people who I assumed had been waiting overnight for a key position. Some were even on stepladders to get the best possible vantage point. I was clearly not the only person trying to get close to the action and as such security was by no means subtle. Quite literally there were police and security guards everywhere.

Before arriving in Cannes, I had envisaged myself strolling along the red carpet, swirling a glass of Cognac in one hand whilst high-fiving celebrities with the other as we laughed and joked about the cost of plastic surgery. Now, metres from the carpet, I recognised that I'd be lucky simply to touch the red carpet without being tasered.

My only option was to try and outsmart the establishment.

With no experience in the art of red-carpet crashing, it was clear that the first step was to research the event; I needed to know what I was dealing with. This information I obtained thanks to a friendly security guard whom I started chatting to outside the front doors to the busy media centre. I asked him what I needed to do to get on the carpet.

He grabbed at a lanyard on his chest and showed off his official pass.

'You need one of these, sir.'

I looked around at the crowd and noticed that everybody near the carpet and official areas had a similar pass draped around their neck. He wasn't lying. Differing levels of accreditation allowed access to different parts of the area. Having no pass was not a good thing.

Plan A, therefore, was to try and get official media accreditation. By doing so, I would hold a pass that would allow me access to all areas of the event. With my very own cameraman, Rob, how could anyone deny me a media accreditation pass?

Alongside hundreds of proper journalists waiting to collect their legitimate passes at the media centre, I queued with a degree of nerves, and sure enough, when it was my turn, I was met with opposition.

'Sir, if you cannot present us with details of your media company, the reason for filming and a journalist résumé, we can't help you,' said one worker in the media centre.

I scratched my head and used my foolproof line, 'But I have a cameraman.' Plan A had failed, horribly.

A nearby journalist, who had picked up that I was essentially trying to scam my way onto the red carpet, approached me to share some advice.

'You can't get onto the red carpet dressed like that, dear.'

She had a point: my attire was definitely un-red carpet. Wearing a T-shirt, shorts and a pair of thongs, I looked like I was in Cannes for a surf rather than a stroll along the red carpet.

'If you want to get on the red carpet, you have to dress the part. Get yourself a tux.'

Perhaps she was right.

It was late by the time we left the media centre so we decided to call it a night and start fresh in the morning. On the opening day, less than twelve hours away, was the premiere of the new *Robin Hood* movie, starring Russell Crowe, a fellow Antipodean. Surely if I made contact with him, he would help me.

We left the main street of Cannes as council workers polished brass statues and touched up pedestrian crossings and other road signs with fresh layers of paint in preparation for the glitz and glamour of the first day of the festival. It was all about appearance.

The next morning it was time for plan B. Worryingly, this meant that we were one step closer to plan C, and plan C involved jumping the fence and trying to run onto the carpet. I wanted to avoid this, so Rob and I hit the streets in order to try and find a ticket, if not Russell Crowe himself.

Arriving at the red carpet at midday, once again thousands of people had beaten us to the main area. They were already lining the fences in a competition for the best view. The premier position of the traffic refuge was heaving with people once again and even more people on stepladders now looked down upon us.

As we walked past the entrance of one restaurant, I spotted a huge piece of cardboard dumped next to a bin. Plan B was falling into place. What if I wrote a plea of some sort on the cardboard and paraded around the Cannes Beach circuit?

A big smile from Rob confirmed the plan was at least unique and after a brief brainstorming session, we had ourselves our greatest weapon yet: a cardboard sandwich board that would advertise my needs. It read:

HELP! I NEED RED CARPET TICKET! INVITE ME PLEASE

By cutting out a hole in the middle of the cardboard, I could pop my head through and wander the streets as a walking advertising board. Surely a ticket would fall into my lap.

Needless to say, as I stumbled along the busy streets of Cannes, I drew a lot of attention, most of it unintended. The cardboard, you see, was a lot wider than I thought and consequently I couldn't help but brush or, worse, bang into, everyone I passed. Luckily, after reading my sandwich board, they found the amusing side of it. At one stage a Japanese TV station even interviewed me. An hour of laughter, however, did not result in me finding a ticket and so we decided to leave the scene, minus both the sandwich board and my dignity.

The previous night, following the piece of advice that the kind journalist offered me about attire, I had googled 'Cannes suit hire' and had written down the details of some shops. I knew that one was nearby. With time running out before the premiere began, Rob and I decided we had little choice but to try it. Once we found the shop (a fancy-dress shop, to be specific), it wasn't long before we found my tux. I'd like to say that it fitted like a dream but in honesty it felt like I'd borrowed it from a person half my size. Regardless, as I was now sporting a bow tie and shiny shoes, perhaps someone would mistake us for a legitimate film crew, or at least me for a TV personality.

With only an hour until the premiere, we walked back towards the carpet noticing a swelling crowd and a rise in anticipation. Understandably, my angle of approaching single females and asking if they wanted a red-carpet date did not work very well, though it did lead us to an entry/exit point where red-carpet ticket holders would go inside to pick up their official lanyards. It was here that I realised that I wasn't the only one looking for help; I was part of a clan of wannabes who were all begging for spare lanyards. The funny thing was that they too were dressed to impress! The men were stylish, the ladies elegant. I was not the only fraud. So cunning were these guys that they had formed a tunnel that the ticket holders would have to walk through in order to exit. It was an act of begging so desperate that naturally I stood at the end of the tunnel and joined in.

After ten minutes and no positive results, I looked at Rob and nodded. We were both thinking the same thing: it was time for plan C. We were now only minutes away from celebrities walking down the red carpet. Plan C was my last and only option. I had to jump the fence.

In preparation for what possibly might be the stupidest thing I'd ever done, I approached a nearby police officer for one final consultation.

'Excuse me, what would happen if I jumped the fence and ran onto the red carpet?'

His response came by way of sympathetic laughter.

After a humorous thirty-second conversation, we had covered topics including wrestling, tasering, imprisonment and fines. In short, if caught trying to make it onto the carpet illegally, the consequences were less than appealing.

With time against us, Rob and I made a beeline for the traffic island, which was the closest point to the actual red carpet, managing to navigate through huge crowds and an ever-increasing number of police and security guards as we went. I was nervous; I'd never been tasered before! After some pushing and shoving, we made it to the fence line closest to the red carpet but once there we noticed that both police and security guards, no more than five metres apart from one another, lined the fence. Awaiting the arrival of the celebrities who would emerge from their limos and walk to the carpet, they guarded the narrow road separating us from the red carpet with authority. My chances of getting to the carpet itself were looking slim at best.

The show soon began and with the onset of music came the stars. Celebrities have never been my preferred topic and when the crowd started cheering and screaming as yet another tall, leggy blonde got out of a car and smiled, I was left scratching my head as to who it was. Embarrassingly I did recognise Jean-Claude Van Damme, though.

As each celebrity made their way from a car to our traffic island to sign autographs and then back across the road to enter the red-carpeted area, the two nearest security guards – let's call them Gustav and Scarface – would scour the crowd for any potential danger. Armed with earpieces, protruding jaws and dark sunglasses, they were the real deal.

The biggest cheer of the evening was reserved for the last car in which sat Russell Crowe. As he left his car and waved at the crowd, I knew I had to talk with him. My theory that he would help me as I too was Australian was admittedly weak, but it was either that or risk my health by jumping the fence. All I had to do was get his attention.

'Russell, it's me – Sebastian!'

But my cries were drowned out by hysterical screams and, within seconds, Russell had crossed the road and vanished onto the carpet for his photos.

This meant one thing: I had to jump the fence.

Wanting to avoid a kamikaze-style run which would potentially lead to any one of the catastrophic outcomes explained to me by the police officer earlier, I needed to pick a moment when Gustav and Scarface were not looking directly at me. If I was able to evade them, perhaps I could walk straight past the other fifty or so security guards who stood between them and the carpet.

Shortly after Russell reached the carpet, Gustav looked to the left whilst Scarface looked to the right. Without hesitation, I ducked under the fence and, remaining calm, began crossing the road. My goal was simple: don't stop unless forced to.

I must have been watching the actions of Gustav and Scarface a little too closely as, after a few paces into the middle of the road, I instinctively placed my right index finger to my right ear as if listening to my own make-believe earpiece. Expecting to get pulled to the ground at any moment, my feet just kept moving forwards as I stared down, passing a group of seemingly unaware French policemen in the process. In my adrenaline-fuelled state, my reality had become such a blur that it didn't register that I'd actually reached the other side of the road until someone suddenly called out at me. My heart raced like it hadn't before as I ignored the voice.

The entrance to the red carpet, which was now only a few metres in front of me, had been narrowed as all the guests had arrived. On either side stood another two security guards whom until then I hadn't noticed. It was too late to change course. Again, a voice called out to me from one of the guards who now looked at me curiously as I approached with my head down. Acting on sheer impulse, my natural reaction was to start muttering random words into the collar of my shirt – I presumed that is where a microphone would be if I actually had a microphone – in an attempt to make them think I was some kind of security personnel.

Surely my luck was about to run out. Bracing myself for an imminent tackle, I took two more steps without slowing, continuing to talk gibberish into my collar as I moved forwards. It was at this stage that the guard who I'd now ignored twice up to this point stepped directly into my path and attempted to make eye contact. Still refusing to acknowledge that he actually existed, my seemingly arrogant behaviour must have somehow confused him into thinking that I was indeed a guest and almost immediately he stepped aside to avoid me walking directly into him. Somehow he'd let me through.

With my eyes still firmly focused on the ground, my heart almost exploded as I gauged the very edge of the red carpet only a few steps in front of me. Two police officers stood in my way but they weren't going to stop me at close range. In one exaggerated step that no doubt made me look like a complete clown, I leaned back and extended one leg out at full stretch in front of me, poking it between the two police officers before it landed right on the red carpet. I almost overbalanced but managed to avoid this before being let through once more.

I was on the red carpet! Not only this, but I was walking around freely.

Having actually made it onto the carpet, I now found myself in a strange position: I had no idea what I should do. I turned around and waved at a distant Rob, who was still stuck next to stepladders on the island back across the road, and then continued my stroll through the crowd and up the stairs where I took a deep breath. I'd done it!

For the next thirty minutes, I managed to chat to a few A-listers, get some photos with the tall, leggy blondes and even have a joke with Benicio Del Toro about eating beetroot. Soon enough the A-listers all entered the Palais des Festivals, leaving me alone on the red-carpeted steps smiling to myself. Against all odds, I had made it onto the red carpet at Cannes on the opening day. I felt amazing.

As I walked back down towards Rob, a throng of fans had made their way to the fence by the edge of the carpet, hanging on to the last glimpses of the celebrities they had come to see. Being the last one left on the carpet, and courtesy of the cheap hired tuxedo, I happened to look as though I might just be famous, and I noticed that people began watching me as if I was someone they knew. I wasn't quite sure what to do, until one man shouted out at me, holding a piece of paper and a pen. He wanted an autograph. I don't know who was more surprised, he or I, but naturally I obliged. I spent the next half-hour signing autographs, and on each piece of paper I wrote down:

Number 98: Crash a Red Carpet – COMPLETE. Sebastian Terry

Chapter 35

IT'S EASY TO TAKE things for granted in life. The places we visit, the events that occur and the people we meet are all pivotal to our experience and, good or bad, these are the ingredients that form our lasting impressions. Perhaps it was the fact that I was alone or that I had had nothing but positive experiences of late, but on a personal level I was becoming more and more appreciative of every day of my life.

Every person that I'd met through the LEL campaign was someone I hoped to see again and every activity I did made me smile. Claudio even picked up on it one day when he approached me with a camera rolling and asked a strange question that caught me offguard.

'Seb, I always hear you say that you're happy. Are you hiding something? I think that maybe you are not as happy as you say.'

It was the first time that someone had ever suggested that perhaps my smile was a facade for darker emotions. After taking a moment to digest the question, I looked straight at Claudio and answered him truthfully: I was just a simple bloke who was happy with life; that's all there was to it. I felt mildly silly for not having a more profound answer but I guess life doesn't have to be complicated for someone like me.

Perhaps Claudio was just after an interesting angle for the documentary, I don't know, but in any case he just smiled when I answered. This conversation did make me sit down soon afterwards and contemplate where I was.

Whether it was from being on the move so frequently or from constantly thinking about my list, I often found my thoughts racing. Compared with my headspace less than one year earlier, the contrast was huge and I felt like I was discovering more about myself than I ever had before. The simple fact of the matter was that with more proactive and ambitious thinking came new opportunities to achieve things that previously I had never considered possible. It was almost as if I'd freed myself of a set of shackles from around my ankles. Whereas previously I was slowly shuffling through life, I now felt like I was ready to run.

I began to appreciate that somewhere along the line I'd managed to overcome a huge hurdle that had limited my achievements before leaving Australia – one of fear. Although I never liked to admit it, I often used things like money, commitments, time and fear itself as excuses; excuses that ultimately acted as self-imposed barriers in my life. Now though, having stood at the top step of the red carpet at the world's largest media event, I was beginning to see that my trip was in fact my way of surmounting these barriers. I was now saying yes a lot more than I was saying no, and with this refusal to accept any excuses, even logical ones, I was achieving more and in doing so, I began to feel that anything was possible.

Hurdles are just that: hurdles. At the age of twenty-eight I was only now learning how to jump them.

Chapter 36

PICTURE A BIRD ELEGANTLY gliding high in the sky, looking down on the land below with only the sound of wind in its ears. How liberating! This was the feeling I wanted to experience when I turned up at the tiny French town of Mauberge in an attempt to tick off Number 58: Skydive Naked.

Why naked? I hear you ask. Well, I'd always envisaged that jumping from a plane and plummeting through the air to be one of the most incredible means of experiencing freedom, but now imagine doing this with no clothes on. Symbolically I could think of no better way to momentarily unshackle oneself. I had to try it.

My only oversight was that since it would be my first skydive I had to have an instructor strapped to my back. So, in the weeks leading up to the filming date, the main problem was not finding a place that would allow me to skydive naked but trying to find an instructor who was willing to have a naked man strapped to his or her chest. Thank God for the French!

And then there were the logistics of filming my naked jump to consider. In addition to following me with two normal video cameras, Claudio and his team decided to attach two mobile cameras directly to me. One of these would be anchored creatively around my chest whilst the other would be positioned somewhat artistically on my inner thigh, facing up. There was literally nothing that wouldn't be caught on camera during this jump. Whilst Claudio would accompany me to film the moment I leaped from the plane, Rob got the job of staying on the ground to film the landing. Given the potential angle of my approach, I'm certain Rob drew the short straw!

As our small plane ascended towards the jump height of 4000 metres, I sat at the rear of the plane staring at the exit from which I would soon be launching myself. With every metre climbed, I became more and more nervous. I suppose this is where I should acknowledge my second oversight. You see, I'd always thought I'd be alone in this little plane as I readied myself to jump, but as it was, the hold was actually crammed with other skydivers. Not only did they differ from me in that they were clothed but by sheer coincidence they were the current formation skydiving world champions, dressed in what I presumed was the latest and greatest skydiving gear. I admit that I felt slightly uncomfortable being stuck in one corner wearing only an instructor by the name of Jorge for clothing. Thankfully, though, Jorge had a great sense of humour and was not nearly as awkward as he could have been. I could also point out that he was clothed! Bearing in mind that we'd only just met minutes before taking off, the friendly local instructor was someone whom I definitely owed a beer when we touched back down on land.

'Sebastian, this is our drop zone. You are ready?' said Jorge.

The answer was yes; I was ready. Claudio, who had found

himself in the unfortunate position of sitting in front of me, turned the camera on me and asked how I felt. This I saw as an opportunity to justify my predicament right away.

'It's cold!' I said.

With that, the door opened and as if casually exiting the front door of a house, the Mauberge skydiving team stood up as one and began streaming out through the door. Having never witnessed anyone actually step out of a plane mid-flight, the vision of a group of ten people being sucked out the door then disappearing into the air freaked me out. It didn't seem natural. A tap on my shoulder meant that it was now my turn to do the very same thing. Placing my hand over my crotch in an attempt to hold onto my last piece of dignity, so to speak, I waddled towards the door whilst Jorge ran me through the basics of arm and feet positioning once more. However, with the noise of passing air filling my ears and my heart pounding, I heard little of what he said.

As I stood at the open door, I was quite apprehensive. Would my parachute work? I suddenly found myself at the point of no return. Without thinking about it, my toes were already hanging over the edge of the doorway and my hands gripped tightly onto the top of the opening as gusts of wind whipped past my face. I looked out towards the horizon and then down at the fields and tiny roads far below. It was surreal.

'Enjoy it, my friend. We jump on one!'

Claudio, cautious not to get too close to the doorway himself, crouched on one knee towards the front of the small plane, capturing every emotion on camera.

'Three! Two! One!'

We jumped. I was at the mercy of the universe.

I screamed for the first five seconds of freefalling through the air, but then it dawned on me that I would be descending at an increasing speed for some time and I soon fell silent. I had lost any sense of control. Quite literally I was naked and helpless. The gravity of Earth was sucking me closer and closer to potential death, leaving my fate to an unknown Frenchman awkwardly strapped to my back. The only option I had was to trust: in him and in the universe. I had to accept that my life was part of something far bigger. My mind cleared with this thought and that's when I felt it – complete freedom. I had let go; both vulnerable and powerless, I plunged towards the earth with a huge smile. I loved it.

Ironically it was without any form of control that I felt most comfortable. All I cared about was the present moment and as I looked around, I saw the world in a way that I'd never seen it before. Likewise, the world was viewing me in an entirely new way: nude and falling quickly from 4000 metres up in the air!

BOOM!

Just like that, the parachute had been deployed. My Continental friend had determined the next part of my life and thankfully he enabled us to stay alive and float effortlessly down towards the ground. We were safe, and I was ecstatic. I was at complete peace with myself; physically and mentally, I was just gliding. There was nothing else I could do. There was nothing else I wanted to do. I was simply going with the flow; that was what my life was becoming.

By the time I hit the ground and put some clothes back on, I'd never felt more liberated. I couldn't think of a better way to finish up the *Live Every Litre* documentary – blistered hands and all.

Number 58: Skydive Naked – tick!

(Note: I should point out that the blistered hands were in no respect caused by the act of skydiving. Instead they were a direct result of swinging a golf club 1000 times in a row as part of my desperate attempt a week earlier to tick off the fifth item: Number 18: Hit a Hole in One. After continuously hitting golf balls for five and half hours from a short par-three tee on a quiet golf course somewhere near to Geneva, the only hole I made was in my right hand! As such, completing this item would have to wait until a later date.)

Chapter 37

Sometime during the LEL experience, my sister Pascale had rung to tell me that she'd finally got engaged to her boyfriend Brett, who was also a good mate of mine from my uni days. I was thrilled. They were planning to get married on the beach in Sydney during the Australian summer and with their plan came a reason for me to return home. Although I joked that I'd have to see if I was free in January, getting home for Pascale's wedding immediately became an event in my diary that I couldn't miss. Until that moment returning to Australia had not crossed my mind but now the timing felt right.

Before embarking on the trip, I had the idea that I wouldn't return home until my list was complete, but by now I'd realised that this journey was in fact my life, and if life took me back to Australia briefly, well, so be it.

After I said goodbye to Pascale, I looked at a calendar. I decided I would go home for Christmas and then the wedding but I still had almost six months to play with – from June to December. Perfect.

And it appeared marriage was in the air. By coincidence, I noticed on Facebook at around the same time that Pete, Creature's brother in San Diego, had announced that he and his girlfriend, Osamu, had got engaged. Having shared some great times with Pete and his family just a year earlier, I was genuinely excited for the couple. I wrote a quick message to him.

Pete,
Well done, buddy. Stoked for you, you legend! Don't suppose you need the services of a fully ordained wedding minister?
Rev Seb

How could I not ask? Since becoming a fully ordained minister, I had almost forgotten about this bizarre qualification, but seeing Pete's news had reminded me that Number 27 on the list was to Minister a Wedding.

It seemed that June was a month for celebrating and with 9 June marking both my birthday and also the one-year anniversary of the begining of my overseas adventure, there was a lot to think about. It had been a lifetime of experiences squeezed into a single year for me and, contrary to what you might hear about time flying when you're having fun, leaving Australia felt like a long time ago. I'd somehow managed to tick off thirty-two items from my list and not once had I ever questioned what I was doing. From leaving my friends and family in Sydney on the morning of my twenty-eighth birthday with only a plan to visit J-Loc on death row, I'd found my way to Switzerland. I had new friends in my life that I valued hugely and had experienced things that had impacted on the way I viewed the world. On top of this my journey had developed into something that although I still couldn't quite define, I knew was amazing. Clearly there was only one way to recognise this significant moment and that was by ticking off an item from the list and, at 6 am on 9 June 2010, Big Matty, Fuzzy and I climbed to the top of Le Salève to complete one of the more symbolic tasks, Number 91: Plant a Tree.

Having found an ideal place a week earlier after an exhausting five-hour ascent, we knew exactly where to go. If you ever find yourself at the top of Le Salève, look for a lush green meadow about 100 metres from the summit. If you walk through this meadow and cross the gorge, you'll see a small cluster of trees on the far rise. Beyond these trees, you'll come to a grassy clearing that drops off the edge of a cliff, presenting a magnificent 180-degree view of the mighty French Alps. This was our spot. It was incredible.

After two hours of digging through tough ground littered with flint rock, we bedded our trees and soaked them with water from a nearby watertank more commonly used by cows to grab a drink. We were tired, dirty and smelt like manure, but together we had done what we had come to do. We had planted three trees in a triangle at the top of a mountain, albeit a small one. It was the perfect way to celebrate one year of my journey as well as my birthday and the three of us promised to meet at the same spot in ten years' time.

Although looking back at the past year and recognising how far I had come made me happy, it motivated me to make the second year even more memorable. First order of business, figure out what was next on the list. But I could never have guessed what would happen just a few days later.

Chapter 38

Seb,
I'm due to give birth to my child on 8 August 2010. You're
more than welcome to come and help out if you can. Let me
know if it helps you tick off this item from your list.
Tara

Many of the items I ticked from my list were the result of
planning, preparation and on occasions even training, but
sometimes the opportunity to complete one would pop up unex-
pectedly. Whether it was the forces of the universe, the power
of committing a goal to paper or even just great timing, these
opportunities were priceless. Number 23: Deliver a Baby was
one of these and for this reason I saw Tara's email as a gift.

Tara was a girl with whom I'd had a fleeting conversation,
no longer than two minutes, whilst working in Canada in
2005. So when I received her email, five years on, inviting me
to help deliver her baby, I scratched my head in astonishment.
It turned out that we had become Facebook friends at some
point through a mutual friend.

Number 23: Deliver a Baby was one of the most asked about items on my list. People often asked how I would tick it off and I always answered honestly: I had no idea. To me, this item was very special. As far as I was concerned, birth was as close to a miracle as you could get – the final stage of creating a human. I'd always wanted to be present at a birth and since I was nowhere near having a baby of my own, delivering someone else's was my only option.

I replied to Tara's email immediately, and said YES! Of course there were matters such as flights, accommodation, money and the act of childbirth itself to think about, but these would all fall into place. This I knew.

The first call of action was to phone Tara and discuss the offer. The conversation was an unusual one, but it was sufficient for both of us to realise that we were serious enough to go through with it. I found it really refreshing to hear that having already had a child, Tara simply wanted to share with someone else what she described as the most amazing experience in life. It was hard to express over the phone how much I appreciated her generosity.

After the call ended, I went straight to my backpack and found my well-worn credit card that had been hiding beneath my clothes. Minutes after wrenching it away from safety, I had bought myself a ticket to Canada. Perhaps in what was an example of me being slightly immature, I must confess that I found it more than fitting that Tara in fact lived in a city called Regina! Thankfully she saw the funny side of this as well.

With two months until my flight, I was free to enjoy what was a beautiful summer in Geneva with friends. My French was improving on a daily basis and I'd even started to speak some French with Mum over the phone. With the scent of progress being an intoxicating one, I began to wonder whether there was an appropriate item to tick from the list in the small window of time that I had left before I flew to Regina.

Of course the answer was yes.

Chapter 39

AFTER A BUSY PERIOD of filming and the prospect of yet another flight, this time to Canada, I felt as though I needed to do something from the list that would provide an escape from schedules and itineraries. I wanted to go walkabout. As it happened, I had just the item: Number 36: Walk Across a Country.

In the past I'd only travelled by plane, train, automobile or bicycle, never considering walking to be an option. Having flown a lot recently for the *Live Every Litre* documentary, I kept finding myself staring out of plane windows wondering what it would be like simply to walk to a far-off destination as opposed to flying there.

One Friday afternoon, after looking at my trusty world map that had guided me well on many occasions through-out my journey, I rang up Big Matty, with whom I'd become great mates at the bar. We were very similar in the sense that we were both open to the opportunities that life presented and were both in a position to do whatever we felt was important to us; Matty, through backpacking, and me, through my list.

'Matty, do you fancy walking across France with me?' I said.

'Yeah, bro – I'm in! When?'

'Don't know. How about Monday?'

'Done!'

Matty, like me, was in the habit of saying yes to things.

We had just two days to prepare for what would be a challenge that we knew little about. The only consideration for me was finishing the journey across France in time to make the premiere of the *Live Every Litre* documentary, which was being shown in London in two and a half weeks' time. This left us with about fourteen days to walk across France. I love a challenge!

Having served in the military, Matty was the obvious choice to be in charge of logistics. He prepared our backpacks and rations and gave me tips on walking techniques. Matty had done plenty of pack marches as part of his training, so I trusted in his confidence that we'd be okay. I, on the other hand, was left to work out the route.

Geneva sits close to the central eastern border of France. For the purpose of walking from east to west across France, this proved very convenient and so when Wizzo offered to drop us off at the border to start our walk, we were wrapped. We would have walked to the border but we figured we'd be doing plenty of that, anyway.

'It's like the blind leading the blind!'

Jiggles's passing comment as he wished us luck on our departure, although said in jest, was worryingly close to reality. Our limited preparation meant that we had no tent (just sleeping-bags) and only a small supply of clothes, food and my ukulele. On top of this, the weather forecast indicated that we were in for a week of temperatures in the mid thirties. If this wasn't enough to laugh at, our method of navigation surely was.

In my wisdom, I'd decided to use Google Maps to plot our route. Ingeniously I had found a walking icon on the site that when pressed would display a walking route. So our directions would lead us street by street, some 650 kilometres across France. Incredible.

Although great in theory, we quickly learned that in reality there were some pitfalls to following Google Maps' directions, one of these being that it failed to acknowledge the presence of mountain ranges. Consequently after walking for just over one day, we encountered our first mountain range. Somehow until that point, we'd neglected to consider that there might be mountains in France.

With our progress stymied by steep and winding mountain roads, we decided to brainstorm other alternatives. The best of these ideas came to us just as a train passed us at speed and disappeared into a tunnel that we imagined cut right through the mountain. We had to follow. The trip was turning into a real adventure. Soon after surfacing on the other side of the mountain, we realised we'd have to sleep on the side of the train track! Sleeping outdoors would be a constant theme.

The mid-thirty-degree daytime temperatures certainly made us sweat and we tried to rehydrate and fill up with food at every little town that we passed. Due to our route slicing fairly centrally through France though, we quickly worked out that we'd be travelling through the remote French countryside for most of the journey. I was proving to be quite the route planner.

After three days of an anticipated fourteen-day walk, morale had gone from high to low. Soreness had set in and, having been thrown off the national freeway by police (thanks, Google

Maps!), we were now largely confined to windy country lanes lengthening our journey even more. But we knew we needed to remain mentally strong. We stopped focusing on the distance to our final destination of La Rochelle; instead, we just concentrated on our daily goal of forty-two kilometres. By doing this, we knew we'd feel like we were making progress and, sure enough, as the days rolled by, we found that we were.

Before this walk, I'd never slept in a public toilet. Nor had I slept in a field next to grazing cattle, but with extreme fatigue and a tight budget came a lack of care where we rested. We simply slept wherever we needed to once the sun set and with the simplicity of walking until nightfall, came a sense of freedom.

On the morning of day five we stumbled upon a shopping trolley at the side of a road. With tiring bodies, it seemed like a good idea to throw our bags into the trolley and start pushing just to offer our bodies a little break. Ten minutes later we felt a lot better and one hour down the road, our feet had stopped hurting. By the end of an entire day of pushing the trolley that at some stage we named Trojan, we saw no reason to part ways and so just like that we were now a party of three travelling across France.

After crossing the mountainous regions, the land quickly became flat. This in fact rarely changed and from freeways to quaint farming roads, Matty, Trojan and I bonded as a team. My ukulele, which sat proudly in the trolley, allowed us to kill time on the longer stretches but more importantly it acted as a safeguard when approached by strangers. I guess it wasn't common to see two adults pushing a trolley along the side of a major freeway and so when we were questioned by the French police, a casual strum of the ukulele would cause them to drop their guard and ultimately allow us free passage in otherwise dubious territory.

'Where are you going with the trolley?' they would ask.

'The Atlantic Ocean,' we'd say.

'Well, that is not allowed, you know! Is that a ukulele? You may pass.'

By the time we'd reached the halfway mark of our trip, we had a routine. Twelve hours of walking per day would be split up by a midmorning break involving roughly four chocolate croissants each, after which a few more hours of walking would lead to a lengthy midafternoon snooze. This would set us up nicely for an early evening walk lasting until there was no more daylight. If it rained, we'd slip into unfashionable bin liners, and when we were bored we'd sing or share stories in which embellishment was not only allowed, but encouraged. We'd kill hours playing games involving getting cars to honk their horns at us and whenever we saw a confused farmer driving towards us on a tractor, we'd just wave whilst pushing Trojan with purpose.

After a while, we even became familiar with some of the passing truck drivers, who, in delivering freight across the country, would pass us by twice a day. They would beep their horns as encouragement and some even invited us into their homes for a cold drink out of the sun.

Spirits were high and we felt invincible. It was amazing what happened in the time it took for the sun to rise behind us, overtake us, and then bid farewell as it dipped under the far horizon, signalling the end of a day. Even when a rogue insect bit my eyelid, causing it to swell to a degree that I was hospitalised for one whole day, we bounced back a day later with a fancy-dress day which involved bright pink clothing that left little to the imagination. (We got a lot of honks that day. If only the drivers knew that we'd showered just once in ten days of walking.)

On day twelve, after an incredibly taxing but rewarding day, we hit a milestone as we noticed the first sign to La Rochelle.

Just 130 kilometres away, we knew that with three big days of walking we'd be at our final destination. We were so close that we both swore we could smell the salty ocean air beckoning us onwards. This was enough for us to forget about the pain in our bodies and so on we limped in shoes that had almost completely fallen apart.

After a few more sleeps and a further thirty-six hours of walking, road signs leading us to La Rochelle were replaced by welcome signs telling us that we had reached the finish line. Somewhat poetically, the first thing we ran into in town was a supermarket and so we had what was a truly emotional farewell to our beloved Trojan. He was no longer just a shopping trolley; he was a friend. Depositing him in a queue of less-travelled counterparts, we clicked him into line and laughed as a one-euro coin popped out of the handle upon return.

We did it! Big Matty and I had walked across France. It took sixteen days and it all ended when we soaked our heavily blistered feet in the warm water of the Atlantic.

Number 36: Walk Across a Country – tick!

Chapter 40

THE WALK ACROSS FRANCE had been life at its simplest: two men, a trolley and an open road. It was an incredible journey and one that would have given many passers-by the impression that we were hobos. To be honest, at times we felt that way too. The humour of it, though, was that with an estimated forty dollars in my bank account, on paper I was broke. But there was always my credit card . . .

About halfway through the walk Matty and I found ourselves resting in a quaint little French town in the middle of nowhere as I nursed a swollen eyelid (from the insect bite). I decided to check my email at a local internet cafe. The first email was from Tank back in Australia and the news I received made me scratch my head in disbelief.

Ring me ASAP. Mate, we sold the business!!!!!!

By virtue of my trip, Tank and I had spoken only a few times in the last couple of months and when we did catch up we spoke only about each other's adventures. The inflatable screen business that we'd paid off over a year ago was a distant memory, so the fact that the business had now been sold was more than a surprise.

The business itself was potentially very profitable; it just needed enthusiasm and commitment, two things Tank and I couldn't offer it. The new owners thankfully could. After working out a fair split that took into consideration all of Tank's hard work, my share was worth $42,000. Considering the amount of money in my bank account at the time, this was like winning lotto.

It felt unbelievable yet somehow inevitable. Since leaving Australia I'd begun to recognise a trend: things were happening at precisely the right moments, such that the journey could continue in what felt to be a very organic way. I honestly felt that if I was to be dropped off in the middle of nowhere with nothing but the clothes on my back, I'd still be okay and able to keep doing what I was doing. (Perhaps this should become an item on the list?)

After excitedly ringing Tank from a payphone and congratulating him on his work, I asked him to explain the ramifications of the sale. Not being one for details, I needed everything spelt out for me and so the rest of the conversation revolved around fantastically confusing terms such as Capital Gains Tax and Professionals' Fees. Tank, of course, was nice enough to give me a full run-down on what these terms actually meant and soon it became clear that even though I suddenly had a lump of money sitting in my account, I'd have to give a large percentage of that to the tax man at a later date.

I quickly calculated that after having to pay $36,000 of my portion in fees and tax, I was left with $6000! Again, I couldn't believe it.

Luckily for me, I'd known for a long time that money wasn't a driving force in my journey and honestly, I found it quite humorous that having worked almost every day for two years on the business, all I had to show was $6000. Matty, who walked beside me as I worked out the maths, was the first to confirm that this was in fact hilarious.

'Mate, that's the funniest thing I've ever heard!'

He was right, but either way the sale of the business gave me enough money to live in Canada without having to work until I returned to Australia in time for Christmas. Perfect!

In what ended up being an unbelievable week of news, I also got an email back from Pete. I'd nearly forgotten that I'd asked him if he needed a wedding minister, and so when he replied saying that he'd love to have me preside over the ceremony, I stood there for a moment stunned. Somehow I'd managed to book my first gig as a wedding celebrant. With this realisation came two considerations: first, what on earth does a wedding celebrant actually do? And second, when was the wedding? With the prospect of a birth in Canada and now a wedding in America, my fingers were crossed that timing again would allow both of these items to happen in unison. But just as my finances seemed to fall into place at the right moment, I trusted that so too would everything else.

For sixteen days as we crossed France on foot, my only focus was reaching La Rochelle. As a result I'd all but forgotten that by the time we reached the coast there was just one day to rest before having to fly out to London for the *Live Every Litre* premiere. Before I knew it, I was on a plane. Just for fun, Matty decided to come along as well.

More than two weeks of beard growth and two backpacks containing nothing but worn shoes and filthy clothes meant that neither Matty nor I were in any state to show our faces at the premiere. The plan on arrival was therefore simple: to freshen up and buy some appropriate clothes for the evening. Now perhaps it was due to the effects of dehydration, or more likely the constraints of time, but for some reason, after thirty minutes of clothes shopping in Camden, Matty and I thought it was a good idea to buy outrageous hippie outfits. Consequently at the premiere, Matty, wearing white flares that hideously complemented his purple floral shirt, stood proudly next to me as I sported tight baby-blue pantaloons and a matching shirt that resembled a curtain. We looked absolutely ridiculous, but the only thing that mattered was that we'd made it.

The event itself was based in the unique setting of the underground tunnels of old-town London. These had been converted on the night to hold a music stage, multiple bars, a cinema and an outdoor events area. It was like no other function I'd been to. Coloured spotlights illuminated the archways of the tunnels and loud music echoed from within. The polished Honda CRZ we had used for filming was displayed just beyond the entrance while official-looking people ran around busily making sure that everything was going smoothly.

Standing in a slow-moving line towards the venue entrance, Matty looked around and confirmed we were the only hippies there. But it seemed no one was looking at us anyway. Instead, they were staring at a large promotional poster looming above our heads at the entrance. It showed a naked bloke skydiving. Under the picture were the words:

What's on your list?

It was, of course, me.

'Jeez, Seb, maybe you should have dressed differently!'

Matty was quite possibly right. At no stage did it occur to

me that the premiere would be such a big deal; if I had known, I might have reconsidered dressing as a hippie.

With no time to come up with a plan B, Jeremy, one of the guys from the LEL team, ran up and shook my hand. He was excited to see me and dragged me through the entrance, anxious to introduce me to various people. Word of the journey and even the walk across France had spread by the time we'd arrived and as we moved about the venue, strangers would stop and stare, occasionally coming up to congratulate me on what I'd done. It was surreal.

'Sebastian, can we have a look at your tattoo?' giggled a group of girls who approached Matty and me.

'Sure!' I replied. 'How did you know I had one, though?'

'We've watched the documentary already!'

Matty laughed as I unbuttoned my shirt and pulled it over my shoulder to expose the tattoo. This was not the only time this happened that night.

Walking further into the depths of the tunnels, I was soon reunited with Nike, Tamsin, Laura and the gang from LEL. It honestly felt like seeing family again and they all seemed so happy. The editing of the documentary had been a long process but this night was the culmination of months of hard work for them. They had done well.

Jeremy grabbed me again and began to lead me into another room.

'Wait till you meet the guy playing you tonight! You'll love it.'

I had no idea what Jeremy meant by this and so I just followed him as he led us into a large room where two massive canvases rested against a wall. At the top of each canvas was the question 'What's on your list?' and on the ground beside each one was an assortment of paintbrushes and pens which Jeremy explained were there so people could write down their personal goals and aspirations on the canvas. So far the canvases had only a small collection of goals written on them. This room Jeremy went on to explain was a tribute to 100 Things. I felt completely humbled by the thought.

I then got a tap on the shoulder from a man dressed far worse than Matty and me.

'G'day, mate. I'm Seb!' he said.

The name Seb isn't all that common and to be greeted by someone with the same name is always a strange thing. The fact that this man was also wearing skin-coloured underwear and a backpack with a parachute hanging out of it made the introduction even more bizarre.

'Hi, I'm Seb, too,' I replied.

'This is the guy playing you tonight, Seb,' interjected Jeremy, who could see that I was utterly confused. Again Matty just laughed.

It took a moment for me to realise what was going on; after all I'd never had someone *play* me before, but the guy with the exaggerated Australian accent was here to act as me for the night.

'Are you even Australian?' I asked.

'No, mate, it's an accent!'

'A bad one at that!' quipped Matty.

After a few drinks and a chance to catch up with the other guys who had appeared in the documentary, the massive crowd that had shown up was ushered into the auditorium. The atmosphere was electric. We were all there to see the documentary and it seemed like I wasn't the only excited one.

Once we were seated and silence had set in, the curtains parted and the documentary began. As it did, the crowd immediately became absorbed as images of people sailing bouncing castles, stripping, headbanging and skydiving naked flicked past on the screen. A narrator pieced together the story and it worked brilliantly. At one stage I looked over to the LEL crew, whom I was seated next to, and noticed that they couldn't stop smiling. They were pumped.

Since I'd never been in a documentary before, especially one in which I played the main role, it was a very weird experience watching the production. The audience laughed, smiled, cried and clapped the whole way through. The biggest applause of the night came when the story was taken to Cannes. Everyone cracked up as I made an absolute fool of myself in attempting to crash the red carpet then went ballistic when I finally snuck onto the carpet untouched. So loud was the crowd's reaction that I felt embarrassed. Never in my wildest dreams did I think I'd be applauded for evading the French police!

After the credits rolled, I – along with the rest of the guys featured in the documentary – was asked to stand up. Everyone again went nuts. I was both proud and uncomfortable. As I've explained, I've never been great with compliments.

Vanity aside, the whole campaign was incredible. To see a collection of people, on and off camera, come together and achieve their goals was such a great experience. I'll never forget it. *Live Every Litre* was a hit and it felt fantastic to be part of such an incredible project. I couldn't stop smiling all night and, judging by the state of the two canvases that were left in the 100 Things themed room, other people had enjoyed the journey too – the canvases now had lots of dreams scribbled all over them.

I could get used to nights like this.

Chapter 41

THE PROCESS OF SAYING goodbye to those I'd become close to on the trip was always a little sad and leaving Geneva was no different. I'd made close friends with those from the pub, the rugby team and also Jenny, who shared the idea of making the most out of every day. I felt like I'd been looked after and had grown into a better person for it. The one thing that set me straight was the thought that wherever I was in the world I was only a day's travel away – a thought that has helped with many farewells along the track.

I also had the bonus of knowing that as one adventure ended, another equally exciting adventure was around the corner and so although it was sad to fly out of Geneva, I was excited about the prospect of the next step in my journey: delivering a baby in Regina.

'Can you please get me on this plane? It's important – I have a baby to deliver!'

Call me dramatic if you will, but I was desperate to get on the flight. Courtesy of Tal's generous buddy-pass offer, I had a cheap way of getting to Regina, but the catch was that it would take four separate flights, and since I was a stand-by passenger, none of them were guaranteed! My best way of squeezing on to flights was to plead my case.

'You're expecting a baby, sir?' asked the check-in attendant.

'Yes, she's due anytime!'

Technically this wasn't a lie; I was expecting a baby. It just wasn't mine. If the truth be known, Tara wasn't due for another three weeks, but I'd heard that at this late stage of pregnancy anything could happen. This was one of the most difficult items on my list so I couldn't afford to miss this opportunity.

After two days of flying across the Atlantic Ocean, mainland USA and Canada, I arrived in Regina. I was exhausted from sleeping in airports and had not changed clothes once. In a way I felt that *I* had gone through some form of labour! The first call I made after I landed was to the expectant mother.

'Tara, how are you? Have you had the baby yet?' I asked anxiously.

'No, let's have a coffee tomorrow,' she said.

This was a huge relief. For the first time in two days, I took a moment to relax.

Having spent about eight months in Regina several years earlier, I actually had a bunch of people who I really wanted to catch up with whilst in town. Two of these people, in fact, Roddy and Janita, had invited me to stay with them as soon as they heard that I was turning up to deliver a baby. I told them I'd explain everything when I saw them in person.

Roddy, a staunch Scottish rugby tragic, was always up for a cheeky act of debauchery. His better half, Janita, was a country girl, as quick-witted and switched-on as anyone you'll meet. If I wasn't laughing at one of Janita's jokes, I would be plotting a game of golf with Roddy or mucking around with their kids.

Since the last time I'd seen them, they had become a family of four with the birth of two adorable children, Jack and Isla. These guys were my adopted Canadian family and to be so close to people on the Saskatchewan prairies – the middle of nowhere, really – was quite strange. Jack, their cheeky four-year-old, even had a cuddly toy dog that he called Sebastian. Janita reminded me later that I had actually given her the dog as a present for the unborn Jack. She loved to laugh at my forgetfulness. I think at times she saw me as her third child.

When Tara and I caught up for the first time, I wasn't quite sure what to say.

'So he's still in there, I see.'

Tara laughed.

A single mother, Tara was a genuinely lovely girl with a heart of gold. It was the generosity of people like Tara that fuelled my trip and I let her know how appreciative I was of this. After catching up on her news and filling her in a little on my own, we marked out the best way to move forwards from here. I was to ring her every morning to see how she was doing and if something important happened, such as her waters breaking, she would ring me, no matter what time it was. I offered to help with anything else she saw fit, such as shopping, but she had most bases covered.

Unbeknown to me, before I had arrived, Janita had spoken about my quest to a friend of hers who worked in the local media. The upshot of that conversation was that the local paper, *The Leader Post*, wanted to run on a story about the crazy Australian who had flown to Canada simply to deliver a baby. This sounded like a fun experience and since I was now just playing a waiting game until the baby's arrival, I said yes to an interview.

Now, perhaps it was just a quiet week for news in the town of Regina, but somehow I made it straight onto the front page of *The Leader Post* the very next day. Laughing out loud with Janita at breakfast, we soon learned that this was just the tip of the iceberg as by midday, the home phone was ringing nonstop. Apparently everybody in Regina had read the story and by 4 pm I had completed three separate TV interviews with various news channels in the province. I wasn't quite sure what had hit me, to be honest, and Roddy and Janita simply smiled in the background as one news van after the other pulled up in their driveway. The neighbours must have wondered what the hell was going on.

By the end of the first week, I had done about ten talkback radio segments, featured in as many newspapers across the country and had even met the mayor of Regina. On a few occasions, I also got asked for my autograph in the streets! This, I think, wasn't so much a reflection of my fame but more so the size of Regina; it was tiny. The story was everywhere and I just went along with it all. Even Tara got involved whenever she felt able enough. It wasn't just local media, either; by the second week I was invited onto *Canada AM*, a national TV breakfast show, and the story instantly went from coast to coast. There didn't seem to be an end to the interest and with every interview I did, I was told that they'd be following up on the story to see the outcome. The story was a hit.

Of all the interviews, the funniest by far was with a French-speaking TV station from eastern Canada. Having heard that I had come from Switzerland where I was learning French, the reporter insisted that we do the interview in French. Now while in theory this made sense, my French, although 100 per cent improved, was still very basic. My pleas that I wouldn't be able to express myself went unanswered and before I knew it the cameras were rolling.

'*Sebastian, qu'est-ce que vous faîtes à Regina?*'

'*Bonjour. Je m'appelle Sebastian. Je suis ici parce qu'il y a une femme enceinte.*'

Awkward pause number one.

'*Pourquoi est-ce que vous voulez livrer un bébé?*'

'*Parce ce que j'ai cent choses à faire avant de mourir . . .*'

Awkward pause number two.

'Sebastian, let's start again in English, shall we?'

'Good idea.'

Janita, who had been standing in the background, erupted in laughter and began clapping like a circus seal. She, unlike the news reporter, found it hilarious!

The media attention certainly didn't matter to me, but I'd be lying if I said it wasn't fun. Not only would Tara and I both have funny stories to tell, but immediately the donations to Camp Quality started rising again. The media had instantly connected me with a huge Canadian audience who I was beginning to learn was amazingly supportive.

In between media interviews, I was trying to reply to what felt like thousands of emails from complete strangers offering to help me, join me, feed me, shelter me and even throw fundraisers on my behalf. For the first few weeks, I also tried to meet up with all the people who had offered to show me around but this ended up being logistically impossible; there were too many. I don't think it's going too far to say that the people of Saskatchewan and furthermore Canada are some of the nicest around.

By the time Tara's due date of 8 August had arrived, there was still no sign that she was ready to give birth. It looked as though the baby was going to be late.

'He's just hanging in there, Seb. He's in no rush, I think,' Tara told me.

With this came talk of inducing the labour but even this

wasn't an immediate procedure. Both Tara and I were just sitting on our hands.

After three weeks in Regina, I found that I had created a unique little lifestyle for myself revolving around replying to emails, spending time with Janita and the family and doing interviews as they popped up. This was all I could do as I waited. I was conscious of not ringing Tara too much as I didn't want to become an annoyance, but this led to a few days where I didn't hear from her at all.

I had to get in touch with her. After leaving several voice-mails over forty-eight hours, I began to worry that I hadn't heard back from her. Then it happened; one night, ten days after the due date of the baby, I received a message from her on Facebook.

She had had the baby the previous night in an emergency procedure and explained that there simply wasn't time to phone me. She apologised that she couldn't help me and promised to call when she got out of hospital.

I felt like my brain had imploded as my worst fear was confirmed. I had missed the birth. I was devastated. It wasn't anyone's fault, of course, but still I'd missed it. I'd travelled all the way from Europe based solely on the offer of a stranger, and only now did I begin to question my judgement. I re-read Tara's message again, trying to look for clues. Had Tara got cold feet? Was she joking? But none of these mattered, it was over.

After a moment of feeling sorry for myself, I sent back a message congratulating her. The most important thing was that the baby was healthy. I offered my help one more time, but other than that, I couldn't do anything. I was left pondering what on earth I would do now. Then I realised that in the morning I'd have to tell the media I'd missed the birth.

While my planning abilities were never my best asset, understandably I didn't have a back-up plan that would remedy this predicament that I now found myself in. All I could do was talk to Roddy and Janita who could see that I was down. They were too. We all felt low, but before long Janita's sense of humour highlighted the funny side of the situation.

In reality, it was bloody hilarious; much like an irresponsible father, I had missed the birth and with this realisation I picked up the phone and rang *The Leader Post*. This was the first of many humorous interviews that I gave in the following days on radio, TV and in print, all of which ended with the simple yet obvious question: What are you going to do now? It wasn't until the male presenter from *Canada AM* asked the same question that I finally made a decision about what I would do, and in part I think it was because of the way he phrased it, followed by a snigger at my failure.

'So, Sebastian, what's the plan now that you've missed Tara's birth?'

Irritating snigger.

'Well, you know what, I came to Canada to deliver a baby and I'm not going to leave until I do it,' I said.

In an instant, without even thinking about it, I had a plan – albeit a brash plan that lacked any forethought – but a plan all the same.

'In fact, if there's anyone watching who's not only pregnant but also has a sense of humour, please let me know. If you're five centimetres dilated or more and you'd like to share your birth with me, just email me. All my details are on www.100things.com.au.'

Just like that my plea had been sent nationally across Canada, courtesy of the most watched breakfast show in the country. I was excited and no matter how outrageous or unlikely my national plea may have sounded, it at least gave me a glimmer of hope. All I had to do was wait, and I was getting good at that.

Chapter 42

Hi Sebastian,
I've been following your story in Regina and saw you on the news yesterday. I'm sorry that you missed the birth but I think I can help you. My daughter is pregnant and is due any day now. We are based in Regina and I think you should ring her. She wants to help you. Her number is ### ### ###.
Regards,
Lorrie

The morning after the *Canada AM* interview, I'd received nine offers similar to that of Lorrie's above. I couldn't believe it! It seemed that my plea had worked and just as quickly as my Canadian adventure had derailed, it was back on track.

Of all the offers – one from England, one from Australia and eight from Canada – incredibly, three were from people in Regina itself. One of these was from Lorrie, another from friends of Janita's and a third from a bloke named Randy.

As excited as I was, it was crucial that I acted quickly and so after thanking everyone for their huge gestures of kindness, I found myself organising to meet with all of the interested parties from Regina.

The first person I rang back was Randy. His email to me demanded an immediate reply.

Seb, my girlfriend is in labour right now at Regina Hospital. Call me on ### ### ###.

The offer seemed too good to be true, yet after ringing the excited Randy, he insisted that I come down.

'She's in the delivery room now, man! Come!'

I jumped into the car and drove like a madman to the hospital with both the speedometer and my heart rate redlining. Running upstairs to the waiting area, I frantically looked around for Randy but could only see a young teenager wearing a baseball cap and hooded jumper standing at the doorway to the delivery ward. He just stared at me as I tried to catch my breath. I turned around to double-check I was in the right area and I heard a voice call my name. I spun around again but still only noticed the young boy.

'Seb?' repeated the hooded youth.

'Randy?'

'Yes, man, thanks for coming.'

I couldn't believe it. Randy was a native American Indian who looked as though he had just skipped school for the day. After a moment of confusion we began speaking and sure enough he was here to become a father. He told me that his seventeen-year-old girlfriend was in the delivery room next door.

'So, Seb, do we get to be on TV with you, now you're helping?'

I was still in a state of shock that this guy was about to become a father and his last question made me wince even more. Before I could answer, he grabbed me and told me that his girlfriend was waiting for me.

Randy opened the door to the ward and began leading me down a corridor. I followed, not knowing what the normal protocol was. To get to the delivery room, we had to pass the check-in desk and as we did, a woman who appeared to be a head nurse called to Randy and asked him what was going on. Her tone was like that of a suspicious teacher. His response, like that of a guilty student.

'Oh, this is my friend, Seb. He's helping us today.'

In a controlled and soothing manner, the nurse then left her desk and approached us asking Randy if his girlfriend knew that I was coming to help, to which Randy offered no answer. Instead, he exhaled loudly and dropped his shoulders.

'Now, Randy,' continued the lovely nurse, 'I just had a word with your girlfriend and she is very uncomfortable in there as it is. She also didn't know that you were inviting someone else into the room and I'd have to say to you that I don't think it would be a good idea to introduce any surprises to her right now.'

By this time I had regained my breath and with it my awareness of the situation. It seemed that Randy had just rung me up without telling anyone, including his girlfriend. I looked at the nurse who could also see what had happened; like any seventeen-year-old, Randy just wanted to be on TV.

'Randy, I think the nurse has a point, mate.' There was no way I could go through with this. It wasn't right. 'I'd love to help you, Randy, and I appreciate your offer but I think you have to listen to your girlfriend today.'

Randy looked at his feet.

'This is crap, man. She got to choose the baby's name, her clothes, her toys, and all I want to do is have you help deliver the baby!'

It could be said Randy was missing the point. With that, he walked back out into the waiting room and on towards the elevators.

'I'm going, man. I don't even want to be here!' he yelled.

The situation was grim. Randy, an expectant father, was walking away from his pregnant girlfriend and all the other duties that you'd hope someone in his position would be aware of.

Instinctively I followed him and stopped him from getting in a vacant elevator. He wasn't angry, more upset, and over the course of a few minutes I managed to calm him down. Somehow I'd found myself in the strange situation of having to convince a father-to-be to stay for his partner giving birth. At one stage I remember thinking, *What would Dr Phil say if caught in this predicament?*, and ended up making a speech about responsibility (minus a Southern accent).

Randy eventually returned to the bedside of his girlfriend and as he did, I had a chat with the nurse who came out to thank me. Although Randy didn't walk out at that stage, it seemed that there was a fundamental issue which would most likely arise again and again. Randy was not mature enough to be having a child. Sadly the nurse told me that this was a common problem in the area.

The second interview, based in Janita's living room with her expectant friends, was surprisingly normal considering the situation, but it was the third interview, that of Lorrie's daughter, that gave me the most hope. The setting was a Friday night family barbecue. In attendance on the night were about fifteen family members, all curious to meet the random Aussie whom Lorrie had contacted. It was enough to scare anybody off but after being given a beer and a burger upon arrival I felt completely at ease with everyone. They, like most others in Regina, were truly kind people.

Carmen, to whom I was introduced first, was an energetic girl. Having been with her partner Dane for a while now, they were excited to be having a baby together. Carmen already had one child, the gorgeous Olivia, from a previous relationship and for this reason the current little human hanging out in Carmen's belly would truly bring their family together as one.

We lit up a big fire in the yard and sat around telling jokes and stories. Carmen, similar to Janita, found great pleasure in laughing at my bizarre lifestyle and swore at one stage that if she laughed any harder I'd be delivering the baby that night. Dane was also a legend and by the end of the evening we had almost forgotten why I was there in the first place; it was just like we were mates catching up for a beer. The night couldn't have gone better. It was a lot of fun.

There was, however, a horribly awkward moment early on when Dane asked me what exactly I wanted to *do* in the delivery room to help deliver the baby. I just told him the truth: I wanted to experience childbirth firsthand and do whatever I could to assist in the process. He smiled and nodded his head. Clearly I had no idea what I could or couldn't do but I think my honest approach was enough to appease any doubts that I was anything other than genuine.

At half past eleven, the party ended and I was given a lift home by Dane and Carmen. I felt very comfortable with them and I think they felt the same. As I was about to step out of the car, Dane turned around from the front seat and said, 'Seb, Carmen and I had a chat earlier and we agreed that we'd love to have you help with our baby.'

To me, it was the best news in the world and I told them so. They'd accepted me. At a time of uncertainty during my journey, they had steadied the ship with their selfless offer. The world, I am convinced, is driven by such generosity.

As I got out of the car, I said, 'Well, anytime you need me, you just ring me. I'll be there!'

With that, I shut the car door and walked into Roddy and Janita's house. The time was just after midnight.

Four hours later, my phone rang. In a daze I picked it up. Could it be?

Chapter 43

'HELLO?'

'Hey, Seb, it's Lorrie!' She needn't have said any more; there was only one reason why Carmen's mum would be ringing me at 4 am. 'Carmen's just rung me and she's in labour at the hospital. Can you get down there now?'

My heart rate doubled instantly. This was it; it was for real! I don't think I've ever jumped out of bed so quickly.

'I'll see you there in five minutes!' I said, as I threw on some clothes.

Four minutes later, I'd arrived at the hospital. I had broken every road rule to get there so fast. Thanks to Randy, I knew exactly where to go. I sprinted through hallways, and found Lorrie sitting anxiously in the waiting room. It had only been five hours since we'd been talking around the backyard fire. I gave her a big hug and got an update on Carmen.

'Well, her waters broke about two hours ago and Dane rushed her here immediately. She's already four centimetres dilated and all the signs are good. Her contractions are three minutes apart and shortening; the doctor thinks it's going to be a quick one!'

Although I nodded, I actually had no idea about half of what Lorrie had said but my loose take on it was that everything was going well. To a man uneducated about childbirth, this was going to be a baptism of fire.

Standing at the doors to the delivery ward, my immediate urge was to charge through them, declaring, 'Did somebody ask for a doctor?', but sanity prevailed. The female doctor was apparently coming back in a second anyway.

All I could do was sit down and wipe my bleary eyes.

During the next half-hour, other members of the family whom I had also met the previous night joined us in the waiting room. With every arrival of a new person came the same update that I was given by Lorrie. The funny thing was that it was me now delivering the news about contractions and the like, as Lorrie had fallen asleep. By the time the tenth person turned up, I had convinced myself I knew what I was talking about.

Soon enough a nurse appeared at the doorway and called both Lorrie's and my name.

'You can come now,' she said.

I woke Lorrie, and we stood and left the group. As we were led through the doors and past reception to Carmen's delivery room, I even got a rise from some of the nurses at the check-in desk who recognised me from my meeting with Randy.

With Carmen's brother, father and daughter all left to wait, I couldn't help but feel slightly guilty that I had taken precedence over them in the delivery room, but they'd already told me that they wouldn't have it any other way, they were happy with Carmen and Dane's decision.

Having never been in a delivery room before, the vibe as we entered was an odd one to say the least. At the far end of the room was an empty bed and around it were various instruments and machines all on hand for the process of childbirth. What these machines did I couldn't tell you but due to their cleanliness and occasional beeping sounds I assumed they were important. The nurse told us to sit on the seats positioned at the foot of the bed while she collected a few things outside. Then she left, shutting the door behind her as she went. This was a scene I still couldn't believe I was in; the silence only added to the suspense. But where was Carmen? Although uneducated in childbirth, I was certain she was an integral part of this process. Just as I prepared to break the silence with the obvious question, a loud moan came from behind a door that I hadn't noticed until then. Aha! It was the bathroom and inside it was Carmen. I could also hear Dane in there.

For the next twenty minutes Lorrie and I just sat there, listening to what sounded like the onset of severe pain. Like Lorrie, I wanted to help in some way, but with such a personal experience for Carmen and her family there was a thin line between helpful and inappropriate. I knew it was a matter of just waiting until I was asked to assist and admittedly the scene beyond the door sounded like something Dane was a lot better qualified for. Lorrie explained that Carmen was being bathed in warm water as a way of encouraging the birth.

My vision when I penned this item down on my list had always been to play an active role in the delivery and not just be a bystander. As I saw it, if I wasn't actually helping with a birth I was just playing a useless and voyeuristic role. Sitting there with Carmen in the other room though, I couldn't help but stare at the ground wondering how on earth the transition from onlooker to assistant might take place. This had the makings of being quite uncomfortable.

The doctor returned to the room to check on Carmen. After the doctor entered the bathroom and had a conversation with the couple, Carmen emerged from the room, physically supported by Dane who led her to her bed. She looked worn in her hospital gown but smiled immediately as she saw her mum and me.

'I'm so glad you're both here!' she exclaimed.

At that moment any ounce of awkwardness or doubt exited the room. Carmen genuinely wanted my help.

Carmen lay down and was able to chat with us. Instantly we picked up jokes from the previous night's conversation. I started by complaining that she hadn't waited until a more decent hour for her waters to break. The feeling in the room was one of great familiarity. Every time Carmen laughed, she winced in pain and told us to stop, but we could tell she liked it. Occasionally a contraction would interrupt the laughter, but seconds later, we returned to laughing. I had never in my life thought that this was what a delivery room would be like and over the course of an hour even the nurse joined in with the jokes.

Carmen's progress was quick – unfortunately with this came a big increase in pain – and before long she had asked for an epidural. Now not knowing anything about an epidural other than the fact that it's used for pain relief, I'd have to say that I was slightly surprised to find that it came by way of a needle, the size of a medieval jousting stick, being shunted directly into the spine! The result was a huge reduction in pain and with it a huge delay in progress. The subsequent six hours of little action and minimal contractions saw us all relax once again. Before long it was clear my role was the class clown, something that Carmen told me made her feel comfortable. It seemed that during childbirth there was help to offer beyond just the physical realms.

In this same down period I also became the messenger between the delivery room and the waiting room, updating the eager family with news that everything was going in the right direction. It was only after returning from grabbing a coffee in the canteen at around midday that the pace suddenly picked up; the baby had dropped. Fearing that not only had I missed the birth but the doctor had actually mishandled the baby, I ran into the delivery room in a panic. With no sight of the baby though, I then learned that the term 'dropping' simply meant that the baby's head had manoeuvred into a favourable position within the uterus for birth. I was relieved.

Carmen was sweating from pain and anxiety but we all willed her on. She was amazing. Screams followed intense contractions and tears rolled down Carmen's face. As the pain level again increased, so too did the realisation that for this to happen, Carmen had to go through one final unavoidable bout of pain. Understandably she was scared. Nine months of development, nurturing and care had led to this moment, and although potentially the most life-defining moment for any couple, the risks involved were deadly.

As I looked around the table at what was a very crucial time of the birth, I noticed that everyone was watching Carmen. Dane, as planned, was holding Carmen's hands at the top end, encouraging her to do her best. He didn't like the squeamish aspect of the birth and wanted to be able to talk to Carmen at all times. Next to him was Lorrie, positioned at Carmen's midsection; her hands slid under Carmen's back offering light massage. Placed in the stirrups at the end of the bed were Carmen's legs which, now wide apart and propped up, allowed the doctor to crouch in between them like a wicketkeeper waiting for a medium-paced delivery. To the immediate left of the doctor was the nurse who had Carmen's right foot placed on her shoulder, which left me in unfamiliar territory on the right side of the doctor, opposite the nurse, holding Carmen's left leg over my shoulder. In terms of being able to experience childbirth firsthand, this was as close as it got without actually having the baby yourself. If Dane didn't like the squeamish part, let's just say he certainly wouldn't have enjoyed my position.

The noise and intensity increased again while Carmen pushed even harder with each contraction and as a climax of some sort flirted with us, we all just huddled around, transfixed.

Looking down the barrel of Carmen's left leg, I watched with my mouth wide open as the doctor did her thing on the frontline. This was like nothing I could ever have imagined and before long I noticed a white object of some sort protruding from Carmen. Crouched on one knee myself whilst still holding Carmen's left foot around the ankle, I peered in even closer and asked the doctor what it was.

'That's the baby's head. He's crowning.' Didn't I feel stupid!

I was amazed and couldn't help but pass on the news.

'I can see your boy's head!' I shouted without realising that I was.

'Push, baby!' said Dane. 'Here comes our boy!'

With that, Carmen and Dane began crying in sheer joy. Lorrie, still to my right, did the same, and without a moment to try to resist, so did I. It was one of the most overwhelming experiences that I'd ever been involved with – the arrival into the world of a human.

As we leaned in, we focused only on the health of Carmen and her baby; nothing else mattered. At that moment, in that room, there was only one goal: a successful birth. Any issues, thoughts or problems unrelated to the moment were cast aside. We all shared a purpose and with that came clarity of thought; life was simple, and yet so magnificent.

Composed and professional, the doctor demanded a few more pushes from Carmen. Dane also urged Carmen on with complete devotion. If given the chance, I have no doubt he would have pushed too if it would have helped. Carmen responded immediately. Back down at my end, the small white scalp had turned into a complete baby's head after a further push and then, as if pulling on a piece of string, the doctor's gentle traction allowed a tiny hand to emerge from within that sure enough connected to a slightly larger arm, a little body and the rest of the extremities of what was soon a perfectly formed mini human lying in the palms of her hands. In the blink of an eye there were no longer six people in the room; there were seven. I helped the doctor place the newly born baby on Carmen's stomach. Only sheer relief overcame the pain and stress of the occasion. The birth had been successful; Dane and Carmen were parents of a healthy baby boy.

Lying there on his mother's stomach, Oakley Sanguin, as he would be named, took his first few breaths in the world. With the umbilical cord still attached, the doctor handed me the scissors and gestured for me to go ahead; the cord needed to be cut. I wasn't sure this act should be left to me and a quick look over to the teary Dane confirmed that he wanted to do the honours. Fair enough too. It certainly didn't matter to me; I, like everyone else in the room, was just happy that all was well. Everything else paled in significance. We were all in disbelief at what we had just been a part of – the miracle of birth.

After being handed Oakley to take to the weighing table, I read out his official weight of 8 pounds 15 ounces then spent some more time with Carmen and her immediate family. I couldn't tell you how long we were in there for, soaking in the moment.

28 August 2010, Number 23: Deliver a Baby – tick! But this experience I had discovered was not about ticking an item from a list; it was about people helping people and being part of something far bigger.

In the days following Oakley's birth I learned something about priorities. In that delivery room we had managed to somehow clear away all the needless clutter that might otherwise have occupied our attention, revealing what was truly important at that moment in time: on this occasion, the well-being of two fellow humans. I believe these moments of clarity allow us a glimpse of life as it should be: pure, unaffected and exhilarating.

Chapter 44

ONE OF THE FIRST people to comment on my website after I announced that Carmen had successfully given birth to Oakley was Peggy – Pete and Creature's lovely mum.

> Rev Seb, this can only mean one thing; you must be ready for the wedding now.

Pete's wedding had been confirmed for early September and as I'd hoped, the timing worked perfectly, leaving me with just enough time after the birth of Oakley to fly to San Diego for the ceremony. To answer Peggy's question, I was more than ready for the wedding; armed with a generic wedding sermon that an unknown Canadian priest had sent me having heard of my plan to wed a couple in America, I was all set for my lead role. During a secret conversation with Pete a week earlier, I'd even managed to make some adjustments to the sermon in keeping with his request that the sermon be 'simple and funny'. Pete knew that I was simple and I thought I was funny.

It was time to say goodbye to Canada, a place in which over the period of six weeks I had begun feeling very at home. Roddy, Janita and their amazing family had looked after me like one of their own and when I wasn't spending time with them, I was out meeting strangers who'd asked to meet me. The Canadians' generosity confirmed my faith in people. If the truth be known, the whole situation made me think about my own family in Sydney, especially my parents whom I now couldn't wait to see.

By virtue of the ridiculous amount of media that I received, I'd even begun accepting invitations from schools to give motivational talks to their students. Like everything else with my journey, I just went with it and even found myself ticking off a few more items in Canada, including Numbers 39: Read the National TV Weather Report and 92: Haunted House. I had a ball to the very last day.

Peggy's email, however, wasn't the only exciting one around that time; I also received an email from a woman I'd never met before titled 'Number 100: Publish a Book'. My heart skipped a beat when I read the email: I'd been asked to write a book by an Australian publishing company!

Janita, who was sitting next to me at the time, noticed that I'd gone silent. Completely shocked, I just pointed at the screen for her to read. Moments later she screamed and then hugged me. She was ecstatic. So was I, although, if the truth be known, this wasn't quite what I had in mind when I first put that item on the list.

You see, I'd always thought that I'd publish a children's book about talking boats. Before leaving Australia the year before, I had written a series of three kids' books based on the boats in Sydney Harbour. A friend had even had one of the stories illustrated and bound for my twenty-seventh birthday. This had been the book that I thought would enable me to tick off item

Number 100 but instead it seemed this publisher wanted me to write about my journey of 100 Things. I was shocked.

I replied to the email instantly, telling her that she'd be one of the first people I saw when I got back to Australia. With an amazing opportunity on the horizon, the next day I headed to San Diego to tick off Number 27: Minister a Wedding.

Whilst transiting through Denver Airport, one of the world's busiest airports, I got a tap on my shoulder from a stranger.

'How's the baby doing, Seb?' the man asked.

'Really well, thanks,' I said.

'Awesome. Love your stuff, man.'

And with that, he walked off, disappearing into the crowd.

It was only a second later that I realised I didn't know this person, by which stage it was too late to chase him down and ask how he knew who I was or what I'd done. Instead, I just stood there scratching my head; it seemed that the news of the birth had spread.

And it had spread far and wide. Even the girls from *The Circle*, who had known for some time about my unorthodox lifestyle, couldn't quite believe that I'd managed to tick off this item. The support these guys showed me was great and following another Skype interview after the birth, the producer asked me if I'd be interested in locking in five live interviews in the Melbourne studio throughout October and November. My chats with the girls at *The Circle* had apparently been very well received.

For me, this was a big call as it meant that I'd be flying home two months earlier than I'd planned, but in the spirit of going with the flow it seemed that this offer was simply the latest event in a trend of things that all suggested it was time to revisit Australia.

On the spot, I booked an early October flight home.

Chapter 45

THE SENSE OF OCCASION whenever a wedding rolls around is something I've always loved. A celebration bringing together friends and family from afar, a wedding is a unique event for most and one that in this instance I felt honoured to be a part of. Of course Pete and Osamu had not only invited me but had trusted in me to perform. Even though I still couldn't believe that my ministerial ordination had come by way of a free one-minute online application, it was a role I took seriously.

The wedding was to be held outdoors in a luscious green park in San Diego overlooking the water at Coronado Yacht Club. On the morning of the wedding, the sun came out to play and it shone down on the guests who were seated in little white chairs that had been placed on the grass in four rows facing the water. A small path between the chairs led straight up to the flower-adorned archway at the front. The elaborate archway sheltered a lectern upon which lay a few pieces of paper with handwritten notes scribbled on them; this was my sermon. Directly behind the lectern stood two men; one wore a traditional black suit and was about to get married, while the other wore a powder-blue safari suit and was about to wed two people. I'm not sure who was more nervous. Having never presided over a wedding before, I'll admit that I wasn't quite sure what to wear. Thoughts of donning a long black cloak, a white collar and a crucifix pendant seemed ridiculous, leaving me with only one option: the eye-catching retro suit that I'd worn on Canadian television as I read out the national weather a week earlier. Pete loved the informality of it.

With everyone seated, other than the bridal party and of course Pete and me, Osamu's bridal car pulled up at the back of the wedding area. When she stepped out and placed a foot on the ground, the crowd hushed and stood as one. The ceremony was about to get underway.

Next Osamu's father emerged from within the car and a moment later began to slowly lead his daughter down the aisle. On cue, the three-man band began playing 'Here Comes the Bride'.

With just half a song left before the ceremony commenced, I took the opportunity to say a quiet word to Pete in an effort to calm us both down. A warm shake of the hand and a nod of the head was all it took before Osamu had arrived at Pete's side. The moment was now upon us. Gripping onto her father's hand as she peered over to Pete on her right, her eyes gave away that she was nervous but Pete's glowing smile instantly settled her. Feeling very nervous at this point myself, I wished that Pete gave me the same smile! After a last moment of contemplation the couple turned and looked at me as did the seventy or so people watching on. This reminded me that it was my turn to do something – speak.

'Do you, sir, give your daughter to be married here today?' I asked.

'I do,' said Osamu's dad.

'Super!'

Having started strongly with a standard question to the father of the bride, I'd have to admit my response of 'Super!' was slightly less professional. I didn't mean to say it – it just came out – but luckily everyone laughed. At Pete's request, my sermon needed to be simple and funny, so laughter so early on was a good sign.

'Osamu, by marrying Peter here today you are hereby declaring to us all that you support all of who he is and all of what he does as a human. This includes his peculiar habit of collecting poisonous and exotic animals such as spiders and snakes that would most likely scare the majority of people present here today.' Smiles from around the area suggested that I hadn't yet offended anyone and with this being high on my list of priorities for the day, I continued with confidence. 'By the same token, Peter, by marrying Osamu here today, you are declaring to us all that although you do own a wondrous collection of creepy-crawlies from all around the world, you recognise Osamu as your prized catch and will treat her as your favourite. This includes Bitsy, your prized tarantula.'

Even at this stage I still couldn't believe that I was midway through ministering a real-life wedding, and the fact that Pete and Osamu were enjoying themselves made it even more special.

The laughter continued as the ceremony progressed and soon all the parts of a wedding that needed to be addressed, including the vows, were covered. For once I'd done my home-work. Not only had everything gone smoothly, but by the time I'd used up all my one-liners, we'd confirmed that both Pete and Osamu were ready to tie the knot. The rings were slipped onto the appropriate fingers, and there was only one thing left for me to do.

'Pete and Osamu, by the authority vested in me by the state of California, I now pronounce you husband and wife. Pete, you may kiss your bride!'

I didn't have to ask him twice.

It was official: Pete and Osamu were married. The crowd, to use a cliché, went wild.

Although seemingly a quirky item from the list, the fact that I'd not only been accepted by a loving family but also asked to be a pivotal part in what was one of the most important days of their lives was very humbling.

Number 27: Minister a Wedding – tick!

Chapter 46

PEOPLE OFTEN ASKED ME throughout my trip whether I missed home, but I never understood this question. I loved my home but I didn't miss it. Over the past sixteen months I'd always felt as though I was exactly where I needed to be, whether that be posing nude in New York or dressed as a giant tiger in a Swiss ice rink.

The fact that the next section of this trip would see me back in Australia was an added bonus. I didn't feel that my impending flight home would signify some kind of end; rather, I felt the complete opposite. I was just continuing my journey on home soil for the next while. I loved the path I was on; I was happy.

With only a fortnight left before I flew home, I began to wonder if there was anything on the list that I could tick off in the interim. Embracing the proactive approach that came so naturally to me now, I found myself sending one of the most extraordinary emails I'd ever written to a man I didn't know. I began with the following:

Dear Miguel,
My name is Sebastian Terry and I have a list of 100 Things
that I'm attempting to complete before I die . . .

When hitchhiking across America, one aspect that I couldn't
quite get my head around was the fact that everyone had a
gun. In Australia you might keep a torch in the glove box,
whereas in the US it was more common to find a revolver
and so often whilst chatting with the driver, they'd offer to
show me their gun. It killed time, so to speak. I found the
act of holding a firearm extremely confronting and on one
occasion I pointed an unloaded gun at myself for no other
reason than to see what it was like to have a gun pointed at
me. The result was immediate; I froze. The mere thought of
what that gun could do freaked me out. Instantly I'd developed a fear of guns.

Staying true to my mantra of confronting all of my
fears, it was only now, many months on from hitchhiking,
that I decided to address this fear. By coincidence, sitting at
Number 73 on my list was indeed to Get Shot and so the email
I wrote was to a man by the name of Miguel Caballero, the
producer of the world's finest bulletproof clothing.

Now this might sound strange but Number 73 on my list
is to be shot whilst wearing a bulletproof vest and I was
wondering if you'd be able to shoot me if I came down to
your factory.

I've always thought that fear has the potential to hold us back
in life. Whether it be a fear of a specific thing or even the
fear of failure, it's easy to allow fear to control, and ultimately
limit, us. Now that I was in the habit of testing boundaries,
even those created by fears, there was only one way I could

face my fear of guns, and that was by being shot. A day later, I had my opportunity to do so.

> Sebastian,
> I would love to help you and it would be my pleasure to shoot you when you come to Colombia!
> Miguel

Did I not mention that the Miguel Caballero factory was based near Bogota, Colombia? It was the first place that popped up after I googled 'bulletproof clothing companies'.

With just two weeks before I was due to return home, I booked a flight to Colombia; this would be my last hurrah.

Rugsy, who was still working in his New York office, had always told me to keep him posted if I ever made it to Colombia. He had some clients down there and liked the idea of combining a needed business trip with a good old-fashioned catch-up with a mate. As such, he was the first person I emailed with my plan. His response was immediate; he was coming and, somewhat disconcertingly, was very excited to see me get shot!

Jokes aside, in the face of what may have been one of the stupidest and potentially most dangerous things I'd ever done, I was extremely happy to have a mate at my side for the shooting; there was an element of comfort in this. Of course I wasn't sure what comfort Rugsy would actually be able to offer if indeed something did go wrong when being shot, but I chose not to think about this.

As it happened, not long after flying to Bogota and catching up with Rugsy, an unexpected business deal back in New York meant that he had to leave Colombia four days prior to the shooting. In a place where I didn't speak the language

I suddenly felt very alone and to make matters slightly worse, I fell ill with some kind of fever that kept me bedridden in the days leading up to the event.

I'm still unsure if there is a *good* way to prepare to be shot but certainly the bouts of shivering and sweating that I endured didn't help my state of mind. With little energy it was hard to get excited about being shot, but deep down I was, even if few people supported my decision.

As the shooting date approached, I received hundreds of messages from family, friends and strangers pleading with me to reconsider this item. Everybody was concerned for me, including my sister, Pascale, who made me laugh with one of her many emails begging that if I insisted on being shot, could I at least wait until after her wedding? Another person, one whom I'd never met, even demanded I tell them the type of bullet and gun being used, just so he could rest easy at night. The funny thing was that I actually had no idea what I was going to be shot *with*; to me it didn't matter. Instead I had complete faith that the bulletproof vest would work; details were unimportant. Ultimately I was in Colombia for one purpose: to face a fear.

Chapter 47

MIGUEL CABALLERO IS KNOWN in the industry as the 'Giorgio Armani of bulletproof clothing'. I could only assume this meant that not only would his clothing be handy if caught up in a militant uprising but it would also turn heads at a post-conflict dinner party. Miguel has provided garments for anyone and everyone including US presidents, royalty and various armies around the world. When he shook my hand and introduced himself to me at his remote factory two hours out of town, I couldn't help but wonder whether he'd add my name to this list at some stage.

After a brief introduction to the man himself, I was taken for a tour of his factory by his girlfriend who just happened to work there as well. I was intrigued to see the operation of what was a very strange place indeed. The massive square factory floor was filled with rows of tables, each one holding a sewing machine. Seated behind each sewing machine was a worker frantically playing their part in what was a production line of a deadly nature. Pieces of fabric flew from one table to the next while the humming of machines filled the room. As the clothing moved closer to the front of the room, the armour was then added to the inside of the garment before the finishing touches turned it into a stylish lifesaving tool.

Produced in the confines of an orderly, safe work environment, the thought that one day these articles might be involved in a gun battle of some sort was sobering. This feeling was complemented by our next stop on the tour: a large table laden with firearms.

Noticing a couple of pistols, a revolver, and a few machine guns as we approached the table, a mixture of childish excitement and nerves struck me. Two open boxes full of ammunition sat next to the unattended weapons. The weird thing was that no one seemed to care; clearly OH&S was not a priority in these parts. It seemed this was the world's most trusting work environment. So trusting in fact that after Miguel's girlfriend described each of the guns in detail, she walked off to fetch something from another room, leaving me alone at the gun table with free rein to do what I liked. Of course curiosity got the better of me, and I couldn't help but pick up the closest gun with one hand and a bullet with the other. Immediately though, the same fear I'd felt playing with that unloaded gun while hitchhiking across America affected me once again and I quickly put both items back down.

Just as I was beginning to feel the tension of the situation, a small girl wearing a pink dress leisurely glided past me on roller-skates. Seemingly unaware of her surrounds, she innocently smiled at me and sang to herself as she headed towards the factory workers. I looked around to see if there were any clues as to why there was an unaccompanied ten-year-old skating obliviously between factory workers and machine guns, but there was none. By the time I looked back around, she had vanished. I was confused. The whole situation reminded me of the scene in Roald Dahl's book, *Charlie and the Chocolate Factory*, when the character of Charlie first laid eyes on an Oompa-Loompa.

A moment later Miguel's girlfriend returned to the table with Miguel in tow. With a friendly look on his face he immediately picked up an unloaded machine gun and pointed it at me before then cocking it.

He must have noticed the confused expression on my face.

'That's my daughter. She likes to play here,' he said proudly, continuing to aim his firearm directly at my chest.

I laughed awkwardly. He put the gun back down and then asked if I was ready to get shot. Again I laughed awkwardly. By now it had sunk in: I was in a bulletproof clothing factory in the middle of Colombia with a man who very soon would shoot me.

The answer was of course yes – I was ready to get shot; my rising heartbeat told me so.

Chapter 48

'DON'T WORRY, SEBASTIAN, EVERYONE you see here in the factory has been shot once by me. It's part of the initiation into the family. They're all members of the survivors club now!'

At this stage I wasn't sure who was crazier: me or Miguel.

As Miguel handed me a stylish bulletproof black leather jacket to put on, the seriousness of the situation began to set in. This jacket would be responsible for stopping a bullet from entering my body. After zipping it up and beating my chest a few times as if that was enough to prove that the jacket would work, I was then handed one of the boxes full of ammunition. Inside were nine-millimetre bullets. Miguel explained to me that in the name of human rights I was allowed to pick the bullet he would shoot me with. How kind!

I randomly selected a bullet that looked 'friendly', kissed it once and gave it to Miguel. He then reached over for the revolver that I had just placed back on the table.

'I will shoot you with this today. It's a .44 revolver.'

He could have said that it was a toothbrush and I still

wouldn't have questioned him. Things were becoming a blur with a million thoughts racing through my mind.

Now with a bullet chosen as well as a gun to shoot it from, Miguel's demeanour changed. No longer was he joking around; instead he became very serious as he began to explain to me what would happen in the next few minutes. In the corner of the room was a large white wall emblazoned with a poster written in Spanish. Somewhat amusingly the translation, as Miguel explained to me, was 'Colombia – the world's safest country'. This was where I would be shot. Next to the wall was a statue depicting the Virgin Mary and on the small table beside this was a Bible.

'Sebastian, listen carefully,' said Miguel. 'Your hands must stay behind your back when I shoot you. I will count to three slowly and when I say each number you will take a deep breath in before breathing out slowly. I will shoot you on three.'

These rules seemed easy enough, especially the part about keeping my hands behind my back.

'In a moment we will walk over in front of the wall but first show me where your bellybutton is.'

From my bellybutton Miguel traced his finger five centimetres to the right and placed a mark at this point on the jacket. This was the spot where he needed to shoot me. At this stage I was feeling a little tense and I didn't think to ask why this position was so crucial, but I trusted him. I had to. There was nothing else to hold onto but the hope that he knew what he was doing.

From absolutely nowhere gathered a small crowd of people around the wall where I'd be shot.

'Let's go, Sebastian,' Miguel said.

This was it; there was no turning back. It was only ten metres to the wall but the walk there felt longer. Miguel strode ahead of me and stopped at the statue of Mary where he made a quick prayer. He then beckoned me over and delicately manoeuvred me into position in front of the wall. In his left hand was my chosen bullet and in his right he held the gun. Taking several paces back so that he stood facing me just a few metres in front of me, he took a deep breath and composed himself in the same way a tennis player would before serving in the final game to win Wimbledon. I just stared at him as he shut his eyes in concentration. Quietly I hoped that they'd reopen before he took aim.

A second later, Miguel opened his eyes and looked to his left out towards the factory floor. He needed silence and so he shouted over to the factory workers still at their machines who instantly stopped what they were doing. A hush engulfed us and all eyes in the room turned to me.

'Sebastian, we practise first,' he explained.

Lifting up the unloaded revolver and pointing straight at the mark on my jacket, Miguel stood there for a moment staring down the barrel of his arm. I looked down at the gun and traced a line from the barrel all the way to myself. With silence still filling the air Miguel then took one big step towards me so that he now stood just more than an arm's length away from me. My instinct was to move back but I didn't. If I had reached out, I could have touched the gun.

'One! Two! Three!'

There was a long pause between each number he yelled and as he'd instructed me, I inhaled and exhaled in time with each number. I noticed that my breaths were short. He was a focused man at this moment and after a brief pause he again yelled out, 'One! Two! Three!', his eyes never deviating from the mark on my jacket.

After my final exhale Miguel lowered the revolver to his side and in a way that made it obvious to all what he was doing, he raised his left hand in which he was holding the bullet and placed it slowly into the barrel of the revolver. He then flicked his wrist to close the barrel and with his left hand, cocked the gun.

We were ready. My hands gripped tightly behind my back as I watched the whole scene in slow motion.

Again Miguel raised the revolver so that it pointed straight at me. His gaze honed in on my midsection. The only difference this time being that when he pulled the trigger, he would actually be shooting me. I was helpless; all I could do was to look the man in the eyes. I had no control of what was about to happen.

As I stood there motionless with my hands behind my back, my mind was racing like it hadn't ever before. The gravity of the occasion had suddenly hit me and with a mixture of memories, emotions and feelings flooding my head, I realised that I was alone, about to do the most dangerous thing I'd ever done in my life. My palms were sweaty, I was nervous, and I could feel my heart pounding beneath the armour. I was well and truly out of my comfort zone.

Up to this point, I'd always been supremely confident that nothing would go wrong but now, only a few seconds away from Miguel pulling the trigger, I considered what might happen if the vest didn't do its job. What were the consequences? In the best case scenario I would get injured, but in the worst there was actually a chance of dying. If for some reason the bullet penetrated the vest (and my body), things could come to an abrupt end. The risk, in this sense, I had never truly considered until then.

It was only at this precise moment, when faced with the notion of death, that for the first time in a long time I took a step back from my reality and thought about the things that were important to me. It was just then, as Miguel drew his breath to start his count of three, that I asked myself the very question that had prompted my entire trip: If I knew I was going to die today, would I change anything? I thought about this for a brief second and instantly felt my head clear. Something had happened. For the first time in my life I was able to answer no; if I knew I was to die today, I wouldn't change a thing. I was truly happy. With this answer came the clear understanding that everything I had experienced in the past sixteen months, if not the last two years of my life, had all contributed towards this feeling. I felt like I'd grown because of it. My trip had come full circle and it took a man to point a gun at me to realise it. This too I wouldn't change.

I was exactly where I needed to be and I had never felt more fulfilled.

It had taken me forty-two items from my list to reach a place that I thought I would only reach when I finally ticked off the hundredth item. I was content.

On top of this I could also feel that my list was the beginning of something far bigger: a positive message underlying all my exploits that I wanted to share with others. I swore right then that if I did survive the shooting, this would become my next challenge.

I just stared into Miguel's eyes with a calmness that took over my body.

'One!'

BANG!

There was no two or three.

Chapter 49

W‌ITH A HOLE IN my shirt courtesy of a nine-millimetre bullet, I left Colombia the same afternoon and flew directly to LA where one day later I would board my flight back to Sydney. But before I left LA, I had one more thing to do.

Whilst in Colombia I had been approached by an LA-based production company that wanted to talk to me about turning my journey into a TV show. It seemed that the production company had heard about me through a few recent TV interviews that I'd done with *The Circle* and also *Sunrise* which had approached me for the first time since I'd left Australia. I think it was the fact that at the time I was talking about getting shot in Colombia that caught their attention.

Shortly after landing in LA, I found myself seated at a meeting table with two people telling me about my potential for TV. Having no comprehension of how the industry worked and not having ever thought about going on TV as a realistic option, I was flattered, of course, and in part excited, but as soon as talk of money, percentages and ownership came up, I began to lose interest.

The idea of sharing a positive and entertaining story on TV appealed to me greatly, but I hated even considering the business side of something that I only ever did because it felt right. I wasn't ready to commit just yet and so I declined signing the contract that was placed under my nose. Like the rest of my journey that had gone before this moment, I believed that a TV opportunity would happen when, and if, it needed to.

As I boarded my Sydney-bound flight at LAX, I tried to put down on paper how I felt. Ultimately my time overseas hadn't been a way for me to escape reality or take a break from other commitments in my life; instead I was trying to answer the many questions I had about the world, myself and all the things in between. This process was not only changing the way I saw the world but allowed me to gain a new perspective and way of life that I'd never experienced before.

I still had fifty-eight items on the list to complete but this feeling wasn't based on numbers; it was based on something more pure and holistic.

On the plane ride home I began to feel an incredible amount of anticipation. The next chapter was about to unfold.

I could tell it was going to be fun.

Chapter 50

SOME PEOPLE SAY THAT adjusting to the weather is the most interesting part of arriving in Australia but I think far more interesting is adjusting to the accents. There's nothing better than hearing a room full of Aussies talking about the cricket, the *bloody* heatwave or taking the piss out of a mate who's standing in front of them after you've been away for a while. We're a unique bunch.

After making my own way across Sydney Harbour courtesy of the Manly Ferry, I headed straight to my mum's place. She'd offered to pick me up but I felt like I needed to make my own way there. The funny thing was that I had nowhere else to go! Seeing Mum after a long time away was awesome and it was good to hug her again, but catching up would take time; there was just so much to tell.

Once Mum had released me from her grip, there was one thing I had to do – something I'd been looking forward to doing since March. I reached into my bag then walked into the living room. Above the television was a dusty framed certificate that had been hanging on the wall for the last seven years. Although the certificate had my name on it, I felt no connection with it; it was my university degree. In my hand, I was carrying another framed certificate that I'd more recently acquired; it too had my name on it but this one meant everything to me. It read:

> The most eggs crushed with the toes in 30 seconds is 24 and was achieved by Sebastian Terry (Australia) at the Ibis Hotel in London, UK, on 13th March 2010.

This was my official Guinness World Record and it was clear what had to be done. In one smooth movement I reached up to the framed degree, dislodged it from the hook and placed it on a nearby table. I then grabbed my newer certificate and proudly hung it in its place.

After taking a moment to step back and admire the certificate, I turned around and gave my mum another hug. This time it lasted a lot longer.

In addition to catching up with friends and family, I hit the ground at full pace back in Sydney. In the time that it took me to fly from LA I had received more emails from various production companies, local media and an array of people, all of whom wanted to meet up in person. On top of this I had a meeting with the publisher who'd contacted me when I was in Canada about writing a book as well as my first in-studio interview with the girls from *The Circle*, based in Melbourne, which meant that I needed to jump on another plane just two days after my return home. For a man who had no job, I was flat out!

The flight down to Melbourne for the interview was an entertaining one. I've always enjoyed talking to strangers if for no other reason than to hear about other people's lives. Likewise it's always nice to try and make someone laugh by sharing a story or two. I have come to love these sorts of exchanges and the varying reactions I get are often priceless. Plane trips are ideal for this. Sitting next to me on the flight was a man wearing a business suit. After some small talk, he asked what I did for a living. Answering this question for only the second time on home soil, the first being over sixteen months ago during Tank's and my lunchtime conversation with the inebriated couple on an awkward date, I gave the man an answer that I'd given countless times whilst overseas: 'I've got a list of 100 Things that I'm trying to do before I die.'

This was the beginning of a lengthy conversation that saw me answering question after question from a man who clearly wasn't quite sure what to think of me.

'So, you got shot in Colombia and flew home via LA?'

'Yes, but before I got shot in Colombia, I actually ministered a friend's wedding in the US.'

'You're a wedding minister?'

'Yep.'

'And this is before delivering your friend's baby in Canada?'

'Yes, but I didn't actually know that person; I only met her the day before she gave birth.'

The conversation continued in this vein for the entire flight.

Now, I don't know if you've ever had the experience of talking about something you know inside out, but for some reason it feels like you're hearing it for the first time. Well, I experienced this during our conversation and even I couldn't believe how strange my story sounded. It was weird to think that something so abstract had literally become my way of life but I loved it and the fact that this man felt comfortable enough to laugh at me made it even better. When we disembarked in Melbourne, he shook my hand and told me to keep going with my journey. This I took as a sign that he didn't think I was completely mental and with that he handed me a card.

'I think you need an agent. Give me a call when you get a moment.'

My first encounter with the girls from *The Circle* was great. They, like their studio audience, were lovely and sitting on their talk-show couch, it felt good to be entertaining an Australian audience with stories from my trip. The girls even offered to help with one of the trickier items from the list, Number 32: Learn Salsa. This would involve a few free lessons that would be filmed. The support was amazing and when I left the studio, the producer and a few others sat me down and gave me some advice on what they labelled as my 'career'. Apparently I needed to consider getting an agent or even a manager of some description who would look after me but in honesty, having just arrived home, I felt like I needed a mother. I felt like a naive kid who had somehow found himself in the limelight.

Without a day to rest I was back in Sydney and suddenly I found myself in a meeting with the publisher to discuss the idea of a book. Of all the recent dealings that I'd had, this meeting was the easiest by far. It became clear straightaway that we were on the same page, so to speak. The potential book was not merely a collection of 100 stories, each one detailing an item on the list; instead it was about something far bigger, a message of sorts. For me, this was the greatest finding of the whole trip and with a book offer now to consider, another item from the list was manifesting.

When I got home from the meeting that day, however, I found that another book publisher had invited me to a meeting.

I attended and one meeting later I found myself in a position I could never have imagined just a week earlier: I suddenly had two book offers on the table.

Flustered by the options in front of me, I took some time to contemplate the offers. This was something I enjoyed doing alone and after a week, I finally managed to make up my mind about which publisher to go with. Now, having made my first decision since my return, I was ready to attack the unknown.

I was about to write a book – that is, the one you're reading!

Chapter 51

ON *THE CIRCLE* FOR the second time in as many weeks, I ended up presenting my own segment which showed my first salsa lesson at a local dance studio. Similar to learning French, the acquisition of salsa would be a long process but the fact that I didn't fall over in my first lesson I saw as promising. After the footage ran, the girls turned to me on the couch and asked what I had coming up with regard to the list. Having asked myself the same question just days earlier, I already knew the answer: I wanted to try and help others. Number 26: Help a Stranger, therefore, was the next item on my radar and so I took the opportunity of live television to make a simple offer.

'If there's anyone out there who would like me to help them with something, no matter what it is, please let me know.'

Ten minutes after the interview had finished, my email inbox began to fill up with strange requests and invitations. I had no idea what this open-ended item might bring, which in part made it even more enticing, but as my inbox flooded with requests, I felt a sense of opportunity once again. It seemed that lots of people wanted help of one sort or another. Some asked me to help them move house, while others wanted me to babysit their children. Some requests were hilarious, others were concerning. After a few days of sifting through hundreds of emails, there was one that I kept coming back to. It was from a concerned mother based in Melbourne.

> Hi Seb,
> I am so inspired by your motivation and zest for life.
> I have a 10-year-old daughter who is beautiful, smart and has the kindest heart, however she is bullied endlessly by kids at school. She cries herself to sleep on a regular basis. My husband, daughter and I would be so grateful if you would talk to her class about your life, I think it would go a long way to stopping the torture she goes through every day.
> Thanks for your consideration.
> Sian

This email stood head and shoulders above the others. While most of the emails asked me to aid in a particular task, Sian had written to me about an issue that was actually affecting a child's life. This was the obvious choice for me and so I rang Sian directly to see what I could do. Five minutes after ending the conversation I announced on my website that I'd be flying to Melbourne to talk at Sian's daughter Billie's school.

In an unexpected twist, the news that I was about to give a talk at Billie's school prompted a flurry of emails from people throughout Australia, all asking whether I'd also be available to do talks at their schools, workplaces or social clubs. Surprisingly, it looked as though there was even enough interest to organise some kind of speaking tour! With no plans other than to write a book, I decided to run with this idea.

The potential of a motivational speaking tour excited me greatly. One thing that had become clear over time was that people enjoyed hearing about an average bloke taking on his dreams with such passion. It wasn't the specific items that were important to people but instead it was the notion that anyone can achieve anything if they put their mind to it. The first step was just taking the time to realise what you wanted to do. From this, it seemed, people drew some form of inspiration. Also the fact that strangers had been writing to me, telling me that they had created and started to tick items from their own lists purely because they'd heard of my journey, made me want to connect with as many people as I could.

By coincidence, I also found out that Dave Cornthwaite, my adventurous egg-placing friend, happened to be in Australia at the same time and, having previously toyed with the idea of doing some kind of motivational talk together, I decided to invite him along. All it took was one email to him and just like that we had an official Australian speaking tour.

Chapter 52

As I FOCUSED ON planning the speaking tour as well as writing a book, I accepted that many of the uncompleted items from the list, such as Numbers 10: Chase a Tornado or 43: Work at an Orphanage, would have to wait for a more practical time. One afternoon though, after a brief look at the list, I noticed an item that I had almost forgotten about: Number 41: Buy a Stranger Lunch. This I could easily fit in to my schedule straightaway. Having been shown generosity from people all throughout my trip, I figured the least I could do was buy someone lunch.

One sunny October morning I took the ferry into the Sydney CBD. My plan was straightforward: find someone who would allow me to buy them lunch. How hard could it be?

After an hour of walking around the bustling streets of Sydney, I was still without a dining partner; everyone seemed too busy with their own thing. Even the act of making eye contact with someone was a tough ask. Not disheartened, I continued to walk up George Street and on to Martin Place, in the heart of the city, where I was certain I would track down someone. This is where I met Chris and Emily.

A bustling thoroughfare for city slickers and tourists alike, Chris and Emily were the only people who were staying put. Side by side, they rested quietly against a wall with a small cardboard sign that read:

Homeless. No family or friends to turn to. Any spare food or money greatly appreciated. Thank you or God bless.

Chris and Emily had been living on the streets of Sydney for a while and, unlike most of the others I'd encountered that day, were open to chatting. They too found that few people were willing to talk and had come to accept this as normal. Of the people who did take the time to stare down at them and read the sign, Emily told me the reaction was mixed. Occasionally, generous people would offer loose change and sandwiches but there were others who would taunt them by shaking their pockets full of change as they strolled by with a spiteful glare.

'Get a job!' was the most common call, but this was hard for someone with no house. Literally, their belongings were held in a few torn bags that they leaned on as they tried to find comfort on the pavement in front of the Martin Place Post Office.

Chris then repeated something that I remember another homeless person had told me a while back.

'You can't get no job with no house, and you can't get no house with no job.'

Within spitting distance of international banks, designer shops and ritzy restaurants, Chris and Emily had nothing. Well, almost nothing, these guys thankfully had each other.

Both having come from similar tragic circumstances, they found themselves homeless from a young age. It wasn't until 2003, when Chris and Emily met in Queensland, that things changed. Sharing much in common, including the fact that neither of them knew their fathers, they ended up spending a lot of time together and, seven years down the track, they could proudly say that they were still together. This, of course, was tricky for a homeless couple as most refuges or shelters don't allow couples to stay overnight.

Centrelink, Australia's social welfare system, gave them each $200 every week, allowing the couple to seek the cheapest accommodation they could find at least two nights a week – but they still had to find somewhere to stay for the remaining five nights of every week. This usually came by way of Central train station, a night-time destination for many of Sydney's homeless people.

'It actually generates a sense of community,' said Emily, who mentioned the names of some of the locals who also sat on the street 'cold-biting', or begging as most of us would know it. As she spoke, another homeless man walked past us and sat down ten metres away in the middle of an alleyway. His look was one of emptiness and I wondered whether it was alcohol or reality that made him gaze indifferently into the street. I think it was the latter. I felt sorry for him.

'The thing is that some of them actually own a house but cold-bite just so they can get money for drugs or something like that. It gives us real homeless people a bad name!'

If you didn't know any better, you would think that Chris and Emily were like any other twenty-something-year-old couple. Sure, on closer inspection there were the longer fingernails and the worn clothes, but self-respect and determination seemed to have helped them along the way. These guys had a goal, Emily said, to get a house. Not just for themselves but for their four kids as well.

As they told me the names of their children, I couldn't help but wonder where they were. Emily produced a framed photograph of the four children together before Emily and Chris had to give them up temporarily.

'They're with their foster parents now,' Emily told me.

'We can't get them back until we have a house,' added Chris.

Emily and Chris were driven by the need to find a place to live. Unlike their own childhood, Chris and Emily wanted their kids to grow up knowing their parents.

'We're saving our Centrelink payments for a deposit on a rental property,' Chris explained.

The money that generous souls dropped in their tin can was considered spending money but with only $12.50 in total collected on this particular day, there wasn't a lot to go around.

'On our best day, we get over $200!' said Chris, grinning. Not much for starting a day at 6 am and sitting in one place until 9 pm.

We soon moved from the end of Martin Place to a nearby restaurant bar. Chris and Emily had accepted my offer of lunch on the proviso that we sit outside as Emily felt embarrassed walking into the restaurant carrying her life's possessions in a couple of bags. Once we placed all the bags and their large cardboard sign on the ground beside us, we ordered some food. I made it clear that we could eat anything from the menu but Chris and Emily simply asked for a bowl of hot chips. I wished that they had ordered something more substantial, but I think they had too much self-respect to take advantage of my offer. I even had to convince Chris that it was okay to have a beer with me.

Once we started to eat, I noticed that Emily was wincing in pain with every bite of her food. I asked what was wrong and she told me that one of her teeth had split in half earlier that morning and without the aid of a dentist, she simply had to let it dangle until gravity took its toll. I felt useless not being able to help.

Over the meal we spoke more about Emily's past, which sounded much like a horror movie, but still she spoke with a positive voice, inspired, I think, by her kids.

Chris, on the other hand, had been in pursuit of his mother for years and only recently, after creating a Facebook account, reconnected with her. She may hold the key to a more secure future.

'No matter how bad it gets, we all help each other on the streets,' Emily said.

This I saw firsthand as, after a brief pause in conversation, Emily asked if I was done with my calamari. I answered yes which prompted her to tip the remaining five or six pieces of calamari onto a piece of paper before approaching the homeless man who was lying down in the middle of the alley near us. As he looked up, she handed him the package, a much-needed meal from a girl who had so little herself.

When she returned to the table, I asked her about a notebook that I'd seen poking out of the top of one of her bags and, after admitting that she had a love of writing, she shared a poem that she wrote entitled 'Think of My Loved Ones'.

If there is someone you really love,
And in days to come they die,
Your love and feelings are strong for them,
And then you begin to cry,
Knowing that they're gone but thinking they're nearby,
Watching from above,
In heaven's only sky.
So the teardrop runs down my face,
And the crying won't stop,
You are the one I love,

And that love for you will never stop.
I know now you're gone,
And you're not coming back,
But I'm always thinking of you, loved ones.
As time goes past, so does life,
And I'm missing you more than ever,
Waiting for the day,
That we'll be joined together.
Right now I'm sad that we're apart,
Right now I have to mend my broken heart,
But I can't wait till we meet again,
But I hope you have fun in heaven till then.

Her dream, she told me, was to write a book about her life and also to have a poem published. I told her I could maybe help with this last wish.

As we finished our meal, the heavens opened up and the rain hit George Street with anger. I paid no attention at first but then noticed how Chris and Emily turned their heads to look at the sky with intent.

'I hate the rain,' said Emily.

While I had a roof over my head when I returned home, Chris and Emily had nothing. In fact with this realisation they told me that they should go. They needed to raise more money.

I topped up their tin of coins with a note donation that I wished would go further, but I knew they'd get at least one night's accommodation.

After a shake of Chris's hand and a big hug with Emily, I said goodbye. This, though, would not be the last time we'd see each other; I promised to stay in touch.

There are moments in life that stop you in your tracks and put things into perspective. This was one of them for me.

Number 41: Buy a Stranger Lunch was complete, but yet again it seemed there was something far more important to consider than a simple tick.

Chapter 53

WITH THREE DAYS TO spare before the start of our speaking tour, Dave turned up on my doorstep, fresh off a twenty-five-hour flight from London. Aside from the fact that we hadn't actually written our talk yet, our speaking tour had taken shape nicely.

The tour itself would see us speaking in three states. Starting in Melbourne, we were to address a number of schools before heading to NSW and on to Queensland where some larger corporate groups had asked us to speak. In total we had about twenty bookings. It was an exciting prospect, and with Jeep, the car manufacturer, jumping on board as a sponsor, we now had a shiny blue Jeep Patriot to get us from A to B. Things yet again had fallen into place perfectly.

For me, this tour was more of an adventurous experiment than anything else. If it worked, it would offer a great potential platform to spread a positive message. I wanted to make the talks unique – humorous and engaging, as well as thought-provoking. Dave, like me, loved talking and we both wanted to create something special.

Our first talk, in keeping with Number 26: Help a Stranger, had special meaning to me as I would be helping Billie out by talking at her school. For this reason I was quite nervous before the talk and by the time Dave and I found ourselves standing in front of a rogue bunch of excitable pre-teens ready to deliver our speech, we could only hope that they'd respond positively to what we had to say.

Thankfully, five minutes into the talk, it was clear that we'd hit the mark. It was incredible to witness a room full of young faces, including Billie's, smiling and laughing as we touched on the important topics of respect, self-belief, problem-solving and of course the notion of dreaming big. Even the teachers standing at the back of the room seemed to hang on our every word. My framed Guinness World Record, which I'd decided to bring along as a prop, became a focal point as it got passed around the room and before long I found myself in the humorous position of giving advice to young kids and adults alike about crushing eggs with toes. We'd managed to connect with young and old and, to my surprise, once the talk was over we were mobbed by kids, all of whom wanted to share their newly formed bucket lists with us. From one young boy who aspired to sleep in a bed of jelly for one week to Billie herself who yearned to swim in the Red Sea, it appeared that everyone had dreams.

As Dave and I took the talks further north, we continued to receive an overwhelming response. From eight-year-olds to eighty-year-olds, everyone seemed to engage with what we spoke about, and for the first time in my life, I felt like I was truly being useful. Complete strangers, having listened to the talk, weren't only left smiling but they would actually begin the process of making positive changes in their lives. I knew this because they'd keep me posted on their progress long after the talks. It seemed that when given a moment to think about it, everyone had at least one thing that they wanted to do. It was just a matter of realising it.

On top of the success of the tour, the fact that we were on the road meant that I could also meet many of the Australian-based campaigners from my website. Being able to say hello to people who'd supported my journey for a long time was something that I valued immensely. The campaigners included people from all walks of life and with all kinds of dreams – such as Declan, an ambitious Year Twelve student who'd decided to start writing the fantasy novel that he'd always dreamed of completing, and Kylie, an inspiring woman who invited me to help her become a human billboard for a day, Number 22 on her list, as a way of overcoming her shyness that she felt had held her back for so long. It was overwhelming to hear firsthand of the positive effects that my journey had had on others' lives.

One of the most incredible campaigners I met was a bloke called Mark, who'd seen a recent interview that I'd given with the girls from *The Circle* and had written me an email asking to meet up. Mark had always had a list of things that he'd wanted to achieve but in his mid twenties he suffered a setback that not only stopped his progress, but almost took his life. After returning from an overseas holiday at the age of twenty-four, a major health complication resulted in Mark falling victim to an unknown neurological disorder that stole all of his physical abilities and ultimately confined him to a wheelchair for life. For years Mark's health was his focus but after seeing me talk about my journey on TV, he decided it was time to revisit his list.

When I met up with Mark on the side of a road, he'd come prepared. His entourage included two full-time carers, a mobility van and a set of hair clippers. It was the last of these items that made us both smile. You see, unbeknown to me, one of the items on Mark's list was to shave his head and he went on to ask if I'd be happy to do it for him as he sat in his wheel-chair on the pavement. Feeling honoured that he wanted me to help – and that he trusted me with an electrical appliance – I accepted. Ten minutes later, after shaving a nervous first line down the middle of his head, I'd quite effectively liberated the majority of Mark's hair from his scalp. As ridiculous as the whole scene must have seemed to pedestrians walking past us, we were both stoked that he'd ticked off an item on his list. But we didn't stop there.

'So what else is on your list, Mark?' I asked.

'Well, I've always wanted to complete a half-marathon,' he said.

'How do you plan on doing that?'

'Well, I need someone to push me . . .' Mark said with a hint of hope in his voice.

'I'm in!'

And just like that we had an agreement. There was nothing else in the world that seemed more important to me than helping such an awesome guy achieve his goals in life. I knew then with certainty that this journey wasn't about my list anymore.

Chapter 54

THE CONTINUATION OF MY journey on home shores was amazing.

In less than two months after arriving back in Sydney such a lot had happened, but the one factor that kept me going was the sensation that things simply felt right. It is this feeling that keeps me going with my journey today.

I'll be the first to admit that initially the trip was based solely on my own desires and dreams and was perhaps somewhat hedonistic, but I think that this was what I needed at that time of my life. No matter what we're led to believe, there is nothing wrong with putting yourself first; in fact, I'd go as far as saying that it's very important. What is just as important, though, is that by doing so, we grow so that we can in turn put other things or people on the same level.

I believe this is what the first part of my journey was all about: learning about myself and building a foundation of sorts. By tapping into what I defined as my core beliefs, I led a lifestyle that tested me on every level, causing me to develop in a positive and meaningful manner. As a result I finally realised that my journey is more than just a list of challenges – it is subconsciously my way of searching for something paramount to all of us on a primal level: purpose. My list in this sense was the vehicle through which I chose to carry out that search. Each time I attempted something from my list, no matter what it was, I felt a sense of purpose. And I still do today. As I see it, purpose is essential in the search for fulfilment.

Although travelling by myself up until this point, I've always been surrounded by people, but as I write the closing chapter of this book, I can safely say that I am in complete isolation: I'm alone, some fifty-five kilometres off the south-east coast of New Caledonia, on a desert island. I've been here for four days of seven so far. Quite literally I'm in the middle of the Coral Sea armed with a ukulele, a hammock, a bunch of coconuts and some writing paper. I am, of course, working on Number 67 on the list: Live on a Desert Island for One Week.

By day I explore my tiny island, swim in the ocean and marvel at the solitude. By night I gaze at the stars, sit next to a small fire and do a lot of thinking. Shark fins, sea snakes and nudity are all part of this desert island experience and as I watch the sun dip into the ocean at what has become my favourite part of the day, I think it's time to start thinking about what's next.

Whenever I give a talk, receive an email from a stranger or help someone tick off a goal from their list, I'm reminded that there's something in what I'm doing that offers a sense of possibility and positivity to others. This makes me want to continue my journey. If this weren't the case, I would stop.

Everyone, I believe, has one thing, or even a list of things, that they've always wanted to do. Whether those things are in our heads, or on a piece of paper, they act as goals. By focusing on these goals, we find purpose, and by linking up our goals, we find direction. As one goal is accomplished, another goal manifests. The important thing is to check in with ourselves every so often so that our lists reflect our growth. In this way our goals – or lists – offer us a constant sense of purpose.

Sadly the easiest part of the whole process is often the one thing that people find hardest to address: taking the time to realise their goals. All it takes is a moment of reflection without which may result in us living a life that isn't orientated towards the things that mean the most to us. Instead we risk going through life working towards goals that we didn't choose.

From the moment I took a step back from my reality when Detho passed away, my life began to change. That day I asked myself the most important question I'd ever asked: If I knew I was going to die, would I change anything? It was a question that led to an enormous shift in my outlook and my entire approach to life. All it took was a moment of clarity upon which I acted.

In a perfect world, you wouldn't have heard of me; in honesty, what have I done that's so outstanding? The answer is nothing. Quite simply, I'm just doing the things that I want to do. Surely we should all be doing the things that we want to do in life? Nothing to me makes more sense.

The fact that my story has garnered attention – even the fact that you are about to finish reading a book that outlines my journey so far – is an alarming reflection of the society we live in. It means that my story is different to the majority. This shouldn't be the case, but having found myself in this surprising position, I see that there is an opportunity to make a positive change.

In Colombia I answered no to that question, that I wouldn't change a thing – I would be happy if I died today – but in line with the shift in my recent journey, I know that there's now a lot more that I need to do to make a positive impact. This is now my challenge; this is my purpose. The last couple of years have taught me that anything is possible.

Having never written a book before, I'm not too sure what I should do at this stage. I guess this is pretty much where I might leave it, for now. I was thinking of ending it by saying, 'Number 100: Publish a Book – tick!', but as you know this story isn't just about me ticking boxes. Instead I think the best way to end would be by asking you one simple question.

What's on your list?

Take the time to consider it. You never know, it could change your life.

What's on Your List?

ALLOW YOURSELF A MOMENT to think about what's important to you. Is there something, or some things, that you've always dreamed of doing? Start writing your ideas down – this is the first step. You may have just one goal or you may have 100, but just remember that everyone's list is different.

1. _____
2. _____
3. _____
4. _____
5. _____
6. _____
7. _____
8. _____
9. _____
10. _____
11. _____
12. _____

13. _____
14. _____
15. _____
16. _____
17. _____
18. _____
19. _____
20. _____
21. _____
22. _____
23. _____
24. _____
25. _____
26. _____
27. _____
28. _____
29. _____
30. _____
31. _____
32. _____
33. _____
34. _____
35. _____
36. _____
37. _____
38. _____
39. _____
40. _____
41. _____
42. _____
43. _____
44. _____
45. _____

46. _____
47. _____
48. _____
49. _____
50. _____
51. _____
52. _____
53. _____
54. _____
55. _____
56. _____
57. _____
58. _____
59. _____
60. _____
61. _____
62. _____
63. _____
64. _____
65. _____
66. _____
67. _____
68. _____
69. _____
70. _____
71. _____
72. _____
73. _____
74. _____
75. _____
76. _____
77. _____
78. _____

79. _____
80. _____
81. _____
82. _____
83. _____
84. _____
85. _____
86. _____
87. _____
88. _____
89. _____
90. _____
91. _____
92. _____
93. _____
94. _____
95. _____
96. _____
97. _____
98. _____
99. _____
100. _____

If you would like to join the growing number of 100 Things campaigners, you can also share your list online by submitting it at www.100things.com.au.

Postscript

BY THE WAY, MARK and I did complete the half-marathon.

In what was an experience that I'll never forget, I pushed Mark for twenty-one kilometres in a time of 3 hours, 38 minutes and 42 seconds at the Run Melbourne Half-Marathon on 17 July 2011. Needless to say, by the end of it I was buggered.

If ever I needed confirmation that Mark was happy, immediately after the race he turned to me and whispered from his wheelchair, 'That was special.' I've never felt better in my life.

With my work seemingly done, two days later I received a phone call from Mark. He had a question for me. I thought perhaps he may have been asking if my muscles were still sore, but instead he dropped a bombshell.

'Mate, do you fancy trying to do a marathon together?'

Doing a marathon just so happens to be Number 86 on my list. But regardless, how could I say no to an awesome guy like Mark?

We're now in training.

100 Things

LIKE LIFE ITSELF, MY list of 100 Things is continuing. From the moment this journey began until the time this book was sent to production, I'd ticked off fifty-one things. Although unable to write about every item in this book, here is the updated list with ticks next to the completed ones.

Of course, there's no set plan but I'm looking forward to knocking off the remainder of the list in the near future. You can also follow my progress at www.100things.com.au.

100 THINGS
1. Running with Bulls ✓
2. Marry a Stranger ✓
3. Bet $1000 on Black (Roulette) ✓
4. Raise $100,000 for Camp Quality
5. Save a Life
6. Complete a Triathlon ✓
7. Feature in a Bollywood Movie
8. Olympic Ski Jump

9. Be in a Dance Video Clip ✓
10. Chase a Tornado ✓
11. Whale Shark Swim ✓
12. Visit a Death Row Inmate ✓
13. Be in a Medical Trial ✓
14. Burning Man Festival ✓
15. Stand-Up Comedy Routine ✓
16. Street Performance ✓
17. Surf Safari
18. Hit a Hole in One
19. Guinness World Record ✓
20. Say Yes to Everything for One Week
21. Speed Dating ✓
22. Participate in a Boxing Match
23. Deliver a Baby ✓
24. Publish an Article ✓
25. Catch a Thief
26. Help a Stranger ✓
27. Minister a Wedding ✓
28. Visit a Fortune Teller ✓
29. One Week's Silence ✓
30. Join a Protest ✓
31. Build Something
32. Learn Salsa
33. Be a Contestant on a TV Game Show ✓
34. Kiss a Celebrity
35. Find My Family Tree
36. Walk Across a Country ✓
37. Be a Horse Jockey
38. Be in a Hollywood Movie
39. Read the National TV Weather Report ✓
40. Sail the Seas
41. Buy a Stranger Lunch ✓

42. Cycle Through Cuba ✓
43. Work at an Orphanage
44. Represent a Country at Something
45. Sumo Wrestling
46. Learn French ✓
47. Go to Timbuktu
48. Act in a Play
49. Be a Matador
50. Throw a Party
51. Endurance Tandem Bike Ride ✓
52. Sports Streak
53. Ice Fishing
54. Scooter Across Australia ✓
55. Own a Company ✓
56. Tantric Lesson
57. Cross a Desert
58. Skydive Naked ✓
59. Attend an Extreme Religious Ceremony ✓
60. Throw a Dart at a Map and Visit the Country It Lands On
61. Ultimate Prank
62. Live on the Streets
63. Get a Tattoo ✓
64. Challenge a World Champion ✓
65. Dad's Dream Car ✓
66. Treacherous Trek
67. Live on a Desert Island for One Week ✓
68. Invent Something
69. Join a Cattle Drove
70. Meet Another 'Sebastian Terry' ✓
71. Naked Rugby ✓
72. Stay Awake for Seventy-Two Hours ✓
73. Get Shot ✓

74. Crazy Bid
75. Pose Nude ✓
76. Surf River Wave
77. Be a Team Mascot for a Day ✓
78. Write and Perform a Song ✓
79. Live with a Tribe for One Week
80. Have Something Named After Me ✓
81. Make a Beefeater Laugh
82. Hitchhike ✓
83. Foreign Aid
84. Face a Shane Warne Over
85. Go on an Adventure ✓
86. Marathon
87. Meditation
88. Grow a Beard ✓
89. Playboy Mansion
90. Land Diving
91. Plant a Tree ✓
92. Haunted House ✓
93. For Auction on Behalf of Camp Quality
94. For Auction on Behalf of Camp Quality
95. For Auction on Behalf of Camp Quality
96. For Auction on Behalf of Camp Quality
97. For Auction on Behalf of Camp Quality
98. Crash a Red Carpet ✓
99. For Auction on Behalf of Camp Quality
100. Publish a Book ✓

You may notice that Numbers 93, 94, 95, 96, 97 and 99 are up for auction. In keeping with attempting to raise $100,000 for Camp Quality, I am now allowing YOU to pick these items for me in return for a generous donation to Camp Quality. If you have an idea and would like to make an offer, I'd love to hear from you. I'd also love you to join me in attempting that item if you wish. Feel free to contact me (my details are below).

DONATE TO CAMP QUALITY

To find out more about Camp Quality, the amazing charity helping kids and families affected by cancer, please visit their website, www.campquality.org.au. If you would like to support the cause, please feel free to donate any amount at the 100 Things Camp Quality donation page, www.campquality.org.au/events/sydney/100things.aspx.

HELP!

If you think you might be able to help me achieve any of the incomplete items, I'd also love to hear from you. After all it's the generosity of others that allows this journey to continue as it does. I thank you in advance.

Contact details
Email: seb@100things.com.au
Facebook Group: 100 Things
Twitter: @Seb100Things

Thanks

FROM SOMETHING THAT BEGAN as just an idea in my head, my journey has now become a way of life for me. It would be ridiculous of me to think that this has happened only because of a positive attitude. As such I'd like to thank everybody who has helped me along the way. Without your support and assistance, I'd most probably be stuck on the side of the road still attempting to hitchhike across America.

To the friends mentioned in the book, being able to write about you has filled me with as much joy as the moments we had together. To those whom I encountered but wasn't able to write about here, please believe me when I say that you were just as important to my growth. I hope I left a positive memory for you also.

To those who took the time to look at my blog and to those who went one step further and emailed to congratulate me, help me and on occasions join me, thank you.

To my family, seeing as I always forget to say hello to you during interviews – hello! I know at first that my plans may have seemed completely crazy (and quite possibly still do), but I hope you can see that as a result I'm happy and in this, you are too.

My dad once told me that it's better to live one day as a wolf than a thousand as a sheep and only now can I really see what he meant.

I should also mention that Pascale and Brett did get married in January 2011 and it was an incredible day. Congratulations.

To the Dethicks, as you know, there were various things in my life that influenced this journey but none, I felt, more so than the passing of Chris. Thanks for being the open and lovely people that you are. To be able to talk to you throughout this writing process has been important for me and I hope you enjoy the message here. You told me that you hoped that the legacy of Chris was something that lives on and this book is certainly testament to that. Detho, you're a legend!

As a side note, I'd like to congratulate my Canadian parents, Janita and Roddy, who have recently had a third child named James Malcolm Sebastian Macleod. Janita contacted me shortly after giving birth telling me the great news. She also informed me that I was now able to tick off Number 80: Have Something Named After Me!

And in case you're wondering, J-Loc and I continue to write to each other. By chance, in his latest letter to me, he finally answered my question of what he'd do if given one more day on the outside. He told me that he'd take his daughter to the beach. This is now something I'm trying to arrange.

A big thanks goes to Emily who allowed me to reproduce her poem in this book. I should also offer a huge congratulations to her and Chris who recently told me they have now found full-time jobs and are renting a house!

It goes without saying that without the support and vision of Sheila Vijeyarasa, Mark Lewis, Virginia Grant and everyone else at Random House, this book would not be in your hands, so thanks to everyone involved with the publishing of my first book. Number 100: Publish a Book. What an experience!

And to you, the reader, thanks for taking the time to pick up this book. I hope that it leaves a positive message with you and a smile on your face. Not only through reading this book have you become a part of my journey, but a percentage of the money from your purchase of the book has now been donated to Camp Quality.

Thank you,

Seb

www.100things.com.au

You've finished the book but there's much more waiting for you at

www.randomhouse.com.au

▶ **Author interviews**

▶ **Videos**

▶ **Competitions**

▶ **Free chapters**

▶ **Games**

▶ Newsletters with exclusive previews, breaking news and inside author information.

▶ Reading group notes and tips.

▶ VIP event updates and much more.

ENHANCE YOUR READING EXPERIENCE

www.randomhouse.com.au